CARE MATTERS

WITHDRAWN

CARE MATTERS

*Concepts, Practice and Research
in Health and Social Care*

edited by
Ann Brechin, Jan Walmsley,
Jeanne Katz and Sheila Peace

SAGE Publications
London • Thousand Oaks • New Delhi

Editorial selection and Introduction © Ann Brechin, Jan Walmsley,
Jeanne Katz and Sheila Peace 1998
Chapter 1 © Dorothy Atkinson 1998
Chapter 2 © John Adams, Joanna Bornat and Mary Prickett 1998
Chapter 3 © Jeanne Katz 1998
Chapter 4 © Stan Tucker and Penny Liddiard 1998
Chapter 5 © Jill Reynolds and Jan Walmsley 1998
Chapter 6 © John Swain and Sally French 1998
Chapter 7 © Moyra Sidell 1998
Chapter 8 © Sheila M. Peace 1998
Chapter 9 © Celia Davies 1998
Chapter 10 © Julia Johnson 1998
Chapter 11 © Linda J. Jones 1998
Chapter 12 © Ann Brechin 1998

First published 1998

SAGE Publications Ltd
6 Bonhill Street
London EC2A 4PU

SAGE Publications Inc.
2455 Teller Road
Thousand Oaks, California 91320

SAGE Publications India Pvt Ltd
32, M-Block Market
Greater Kailash – I
New Delhi 110 048

British Library Cataloguing in Publication data

A catalogue record for this book is available
from the British Library

ISBN 0 7619 5565 8
ISBN 0 7619 5566 6 (pbk)

Library of Congress catalog card number 98–060536

Typeset by Mayhew Typesetting, Rhayader, Powys
Printed and bound in Great Britain by Athenaeum Press,
Gateshead

CONTENTS

ACKNOWLEDGEMENTS

The editors and publishers wish to thank the following for permission to use copyright material: *Acta Sociologica* for Celia Davies (1995) 'Competence versus Care? Gender and Caring Work Revisited', *Acta Sociologica*, 38: 17–31.

We were particularly pleased to discover Muriel Bell's previously unpublished poem, 'Convalescence', which was provided for us by her daughter, Sheena Rolph. Muriel Bell had written poetry all her life and began to have some published in her 70s, including a booklet of her poems *The Coral Seekers*, published by Lilliput Press, Norwich. 'Convalescence' was her last poem and seems to us to speak volumes.

We would also like to thank our co-contributors and colleagues for their patience in staying with this project through many delays and despite intense pressures on their time. We would like to thank them also for their continued enthusiasm, encouragement and support in what has been very much a shared venture.

Our thanks in particular to Serena Stewardson, who somehow stayed abreast of which version of each chapter was the most recent, and what the latest view on chapter order might be, while handling floppy discs, e-mail attachments and hard-pressed authors with equal aplomb.

CONTRIBUTORS

John Adams is a senior lecturer in Health Studies at Homerton College, Cambridge, and Editor of the *International History of Nursing Jounal*. He has a special interest in reminiscence work with older people.

Dorothy Atkinson is a senior lecturer in the School of Health and Social Welfare at the Open University. Her background is in social work and includes several years' experience of working with people with learning disabilities. She is co-editor of the *British Journal of Learning Disabilities*. Her research interests include the use of oral history and auto/biographical approaches to enable people with learning disabilities to relate, and reflect on, their lives and experiences.

Joanna Bornat is a senior lecturer in the School of Health and Social Welfare and has researched, written and taught on issues relating to memory, biography and ageing over a number of years. She is joint editor of the journal *Oral History*.

Ann Brechin is a senior lecturer in the School of Health and Social Welfare at the Open University, where she has worked for 20 years. Her previous work as a clinical psychologist led to an interest in learning disability, which has remained the focus of her research and teaching.

Celia Davies, Professor of Health Care in the School of Health and Social Welfare, was previously Professor of Women's Studies and Director of the Centre for Research on Women at the University of Ulster. She has a long-standing interest in gender and the caring professions with particular reference to nursing.

Sally French is a senior lecturer in the Department of Health Studies at Brunel University and has a background in physiotherapy. She has researched and written extensively in the field of disability studies and the social sciences relating to health and illness and was a member of the Open University course team for 'Disabling Society – Enabling Interventions'.

Julia Johnson is a lecturer in the School of Health and Social Welfare at the Open University where she has worked for the last six years. She has a background in social work and has taught and undertaken research in social gerontology for many years.

Linda Jones is a senior lecturer and Dean of the School of Health and Social Welfare at the Open University. Her research interests lie in the field of health policy. She has published widely on health promotion issues, most recently on young people's quality of life.

Jeanne Katz has been a lecturer in the School of Health and Social Welfare at the Open University since 1990 and has been primarily involved in working on the 'Death and Dying' course which she now chairs. Her research includes Department of Health funded studies of the care of dying residents in nursing and residential homes.

Penny Liddiard is Course Presentation and Marketing Manager in the School of Health and Social Welfare where she has worked for 20 years. She has managed and written for courses on disability and her research interest include 'felt needs' in relation to health, and the experiences of young carers.

Sheila Peace is a senior lecturer and Sub-Dean (Research) in the School of Health and Social Welfare. She joined the Open University in 1990, prior to which she was a senior research officer and founder member of the Centre for Environmental and Social Studies in Ageing at the University of North London. She has been involved in a wide range of research with older people, particularly in areas of residential care and environment.

Mary Prickett is a senior staff nurse at Kettering Hospital. She took her BA degree at the Open University, later completing a postgraduate Diploma at Nene College, Northampton where she is completing an MSc in Nursing.

Jill Reynolds has a background in social work with statutory and voluntary agencies, social work education and training. She is a lecturer in the School of Health and Social Welfare at the Open University and course Chair for 'Mental Health and Distress: Perspectives and Practice'. She has research interests in mental health care, work with refugees and women's issues.

Moyra Sidell is a senior lecturer in the School of Health and Social Welfare at the Open University. She has been an author for courses on 'Health and Wellbeing', 'Death and Dying' and 'Promoting Health'. She has researched and published in the field of women's health, the health of older people and her current research is on the care of dying older people in residential and nursing homes.

John Swain is a reader in disability studies at the University of Northumbria. He has a particular interest in learning difficulties, and has worked on a number of Open University courses in disability studies.

Stanley Tucker is a lecturer at the School of Health and Social Welfare at the Open University. Prior to that, he worked in the youth service for almost 20 years. His main research interests are concerned with the impact of social policy developments on the lives of young people.

Jan Walmsley is a senior lecturer in the School of Health and Social Welfare at the Open University, and co-editor of the *British Journal of Learning Disability*. Her main research interests are in the area of learning disability with a particular focus on women's issues.

Convalescence

My life is not my own any more,
My life is not my own.
Strangers come and sweep and clean
Our house, fetch and carry for me –
Most are sweet and caring
But they are not mine.
I sit alone a lot, and think.
Still the branches of the cherry tree
Move with the wind.
And move with my thoughts
In never-ending circles.
The 'phone rings
But it is not mine
And is answered by another
In some other room –
So who can tell?
While I sit and wait –
This is hell.
And my life is not my own any more
My life is not my own.
For many days the rain has fallen
Softly, gently,
Hiding in mist the Downs
Hiding my innermost thoughts.
These mist-covered days
That bring depression and sadness
Frustration and impatience
Which have to be conquered.
Then I look at the wonder of roses
In full bloom. And the happiness
Of birds – the kindness of people.
And my life seems my own once more –
My life seems my own.

Muriel Bell

INTRODUCTION

Ann Brechin

Care and Humanity

> 'Don't care' was made to care,
> 'Don't care' was hung.
> 'Don't care' was put in the pot
> And boiled 'till he was done.'
>
> (Anon)

Such ferocious sentiments reflect the importance attached to 'caring'. Other versions include him being variously 'trussed up', 'put in the box', 'drowned'. Clearly the message is that 'not caring' brings you to a sticky end, one way or another. Maybe old chants such as these refer to a broader sense of caring than the one we are concerned with in this book, namely caring for other people, but perhaps not. There may well be a link worth attending to. 'Don't care' is about resisting responsibilities, resisting appeals to comply with social expectations. It is about adopting a position of alienation and refusing to accept the moral imperative to co-operative, mutually rewarding behaviour. Refusing to care what others think, what others want, what others need from you, is ultimately to turn your back on society and social engagement. To 'care', on the other hand, is to accept a host of moral responsibilities for your own and others' well-being. It is to accept that people matter. At the extreme, care can sustain or extinguish life itself. Even at its more routine, it can influence how people live their lives and the kind of people they become. Caring, therefore, really matters. It is fundamental to the pact involved in being human.

The concept of care has become an increasing focus of attention of late, generating a wealth of books and papers, not to mention legislative and policy changes. So why another book on care? Our purpose as editors and contributors, with a common base or close association with the School of Health and Social Welfare at the Open University, has been to explore care across a wide range of settings and interpretations of care. We have set out to look at both family and paid care; at health and social care; at the implications of being labelled as a 'carer' or as someone to be 'cared for'; at the meanings of care itself. The book draws on research and wider debates about how care is defined and understood and considers the changing ways in which care is offered, as policies and practices change. Organisational divisions have traditionally led to separate analyses and practice in relation to formal care and informal care has only recently become a feature in such debate. Our particular project in this book has been to explore whether common ground or shared meanings can still be found across such differences and in such varied contexts.

The book asks how we can make sense of such varying concepts of care and of the many forms care takes in practice. In addressing such questions, we found ourselves engaged, in a variety of ways, with a range of key themes and debates, which are current in the field of care and which came to the fore for us.

Care tends to be idealised as something spontaneously occurring within families and kinship systems and indeed this is the primary, everyday route by which care is made available. Shared assumptions about family responsibilities for looking after young, old, sick or disabled members of society are common across cultural boundaries and throughout history. Families, despite their varying forms and functions, are expected to 'look after their own' and generally they do, although the nature of that caring and the family structures underpinning it vary greatly. Family-based care experiences will vary with the nature and extent of care required, but the recognition of the potential stress involved, for both parties to the care, can be set alongside an exploration of coping strategies and reported satisfactions arising from caregiving (Nolan, Grant and Keady, 1996). The capacity of families to care will also be subject to the same range of influences as affect lifestyles and relationships generally – the social, cultural and economic environment, including wealth distribution, the community, the neighbourhood and friendship networks, in the context of high geographical mobility, as well as the prevailing political, policy and belief structures.

Such factors will also, of course, influence the nature and basis of formalised and regulated care systems as well as any charitable or private sources of care or support. Paid and regulated care, however society organises the paying, is by definition a form of care that is assumed not to arise spontaneously as a result of a naturally occurring, affectional relationship. Regulation and payment is seen as necessary to engender and sustain it. Raising questions about whether 'stay-at-home' mothers, for example, should be paid, generates heated debate precisely because it appears to challenge deep-seated assumptions about obligations to provide and rights to receive spontaneous care. Forms of regulation or checking, even at the extreme as with children at risk of abuse, for example, are fraught with emotional conflict. Family care is widely seen as the ideal with paid care as second best – a substitute, as it were, for the genuine article.

The current emphases in community care involve sustaining family-based care and modelling substitutes on a notion of family care. This approach tends now to be seen as the best option in the wake of institutional abuse scandals and exposés. More exploration of the assumptions underlying this is needed. Sheila Peace, Leonie Kellaher and Dianne Willcocks begin to address this (Peace, Kellaher and Willcocks, 1997). They ask how far residential care models can ever meet the needs of ageing generations where an increasing premium is put on privacy and on individualised, and privatised, lives. Domestic-scale living with sufficient support seems increasingly an option for those with means, while a majority are effectively still institutionalised. The notion, however, that 'good care' should be modelled on an idealised western version of family and home may be ultimately misleading. (See, for example, Dalley, 1996, for an extended discussion of this.) It may restrict vision in reflecting on factors which contribute to overall quality of life.

Care, whether good or abusive, is hard to define precisely. Interpretations may range from care which involves an intimate physical dependency to care which is more akin to support and encouragement. It may also be seen as a disempowering, dependency-inducing process, or at the opposite extreme, as a wholly enabling, non-possessive form of assistance. Such variations in perception are only partially related to the needs and care tasks involved. More significant is the nature of the relationship and the underlying assumptions, reflected in part in the language used. An individual in control of his or her life with adequate funds is more likely to think in terms of buying in some support or personal assistance than to think of buying care. 'Please would you care for me', has an odd ring to it, rather reminiscent of trying to buy friendship with sweets.

Meanings and language grow up alongside changing ideas and practices. New ideas, new policies or new research evidence can hijack existing meanings and shift them in subtle but different directions. Language is political in the sense that it can have a powerful influence on how people's circumstances are interpreted and on what happens as a result. The feeling is growing amongst some service-user groups, that the term 'care' itself, as in 'community care' or 'social care' is highly undesirable because it portrays an image of people as dependent on others. We argue that the way the concept of 'care' is used and understood reflects as well as influences actual experiences of care and caring and the consequences for quality of life.

The complexity of the term 'care' is acknowledged throughout the book, but we have chosen to retain it in view of its current significance in health and social policy legislation. We also value the appeal of the broader sense of caring as an acceptance that people and their circumstances matter. Tom Kitwood, for example, says 'to have concern for another person is above all else, to experience a feeling, a "movement of the soul", in which that person's being is honoured and respected as if it were one's own' (Kitwood, 1990). Such caring would seem to have the potential to include direct personal care, practical or emotional support and a range of forms of personal assistance. It also has the potential to have a significant impact on people's quality of life.

We try in the book to keep sight of such fundamental aspects of care, without getting too lost in the realms of abstract discussion. Clarifying core principles and setting broad theoretical frameworks are important tasks, best achieved, we believe, by maintaining a base in real experiences. The chapters in this collection take different approaches, but all set out to integrate a more theoretical analysis of the concept of 'care' with attention to direct experiences of care in a wide range of settings and contexts.

Multiple perspectives

The framing and impetus behind this book stem largely from a commitment to exploring this kind of direct experience. In particular the editors set out to bring together ideas developed in relation to different client groups. The interests of the authors span a wide range of care-related issues and draw upon different academic backgrounds, including sociology, social policy, psychology, history, geography, social work and nursing. Research and teaching in the School of Health and Social Welfare at the Open University involves an explicit effort towards the inclusion of service-users' voices. Older people, people with learning difficulties or mental health problems, disabled people as well as those involved in supporting or providing care all have some voice in the planning and development of courses on health and social care issues. Multi-disciplinary teams and a multi-professional focus in the courses create a continual pressure towards inclusive thinking and analysis. The authors have been able to bring their diverse academic backgrounds to the writing of this book alongside a shared interest in seeking out common frameworks and conceptualisations. The book sets out to draw different perspectives and paradigms into the frame and to discover what, if anything, flows from that.

It has been suggested (Gubrium, 1995) that the time has come to allow for 'multiple discourses of "caregiving"'. Research and writing about care has, Gubrium suggests, become so all-embracing and voluminous that it is 'virtually impossible to contain within a coherent scheme of understanding'. The difficulty stems in part from the absence of any such overall scheme. The conceptualisation, as well as the practice and policy in relation to care, has inevitably evolved from different starting points bringing a number of different agendas to the debates, as the following examples illustrate.

For the nursing profession, discussion of 'care' has been profoundly influenced by the drive towards the creation of a new identity for nurses (see, for example, Clay, 1987; Maggs, 1987; Carper, 1978; Porter, 1993), distinct from that of doctor's handmaiden and including professional nursing care as a central element.

For feminists, 'care' debates have involved paradoxically both the owning of 'caring' as an emotional and task-based role to be valued more highly by society (Parker, 1981; Ungerson, 1987; Dalley, 1996; Qureshi and Walker, 1989), and in parallel the highlighting of caring as a 'burden' falling primarily on women, from which women need some protection (Kahana and Young, 1990).

Dalley in particular, in her revised edition (Dalley, 1996) strives for a collectivist model of caring in which the needs of all parties are taken into account.

For disabled people, the debates are about the need to struggle against the imposition of a disabled identity and dependency-inducing care relationships (e.g. Abberley, 1993; Morris, 1994). The confusion and conflicts between such agendas are highlighted when disabled feminists, such as Jenny Morris, point up the issues.

Anti-racist commentators have highlighted concerns about ethno-centric formulations of care, racist labelling, exclusion and inappropriate care services. Following the Wagner Report (Wagner, 1987), which was felt to have addressed these issues inadequately, a Black Perspectives Group was set up to review the situation. The findings in their report (Jones, Philips and Maynard, 1992), (also summarised in Allott and Robb, 1998), stress the importance of black leadership in providing appropriate residential and personal care.

For social policy analysts, on the other hand, the debate has been about market forces in the name of diversification and choice and the construction of individually tailored and community-based care pack-ages (albeit in the context of dwindling resource and increasing need).

Amongst such diversity of interests, it is hard to discover a coherent scheme of understanding. If multiple discourses are to flourish and to draw critically and constructively upon each other, however, there needs to be some common analysis as a starting point. Gubrium (1995) calls for a critical assessment of the field to include three features: 1) an exploration of the language, epistemology and ideology of caregiving; 2) the lived experience of caregiving and receiving care, including processes involved in the constitution and transformation of social relationships as 'care relationships'; 3) the inclusion and critical theor-etical appraisal of a wider range of participating voices, recognising that different models may be needed to allow for distinctive differences.

The approach of this book has much in common with this analysis. It looks, for example, *at similarities and differences in the conceptualisation and language of care across time*. It looks at shifts in relationships, value base, personal and professional roles and assumptions, and at changing emphases in social policy. This falls in Gubrium's first category as an exploration of the language, epistemology and ideology of caregiving.

In terms of Gubrium's second category, 'the lived experience of caregiving and receiving care', the book looks *across different care roles and contexts*. It looks at family-based care, community care, institutional care and across the health and social care divide. It looks at how the setting in which care is delivered may make a difference to the roles that are played out and the nature of the care provided, whether care, support or something else. As to the implication that people will belong either to the category of carer or cared for: the reality is rather one of shifting, fluid boundaries in which roles form and reform. A child may care for a disabled parent. A person with learning difficulties may care for an older relative. An elderly person may care for a mentally distressed spouse. Carers of any description may equally be in need of care themselves. In the broader sense of care, everyone is dependent upon some care from others throughout life for both physical and emotional health and development.

Finally, Gubrium's 'wider range of participating voices' is addressed as the book looks at *issues associated with different 'client groups'*. Does it, for example, make a difference to the meaning or purpose of caregiving or receiving if people are disabled, have mental health problems, are chronically sick or dying or are elderly? The book considers the issues which arise for family or paid carers or professionals; raising the question, what, if anything, does formal care have in common with informal care.

Assuming the book succeeds in drawing some of these multiple perspectives into the frame, what kind of critical scrutiny can be brought to bear; what kind of analysis may help towards the development of useful theoretical frameworks? What, in other words, do we learn from the exercise? A tentative answer might point to the identification of some shared agendas as the primary purposes of care and caregiving, with notions of empowerment and the enhancement and facilitation of choice and control as prime motivations. Such analysis seems often to emerge from a balanced recognition of common human needs and a respect for human rights.

Promoting rights and choices for some brings the risk of increased responsibilities and decreased resources for others. The inevitable conflicts appear to be highlighted and sometimes heightened by care relationships and transactions. The power imbalance, which is almost intrinsic to caregiving, plays into such difficulties. Any analysis or theorising, it would seem from this, needs to take account of the role of caregiving as part of a mediating and negotiating process around power, the meeting of human needs and the promotion of rights and choices. A recognition of the conflicts intrinsic to care or support, as well as the common agendas, will be essential if a balance is to be struck across the interests of the many participants in the process.

Exploring care

Messages from direct care experiences, as well as a concern with more theoretical issues, flow through all of the chapters in this book. Having said that, the ordering of the chapters moves the book primarily from the particular, direct care experiences to the more general and theoretical debates. Some chapters particularly provide valuable insights from the 'wider range of participating voices' called for by Gubrium. In the first chapter, *Living in residential care*, for example, Dorothy Atkinson asks what can be discovered about the quality of life in residential homes for people with learning difficulties as she poses some challenging questions about the models of 'home' on which much residential care practice is based. How far, she asks, can we hear their voices? How far can we go towards discovering the quality of their lived experience and what 'care' feels like for them?

The second chapter, in a different, more institutional setting, is also trying to find out what people, this time older people, feel about the care they receive. In *Discovering the present in stories about the past*, older people in institutional care are shown to have considerable awareness of the care context. Their constructions and interpretations of care and their expectations of it belie the passive dependency relationship they may appear to have. Using 'asides' from life history interviews, the authors, John Adams, Joanna Bornat and Mary Prickett, open a window on the meanings such older people attach to caregiving processes and to the roles they are expected to occupy within them.

In *Terminal care or terminal carelessness*, Jeanne Katz examines what can be learned about care experiences from developments in hospice care for dying people. Although seen as a rather specialist area, Katz shows that there is potential for generalising to more diverse settings. The experiences underlying such care are equally relevant to our understanding of hospital or home settings where death may occur. At such an acutely stressful time, emotions are heightened, but the care still needs to embrace a range of needs and wishes of the individual balanced with those of the relatives. Acknowledging and working with different voices and roles is at the heart of such work. The role of the professional nurse-carer has gone through quite profound shifts to achieve this.

In all of these chapters, the impact on social relationships is implicit in the discussions of people's experiences. In the next few chapters, which continue to reflect a range of participating voices, the emphasis shifts more explicitly onto this aspect. *Young carers* by Stan Tucker and Penny Liddiard focuses on the experiences, needs and rights of young carers. This challenge to more conventional stereotypes of 'carer' or 'cared for' reminds us that caregiving roles may be continually shifting across boundaries. This is a powerful example of turning assumptions about power and responsibility in care relationships on their head. Issues about the need to balance needs and rights also emerge.

In *Care, support or something else?* Jill Reynolds and Jan Walmsley discuss the possibilities and implications of replacing the concept of care with models of support for independent living. Listening to the experiences of adults with learning difficulties and adults with mental health problems, they highlight the potential conflicts of interest in the relationships between carers and those who are cared for. They also explore the similarities and differences in the experiences of these two 'client groups'.

Normality and disabling care, by John Swain and Sally French, takes such challenges further. To be cared for, they argue, involves the imposition of a dependent identity, and frequently the taking over of responsibility by another. It creates a 'them' and 'us' relationship in which normality/abnormality are the valued and devalued opposites. A preferred alternative is presented in which the concept of 'difference' is pivotal. This creates an interesting link forward to Ann Brechin's chapter at the end of the book and the discussion of 'difference' there.

Moyra Sidell addresses another kind of challenge to more conventional concepts of care. In *Treatment or tender loving care*, she considers some of the influences and traditions which hamper the capacity of orthodox medicine to provide effective care to people with chronic illness. The emphasis on cure still casts chronic problems as medical failures and the repertoire and approaches of medicine make the achievement of symptom relief difficult, if not unlikely. Alternative therapies, drawing upon quite different conceptions of health and 'disease', appear more ready and more able to offer appropriate care geared to the needs of the whole person.

Taking in some ways a step back from particular relationships and experiences, Sheila Peace, in *Caring in place*, examines the interactions between experiences of care and the setting in which the caregiving occurs. Looking at both family and residential care settings, Peace develops a framework for understanding the influences of environment, private and public space and the pressures and expectations on roles and relationships which arise from such factors. In a sense this chapter is transitional in moving the book on towards chapters which begin more explicitly to address theoretical frameworks of care and caregiving, and to explore the underpinning language, epistemology and ideology of care. The conflicts between the needs and rights of different participants in giving and receiving care are negotiated and resolved in a myriad of ways and different interpretations and different power bases hold sway. The earlier chapters have provided illustrations of some of these agendas and conflicts in process. The later chapters continue this exploration, beginning to draw out some more explanatory frameworks.

In *Caregiving, carework and professional care*, Celia Davies draws out some of the elements, both historical and current, which affect our understanding of care. In particular, she draws attention to the influence of the language of care. She highlights the gender issues reflected in such language and consequently embedded in our asssumptions about the nature of care in practice. Her focus is primarily on professional care and nursing in particular, where she draws on some highly evocative descriptions of caring in action. In examining these, she traces the meanings of caring, caregiving and carework and tackles the issue of conceptually integrating the relational 'caring about' aspects with the task-based 'caring for'.

The emergence of care as a policy takes an even broader and more historical perspective. Julia Johnson traces the evolution of care as a legislative and social policy concept with a focus on the historical developments and shifts leading up to the current policies of community care. She explores some of the origins of care and how things used to be. It is easy to think back to an imagined golden age, but the realities have often been very harsh. Equally it is often tempting to think that we have now learned the lessons of the past and will not make the same mistakes again. Rather, in focusing on the past, it becomes easier to see that care has a history, of language, of meaning and of ideology, which inevitably continues to influence the present.

Linda Jones also takes a historical perspective in *Changing health care*. Here she considers the implications of the new terminology of 'healthcare', which seems to have replaced 'health care'. What this shift in language reflects and what it implies about changes in the meaning, ideology and practice of care, are explored in this chapter. If 'healthcare' is something which is bought and sold in a market, what impact does that have on the delivery and experience of care at the personal level? The conflicts and negotiations reflected in this and in the previous chapters are essentially a feature of society's struggle to arrive at acceptable solutions to the provision of caregiving in society. As ideology and power balances shift, so will the perceived appropriateness of different styles of caring. A shift towards a more compassionate society, for example, inevitably brings issues of human needs and human rights more to the fore.

In the final chapter, *What makes for good care?*, Ann Brechin considers approaches to evaluating quality of care. In exploring what might be seen as the shared agendas of 'good care', however, the potential conflicts between different people's needs and rights become apparent also. To understand how 'good care' can be achieved, it is necessary to understand these conflicts and how they may best be approached and resolved. There are influences at work at policy level and in terms of work practices, training and support for professionals. These alone profoundly affect the nature of care relationships and the assumptions and expectations on both sides. There are also, Brechin argues, important factors at an individual and interpersonal level, particularly in relation to perceptions of 'difference'. Negotiating caregiving processes and relationships involves psychological processes which can support or challenge such interactions and make for 'better' or 'worse' care experiences?

From perspectives to principles

What conclusions, then, can be drawn from this book? Quite different kinds of rationale co-exist to 'explain' care: human instinct of the 'mother love' variety; religious teaching – 'love thy neighbour'; social justice; economic arguments; human rights arguments. Ultimately these reflect different paradigms. The book makes clear that even within the context of the current welfare state, there are quite different ways of understanding and talking about care, in relation, for example, to health care as opposed to social care.

Informal or family care shares a common purpose with socially organised care in that both are concerned with caring for or supporting others. And yet, there are important differences too, most clearly in the nature of the relationship and the direct link between the relationship and motivation to provide care. In family care it is the relationship which determines the care; in formal care it is the provision of care which creates the relationship. It is not as simple, however, as one involving 'caring about' and the other involving 'caring for'. There are overlaps in both. But the differences are important and need to be better understood.

Does this book take us to any conclusions about the relative power of different paradigms? Or about commonalities or differences across health and social care, across family and paid care, or across the carer/cared-for dichotomy? Perhaps the clearest message that emerges consistently across all the chapters in this book, to be developed most fully in the final chapter, is about the importance of attending to the needs of all participants in care. Offering and receiving care, even if it is reconstructed as support, involves an interpersonal relationship which impacts on people's identity and sense of self, for both caregivers and those receiving care. The processes are value-laden and carry meanings and implications about roles and expectations, often at a very deep level.

Common agendas for 'care' or 'support' emerge and can be described in terms of quality of life. Concerns include personal empowerment, the promotion of choice and of self-esteem, the creation of opportunities for a desired balance between independence, interdependence and dependency; between comfort, safety and protection from harm on the one hand and the right to choose and live an ordinary life until death with commensurate risks and freedoms on the other. What is often lost in identifying such agendas is the relevance of such issues for the caregivers also. In a just society, with a commitment to equal rights, it may be assumed that everyone's rights and needs should be of equal concern. The same template of agendas can therefore be applied to carers.

It is reasonable to point out, however, that a life spent in care is a very different matter from someone whose paid job involves a set number of hours per week providing care for others. And there are indeed significant differences not just of degree, but also of kind between giving and receiving care. It may, nevertheless, be helpful to notice the common human framework within which obligations, needs and rights are negotiated. This applies not only to frameworks of human interaction, but equally to the common human settings and contexts, within which caregiving will occur, and to the social and political structures which will both reflect and determine care experiences in practice. The mediation and transactions involved in caring are at the core of humanity and civilisation.

It may be more helpful if people are not stereotyped into carer or cared-for roles, but rather are seen as having more fluid, flexible and complex identities in which care relationships and functions are but one element. At the same time, care relationships for all parties involved can have a profound impact on identity and self-esteem as well as on life opportunities and experience. This points up the importance of continuing to learn directly from real experiences of giving and receiving care, drawing out any core principles cautiously against the backdrop of this wide range of participating voices.

References

Abberley, P. (1993) 'Disabled people and normality', in J. Swain et al. (eds), *Disabling Society – Enabling Environments*. London: Sage.

Allott, M. and Robb, M. (eds) (1998) *Understanding Health and Social Care: An Introductory Reader*. London: Sage, in association with The Open University.

Black Perspectives Sub-group (1997) 'Black perspectives in residential care', in M. Allott and M. Robb (eds), *Understanding Health and Social Care: An Introductory Reader*. London: Sage.

Carper, B. (1978) 'Fundamental patterns of knowing in nursing', *Advances in Nursing Science*, 1 (1): 13–23.

Clay, T. (1987) *Nurses, Power and Politics*. Oxford: Heinemann Medical Books.

Dalley, G. (1996) *Ideologies of Caring: Rethinking Community and Collectivism*, 2nd edn. Basingstoke and London: Macmillan (in association with the Centre for Policy on Ageing).

Gubrium, J.F. (1995) 'The caregiver relationship – introduction', *Qualitative Health Research*, 5 (3): 267–9.

Jones, A., Philips, M. and Maynard, C. (1992) *A Home from Home*. London: NISW.

Kahana, E. and Young, R. (1990) 'Clarifying the caregiving paradigm: challenges for the future', in D.E. Biegel and A. Blum (eds), *Aging and Caregiving: Theory, Research and Policy*. Newbury Park, CA: Sage.

Kitwood, T. (1990) *Concern for Others: A New Psychology of Conscience and Morality*. London and New York: Routledge.

Maggs, C. (1987) *Nursing History: The State of the Art*. London: Croom-Helm.

Morris, J. (1994) 'Community care or independent living?', *Critical Social Policy*, 40 (14): 24–45.

Nolan, M., Grant, G. and Keady, J. (1996) *Understanding Family Care*. Buckingham and Philadelphia: Open University Press.

Parker, R.A. (1981) 'Tending and social policy', in E.M. Goldberg and S. Hatch (eds), *A New Look at the Personal Social Services*. London: Policy Studies Institute.

Peace, S., Kellaher, L. and Willcocks, D. (1997) *Re-evaluating Residential Care*. Buckingham and Philadelphia: Open University Press.

Porter, S. (1993) 'Nursing research conventions: objectivity or obfuscation', *Journal of Advanced Nursing*, 18: 137–43.

Qureshi, H. and Walker, A. (1989) *The Caring Relationship: Elderly People and their Families*. Basingstoke: Macmillan Education Ltd.

Ungerson, C. (1983) 'Why do women care?', in J. Finch and D. Groves (eds), *A Labour of Love: Women, Work and Caring*. London: Routledge and Kegan Paul.

Ungerson, C. (1987) *Policy is Personal: Sex Gender and Informal Care*. London: Tavistock.

Wagner, G. (1987) *Residential Care: A Positive Choice*. London: HMSO.

1

LIVING IN RESIDENTIAL CARE

Dorothy Atkinson

This chapter attempts to explore residential care from the viewpoint of the people most centrally concerned; those who actually live there. Although it focuses in particular on the experiences of people with learning disabilities, it draws on the wider literature of residential care, especially for older people, and it has implications too for 'good practice' in residential care settings across the board. My primary focus is, however, on residential care in relation to people with learning disabilities and my mission is to explore, insofar as this is possible, what it is like to live in a residential setting. The chapter can be seen as a detailed case study of one of the themes raised in Chapter 8: how far can 'home' be re-created in a residential setting?

The term 'residential care' here refers to staffed accommodation which operates outside the remaining network of long-stay hospitals. It includes hostel-type accommodation, catering for relatively large numbers of people (from around 10 places up to settings of 20–30 or more places) and 'ordinary housing' catering for small groups of varying sizes, but typically four to six (and up to 10) people. Residential care in the learning disability field has a relatively short history. It has, by and large, grown up alongside hospital provision, becoming more and more an alternative form of care. Indeed hostel care – as it then was – was seen as an important manifestation of 'care in the community' in the 1960s and 1970s. Now residential care, in its widest sense, has largely replaced institutional provision in many areas.

This chapter will start with a brief look at the history of residential care and then look at its current place in the lives of people with learning disabilities. What is it like to live in a residential home? Is it possible to find out what people themselves feel about their experience of residential care? As part of a *care audit* of 12 residential homes, run by a not-for-profit trust, I set out to find answers to those questions. This chapter will look at the possibilities, and the pitfalls, of research which involves informal contact, participant observation and simply 'being there' as ways of finding out about everyday life in a residential home.

Although a picture emerged of what life was like in each of the homes, I was often left wondering whose picture this was. Was it mine? Or did it truly reflect what people thought and felt about their own experiences? There are no easy answers to these questions either, although this chapter will look at the implications of having to ask them. Put together, though, the detailed accounts of 12 residential homes begin to form a bigger picture of residential care and, perhaps, one that is more reliable. This chapter will look at how the homes in this study cared for, or cared about, the people who lived there.

What is residential care?

For many people with learning disabilities 'home' is a residential unit in the community, run by paid staff. Such homes vary in size and ownership, but they are the essence of residential care. Although residential care is a product of an earlier policy of 'care in the community', it survives today as part of current provision for people with learning disabilities.

Although small Board of Control approved institutions and hostel-type annexes to hospitals were around on a modest scale from the 1930s, residential care really began to emerge in the 1960s as an alternative to the family home or the long-stay institution. Thirty years ago, residential care for people with learning disabilities meant hostel care and, as the hostels had evolved from institutional care, they retained many of the organisational and staffing features of the long-stay hospitals. They were, nevertheless, seen as a major advance on hospital care because of their relatively small size and their location in the community. These features were not in themselves enough to mitigate the institutional practices that prevailed and, by the 1970s, the phenomenon of the 'mini-institution' was being discussed (Tyne, 1978). This term is still in use, and is being applied to many present-day residential homes especially those which have been set up by NHS trusts to replace the hospitals which are closing down (Collins, 1993). The term 'micro-institutionalisation' has also been coined to reflect the real-life experiences of people with learning disabilities in the 1990s (Sinson, 1993).

No one set out to build and run mini-institutions, either in the 1960s or subsequently. Indeed the move away from institutional care, at first in a small way but now on a large scale, has been welcomed at every stage as a positive move forward. The 1959 Mental Health Act, which replaced the 1913 and 1927 Mental Deficiency Acts (with their emphasis on institutional provision), took the enlightened view that many people with learning disabilities could, with support, live outside the long-stay hospitals. The 1959 Act encouraged local authorities to provide residential care for those people who did not need hospital treatment. Residential care in those days meant hostel accommodation, but in fact few new buildings appeared and there was no wholesale move to community care. In practice, the large hospitals continued to be the main providers of accommodation outside the family home.

A major boost to community care was the 1971 White Paper, *Better Services for the Mentally Handicapped*. It was published against the backdrop of the first reported hospital scandals at Ely and Farleigh and the publication of Pauline Morris's book, *Put Away* (1969), which highlighted the poor conditions prevailing in the long-stay hospitals. The White Paper aimed to speed up the 'shift in emphasis from care in the hospital to care in the community'. It regretted that only a small start had been made towards providing residential care for people with learning disabilities. The total number of places in residential homes for adults in England and Wales, in 1969, was 4,350. This compared with a total of 52,450 adults who were then living in hospital.

This was a huge imbalance, and subsequent policy statements and documents continued to argue the virtues of community care over hospital care. (See, for example, the 1980 *Review of Services*; the 1981 *Care in Action* guidelines; the 1981 Consultative Document, *Care in the Community*; the 1983 document, *Care in the Community*; and the 1985 House of Commons Social Services Committee Report on *Community Care*.)

Residential care really took off in the 1980s. This was the result of the various policy initiatives together with some modest financial incentives. Later on, a framework was provided by the Department of Health White Paper, *Caring for People* (1989) and the 1990 NHS and Community Care Act which followed. Residential care grew rapidly in the 1980s. In the years 1979–1989, for example, the number of places in residential homes more than doubled, from 15,154 to 31,344 (Department of Health, 1992).

Although this is a continuation of a trend which began seriously 30 years ago, it has been accompanied by major changes both in who provides the care, and how. The providers now increasingly include the voluntary and private sectors, as well as local authorities and NHS Trusts. In fact, residential places in the private and voluntary sectors have increased more rapidly in recent years than other sectors. In 1986–1989, for example, places in private homes increased from 1,653 to 7,588 (Department of Health, 1992).

Residential care initially evolved from institutional care. It has subsequently evolved in others ways too. The influence of normalisation (Wolfensberger, 1972) and the focus on 'ordinary life' ideas (King's Fund Centre, 1980), have led to changes in the philosophy and underpinning values of many residential services. In some instances this has meant the development of much smaller residential homes, often using ordinary housing. Even the remaining larger homes and hostels are increasingly likely to divide their large groups and groupings into smaller family-size groups of residents, with a view to encouraging personal and social development both within the home and outside. In spite of these changes, there is evidence to suggest that even the smaller homes can be run as 'mini-institutions' for the benefit of managers and staff rather than residents (Collins, 1993).

What makes a residential home into a 'mini-institution'? And more importantly when does residential care become a real home for the people who live there? The quest for a 'real home' for people living in residential care has proved an elusive one. The 1971 White Paper proposed that the term 'hostel', which suggested impermanence and austerity, be dropped in favour of the term 'home'. It advised that such homes should become 'homely'; in particular they should be small (no more than 25 adults, or 20 children) and mixed-sex. Homes should create a 'substitute family group' and have a 'family atmosphere'. The Jay Committee Report (1979) echoed this advice in its recommendation that people with learning disabilities 'should live in small family-type groups', and be accommodated in ordinary homes.

What makes a 'real home'? Is it the size and the nature of the accommodation? Is it some recourse to 'family values'? Many attempts have been made, over the years, to recreate a more domestic environment in residential settings across the board. This has been the case particularly in relation to older people whose admission to a residential setting almost always follows the loss of their real home and possessions. Policy makers, analysts, researchers and regulators have sought to define – and create – 'homely' environments based on principles such as fulfilment, privacy, dignity, choice and autonomy (Centre for Policy on Ageing, 1984; NISW, 1988).

A residential home can simulate some aspects of home life but it cannot be that 'real home' which offers sanctuary, space, occupation and identity. Any residential setting requires compromises – the individual is a member of a group, after all, and is only one small part of an organisation. Inevitably the needs of the group, and the interests of the organisation, will prevail at times at the expense of the individual. In the end, as Higgins (1989) argues, 'the real sense of home is essentially a metaphysical concept' (p. 172). 'Home' cannot be replicated through 'more single rooms, more privacy, more resident involvement . . .' (1989: 172); but still 'home' remains a goal in residential care. The aim continues to be to provide as homely and home-like a setting as possible, with some semblance of a real home life for the people who live there.

Can residential settings be evaluated in terms of their homely and home-like qualities? Are some more like 'real homes' than others? And how do we tell? Only the people who live there, presumably, can assess the metaphysical 'sense of home'. The trouble is, they may not be in a position to say – as I and many others have discovered.

Finding out about the quality of care

Is residential care a 'positive choice' for people with learning disabilities? Does it provide a 'positive experience'? And does it ensure a 'better quality of life than the resident could enjoy in any other setting'? These are essential aspects of residential care, according to the Wagner Report, *Residential Care: A Positive Choice* (NISW, 1988). But how far do these recommendations fit with the experiences of people with learning disabilities themselves? And, more importantly, how do you find out?

It is not a straightforward task to find out about the quality of residential care – although I was asked to do so by the Fremantle Trust (a not-for-profit Buckinghamshire-based community housing trust). As part of a series of commissioned studies (for example, on buildings, costs and staffing) of the residential homes they had taken over from the local authority, the Trust also wanted a detailed audit of the quality of care in a sample of the homes concerned. Three care auditors, myself included, were commissioned to carry out *care audits* of residential homes for elderly people and people with mental health problems or learning disabilities. My task was to find out about the quality of care in residential homes for people with learning disabilities from the point of view of the residents themselves.

Finding out is not simply a matter of running a series of interviews, and asking everyone what they think of the home they are living in – or working in. One's home, or one's livelihood, may be at stake, so there may be a natural reluctance to speak out about anything that is less than satisfactory. Several studies of residential homes for older people, for example, have found residents to be reticent in talking about their experiences. (See, for example, Willcocks et al., 1987; Peace et al., 1982; Weaver et al., 1985).

Added to this is the fact that most people living in residential homes have never been asked their views before, and have little experience to draw on in this respect, a point made by Youll and McCourt-Perring (1993). There is also evidence to suggest that the long-term effect of residential care, for some people, is 'inertia or apparent helplessness', especially in regimes where everything is decided and done by other people, (Youll and McCourt-Perring, p. 162). This view is echoed by Tim Booth (1993) who suggests that residential living can lead to 'unthinking compliance', 'inertia' and 'a kind of enforced helplessness' (1993: 161). Compliance can only be counteracted, he argues, by more responsive services where residents feel free to speak their minds. Similarly, Kellaher and Peace (1993) have found that the right 'climate' is necessary in a residential home for people to be themselves – and, presumably, to speak for themselves.

The methodology used in the care audit had to take account of these factors. It was not possible to rely solely on conventional interviews, as all the evidence suggested they would be threatening and therefore counter-productive. In the learning disability field there are evaluative guidelines such as the checklist devised by Lesley Hoyes for assessing residential care (Hoyes, 1990). However, we wanted to tap into people's subjective and qualitative experiences of care, both the giving and the receiving of it, rather than to focus solely on objective criteria such as the location of the home or its links with the community. Other ways of finding out from people with learning disabilities have been pioneered by Julie Wilkinson and Anne Chappell. The 'being there' approach, devised by Wilkinson, involved her in shadowing (one at a time) the residents of a small residential home as they went about their everyday lives (Wilkinson, 1989). Anne Chappell's ethnographic study of four private residential homes involved her in participant observation and informal conversations, as well as interviews (Chappell, 1993).

The approach devised for the care audit was a 12-hour immersion in the life of each home. The 12 hours were usually split, rather than continuous, and were intended to cover different staff shifts and hand-overs: key points in the typical day, such as getting up and meal times; and, where possible, to cover two or more days. The immersion principle was simple. We watched, listened, took part and joined in whatever was happening, and we took every opportunity informally, and sometimes more formally, to speak to residents and staff, individually or in groups or casual groupings.

My remit was to visit 12 residential homes for people with learning disabilities. They ranged in size from a 37-bedded hostel, and two large-ish homes of 18 and 25 beds, to seven staffed group homes, each with seven or fewer residents. The 12-hour immersion approach was applied in each home, regardless of its size. Every effort was made to engage people in conversations about 'their' home, and these conversations could take place formally or informally, in private or in public, in a quiet corner or in a group discussion – and at any point in the home's waking day. More focused interviews were held with home managers and staff (including domestic, clerical and catering staff as well as residential workers). In all, the residential units were the workplace of 120 staff (all categories) and were 'home' to 147 people with learning disabilities. I met most people in both categories, and spoke directly to as many as possible.

As well as talking to staff and residents I was observing what was happening around me. I wrote detailed field notes on my observations at every opportunity. What I *saw* counted just as much as what I *heard* – especially given the constraints that prevent people in residential homes from speaking freely. Observation is an important skill in this context. Although it is impossible to see 'the objectives, the aspirations and intentions of all who live and work at a home', those intangible aspects of life are influential in shaping the residential experience. They need to be recorded, therefore, but this can only be done through the careful observation of the everyday events, incidents and interactions which provide the clues to their meaning. (Observation is discussed in the Department of Health programme *Making Sense of Inspection*, 1990.)

Did the immersion approach work? In one sense it did, in that very detailed pictures emerged of each home. Wherever possible, staff and residents' views were incorporated into the accounts but, as predicted, residents' views were not always forthcoming and, if they were, they were often of the 'It's nice' and 'I like it here' variety. The assessment of the care offered in these homes, and how it was experienced by residents, thus had to rely to a considerable degree on my observations – on my experiences, in fact, just as much as other people's. This was not for want of trying, however, as I took every opportunity to engage with residents and find out what they really thought. The following extract from my research diary illustrates this:

> I spent a lot of time with residents, chatting in the public areas and, by invitation, talking more privately with some people in their rooms. It was difficult, in a group of this size [seven residents], not to seem intrusive and my way of mitigating this was to move around between groups and individuals. Even so, one anxious resident decided that I must be a plain-clothes policewoman come to collect evidence on what he saw as a recent misdemeanour.

Twelve hours is long enough for most people to relax, and get on with their everyday activities. Even if residents were unable or unwilling to talk in detail about their experience of life in 'their' home, (and this was by no means universal) they would often demonstrate some of their feelings about it. Just 'being there' for long periods meant that, inevitably, I got involved in such events as meals, trips out, meetings and home days, and had many opportunities to see for myself what life was like in a particular home. In addition, most members of staff were happy to talk about 'their' home/workplace; its aims, philosophy, practices and regime. Their detailed accounts of what should and does happen, were invaluable commentaries against which to assess the actual working of any particular home.

The commentary and the observation did not always match up, however. In one home where the staff talked about the importance of 'respect', 'dignity', and 'adult choices', I observed what happened at supper-time and wrote this in my field notes afterwards:

> Good practices fell apart at this point. 'Daphne' [not her real name] served food out to the already-seated residents and to me. No-one waited for anyone else, they simply ate. There was no real conversation, though one or two people spoke occasionally, not necessarily to anyone in particular nor expecting anyone else to take any notice. I tried to initiate a conversation by asking about tonight's club, but failed. I got no reply. Daphne didn't join us, she stood by and watched, and ate later. When they'd finished, each person took their own plate to the sink and rinsed it separately.

This lack of fit between what staff say and what they do has been reported elsewhere in relation to studies of homes for older people (Kellaher, et al., 1990).

Experiencing the residential 'climate'

As a care auditor I was, of course, an outsider to the residential homes I visited. My remit was to listen, and to observe, and to report on what I heard and saw. But supposing some people could or would not speak about their experiences, or their views about their circumstances differed from those of other – more powerful – people? How was I to make sense of silences and omissions, as well as discordant voices? And how was I to be objective in my observations? How could I really know what it was like to live in any of the 12 homes?

The supper-time scene, above, was my description of a meal-time, and clearly it did not meet my expectations of a convivial social occasion. It was my view which prevailed and was recorded, however, whatever anyone else thought about the (non) event. It may indeed have met the expectations of the other participants. Perhaps people who ate together every day no longer had anything to say to each other; or maybe they were bored with one another's company or were overawed by the presence of a stranger, or were simply engaged in getting on with their meal.

Some research studies into the quality of life in residential homes for people with learning disabilities have sought to avoid these difficulties by taking an 'objective' approach, and relying on measurements and rating scales. (See, for example, Felce and Perry 1993, Perry and Felce, 1995.) These have generally focused on client satisfaction with the service, and/or have looked at the physical, material and social well-being of residents. Such studies may be limited in practice by the reluctance or unwillingness of people with learning disabilities to make evaluative comments about their circumstances, and they may need to be supplemented, therefore, by direct observations of life in the home (McVilly, 1995).

My visits included the finding out, and recording, of basic facts about each home: for example, the number of residents and staff, and the ratio of one to the other; the shift patterns in the home; handover times and procedures; rules, routines and record-keeping. However, the real challenge was to get behind the facts of a home and see, or even feel, what it was like to live there. A care auditor, like an inspector or regulator, has to rely on art as well as science (Clough, 1994). The 'scientific' use of guidelines and checklists is relatively straightforward compared with what the 'artist' has to do: 'to make creative leaps about what it would be like to live in that place and use imagination in searching for clues' (Clough, 1994: 96).

These creative leaps are based on 'intuitions, impressions and sub-jective understandings' of a home (Department of Health, 1990: 66). They take us into the realm of those intangible aspects of residential life which are so important yet are impossible to measure. One such intangible feature is the 'climate' of a home, its atmosphere or the feel of the place (DoH, 1990). This is experienced or sensed, it cannot be formally rated or ranked; it relies on observation or judgement, not on objective certainty.

The following extract from one of my reports focuses on what felt to me to be a free-and-easy atmosphere, or climate, in the home in question:

> During my evening visit there, a small group of people went with two staff to have a drink in the local pub. This is within easy walking distance, so a pub trip can be quite easily, and spontaneously, arranged. There was a very jolly and free-and-easy atmosphere during my visit. Someone put the kettle on to make tea for the TV-watchers; someone else (who normally speaks in a whisper) sang loudly from her bath; someone else demonstrated his gymnastic skills on the lounge floor. Bedtime is usually between 9.30 and midnight, although the resident who enjoys falling asleep on the settee in front of the late night film was already in place when I left at 11 o'clock.

This home was free-and-easy enough to tolerate, even encourage, its residents to express their individual needs and preferences within a group setting. This was not the case everywhere. Balancing the needs of the individual against the needs of the group could prove difficult, and this was reflected in the climate of the home. When the two sets of needs were, more or less, in some sort of equilibrium then the climate seemed fair and settled. When the balance swung rather too much towards the needs of the group, then the atmosphere changed and disgruntled individuals spoke out, or 'acted out', against it.

I was struck during some of my visits, by the use of 'the family' analogy by staff to describe the everyday working and atmosphere of their home. These comments were made by staff at one of the largest homes on my list:

> It's a well-organised home, like a family.

> There's a nice family atmosphere. It's as family-orientated as possible.

Residents at the same home ventured to me, in private, their own views:

> I get shouted at. I don't like it.

> Some of the staff don't know how we feel. They don't have patience, they lose their tempers.

The rhetoric of 'the family' can sound good. It suggests warmth and care, and the prospect of doing things together. The other side of family life, at least when it is applied to a residential home, is that it can be limiting, restrictive and even 'infantilising' (Chappell, 1993).

What is it like to live in a residential home?

Although the process of finding out about residential care had its drawbacks, nevertheless it seemed to work well enough to build up detailed composite pictures of individual homes. Not only this, but the care audit also provided enough information to build a bigger picture about the nature of residential care for people with learning disabilities. What makes a residential home into a mini-institution – and when, if ever, does it become a real home for its residents?

Perhaps the best place to start answering this question is with the physical location, appearance and layout of the homes. The 12 settings varied a lot in size and appearance. They reflected the passing fashions in residential care, from purpose-built hostels to 'ordinary homes'. The physical appearance and layout of the typical hostel was not conducive to ordinary life, as the following extract illustrates:

'Meadow Lodge' is situated on a campus of special facilities. It is adjacent to the hospital and not far from the prison. As a building, Meadow Lodge is far from being homely or home-like. It has several institutional features such as long corridors, a wide staircase, and heavy-duty lift, imposing hallways and landings, and large sitting and dining areas.

Even the recently designed 'Hollytrees', although physically situated 'in the community', was far from ordinary:

It is an end house, set at the corner meeting point of two streets, and is larger in size than the houses in either street (or, indeed, the whole estate). It is built in different brick, faces a different way and sits within its own perimeter wall. No-one visiting the area would have any doubt that this is a residential home of some sort.

Other factors matter, too, of course, as the discussion on 'climate' above indicated. Evidence from the 'Caring in Homes Initiative' (commissioned by the Department of Health to take up some of the recommendations of the Wagner report, and its associated review of research) suggests that people do best in residential care when there is an emphasis on individuality, and the 'whole person', rather than on collective provision for whole groups. People fare far worse when a too-protective or over-controlling regime of 'care' takes away their power to act, to decide or to speak out (Youll and McCourt-Perring, 1993).

Is there a continuum of care then? Can we identify regimes which, on the whole, relate to their residents as individuals? And can we identify those regimes which are more likely to respond to the group(s) of people who live there? The picture built up from the accumulated evidence of the 12 homes in this study suggests that homes do vary along this dimension. It is not a straightforward either/or picture, however, more a tendency in one direction rather than the other. The homes which took the individual as their starting point were likely to differ in several respects from the group-orientated homes. The former type of home afforded its residents some semblance of a 'real home' whilst the latter took on some aspects of the mini-institution.

The nature of the care regime determined many other aspects of the home. Thus a manager and staff group who stressed individuality, and worked with – and became close to – individual residents, were likely to encourage independence, financial autonomy and risk-taking. They would involve people in making everyday and far-reaching choices. Most of all, they fostered and acknowledged feelings of *reciprocity*. Staff felt they gave a lot in these circumstances, but got a lot back. Often these homes enabled people to adopt whatever appearance or lifestyle suited them best. Typically, individualised holidays, hobbies and outings were encouraged and supported.

The following extract reflects one aspect of the Hollytrees approach to the people who lived there, and came under the heading of 'respect':

All residents have their own rooms, and their privacy is respected. Residents' rooms are kept to individual standards of tidiness not to any real or notional house norms. I was struck by the respect shown by staff in two other ways. Respect for people's feelings is apparent, and this was demonstrated by the understanding of, and support for, individual reactions to a resident's sudden death. This was partially re-lived when I was shown the home video featuring the young woman concerned and one or two residents remembered how they had felt, and how they had been comforted at the time. Staff, too, remembered their own tears and sadness, and how they had supported each other and then residents – in reactions ranging from 'floods of tears' to 'getting stroppy'.

Respect for residents is also shown through positive attitudes on the part of staff. This was put very nicely, and very coherently, by a residential worker who sees the relationships at Hollytrees as *reciprocal*. She told me: 'Being here has changed us. The residents have changed us, and how we see things. They've taught us a lot. We've learnt from them.'

The emphasis in the group-orientated homes was more on the needs of the group or 'the family'. People not only lived and ate together, they went on trips, outings and holidays together. Residents were discouraged from taking risks, and choices were made from pre-set 'menus' of the clothes or supper dishes on offer. These were the homes where I was most likely to find gleaming surfaces and well-scrubbed residents. Some of the characteristics of a mini-institution identified by Collins (1993), such as an emphasis on 'rules, order and pyramidal power-relationships', were in evidence.

One such home was Peartree Cottage. This was run on family lines, a household which by and large did things together. However, there was another side to 'family life' as the following extract reveals:

> The reality is that six unrelated and very different people are, by chance rather than choice, living under the same roof. Inevitably there are differences of opinion, and tensions between people. There are emotional, sometimes violent, scenes when feelings of rage, frustration and jealousy come to the surface. The group is too small for retreat from 'the family' group or a change of company, yet too large to meet everyone's needs for attention and affirmation.

> This is a 'family' group and, whilst individuality is acknowledged, there is also an emphasis on getting on, sharing and doing things together. Individual feelings sometimes find expression in a negative way, through abusive language, for example.

Conclusion

The immersion approach worked in that it gave me an opportunity to see, hear, and even to feel, what a residential home was like. It had its limits, of course, as every attempt to study residential homes from the outside must be limited. I could only see, hear and feel so much and, at the end of my visit, I had my own home to return to.

The outcome of the care audit was twofold: a set of 12 long and detailed reports, and an overview of the findings across the whole sample of homes. It is in that overview that the individual versus the group dimension comes into sharper relief. Looking back now, it seems that those homes which took a more individualised approach were, on the whole, more outward-looking and dynamic. This had a positive effect on everyone as life was often rich, full and varied – for staff, as well as residents. The group approach could, on the other hand, lead all too easily to a static environment, where nothing changed and life became all too predictable and boring. This meant less satisfaction for all concerned, locked as they were into long-term but direction-less contact with each other. One problem for residents in this situation was how to be seen as special and separate from the group without recourse to threatening or even violent behaviour.

The need to feel valued and special is universal, as is the need to belong. That balance between individuality (being special) and the group (feeling a sense of belonging) is difficult to achieve and to maintain. A residential home takes on the semblance of a real home insofar as it gets that balance right.

Acknowledgements

Thanks are due to the Fremantle Trust for setting up the care audit, and for supporting the work involved at all stages. The Trust's commitment to developing good practices in residential care was amply demonstrated in their willingness to disseminate and implement many of the ideas arising from the project.

References

Booth, T. (1993) 'Obstacles to the development of user-centred services', in J. Johnson and R. Slater (eds), *Ageing and Later Life*. London: Sage Publications.

Centre for Policy on Ageing (1984) *Home Life*. London: Centre for Policy on Ageing.

Chappell, A.L. (1993) 'Beyond the normalisation principle: the experience and perspectives of adults with learning difficulties living in private residential care'. Unpublished PhD thesis, University of Bristol.

Clough, R. (1994) 'Being an inspector', in R. Clough (ed.), *Insights into Inspection: The regulation of social care*. London: Whiting and Birch Ltd/SCA (Education) Co-publication.

Collins, J. (1993) *The Resettlement Game. Policy and procrastination in the closure of mental handicap hospitals*. London: Values into Action.

Department of Health (1989) *Caring for People: Community Care in the Next Decade and Beyond*, Cmnd. 849, London: HMSO.

Department of Health (1990) *Making Sense of Inspection*. London: HMSO.

Department of Health (1992) *Guidance on Standards for the Residential Care Needs of People with Learning Disabilities/ Mental Handicap*. London: HMSO.

Department of Health and Social Security (1971) *Better Services for the Mentally Handicapped*, Cmnd. 4683. London: HMSO.

Department of Health and Social Security (1980) *Mental Handicap: Progress, Problems and Priorities*. London: HMSO.

DHSS (1981) *Care in Action*. London: HMSO.

DHSS (1981) *Care in the Community – A Consultative Document on Moving Resources in England*. London: HMSO.

DHSS (1983) *Care in the Community*. London: HMSO.

Felce, D. and Perry, J. (1993) *Quality of Life: A Contribution to its Definition and Measurement*. Cardiff: Welsh Centre for Learning Disabilities, Research Unit.

Higgins, J. (1989) 'Homes and institutions', in G. Allan and G. Crow (eds), *Home and Family Creating the Domestic Sphere*. Basingstoke: Macmillan.

House of Commons (1985) *Second Report from the Social Services Committee, Session 1984–85. Community Care with Special Reference to Adult Mentally Ill and Mentally Handicapped People*, Vol. 1. London: HMSO.

Hoyes, L. (1990) *Promoting an Ordinary Life. A Checklist for Assessing Residential Care for People with Learning Difficulties*. Bristol: University of Bristol (SAUS).

Jay Committee (1979) *Report of the Committee of Enquiry into Mental Handicap Nursing and Care*, Cmnd 7468. London: HMSO.

Kellaher, L. and Peace, S. (1993) 'Rest assured: new moves in quality assurance for residential care', in J. Johnson and R. Slater (eds), *Ageing and Later Life*. London: Sage Publications.

Kellaher L., Peace, S. and Wilcocks, D. (1990) 'Triangulating data', in S. Peace (ed.), *Researching Social Gerontology. Concepts Methods and Issues*. London: Sage Publications.

King's Fund Centre (1980) *An Ordinary Life: Comprehensive Locally-based Services for Mentally Handicapped People*. London: King's Fund Centre.

McVilly, K.R. (1995) 'Interviewing people with a learning disability about their residential service', *British Journal of Learning Disabilities*, 23: 138–42.

Morris, P. (1969) *Put Away: A Sociological Study of Institutions for the Mentally Retarded*. London: Routledge and Kegan Paul.

National Institute for Social Work (1988) *Residential Care: A Positive Choice* (the Wagner Report). London, NISW.

Peace, S., Kellaher, L. and Willcocks, D. (1982) *A Balanced Life? A Consumer Study of Residential Life in 100 Local Authority Old People's Homes*. London: Polytechnic of North London.

Perry, J. and Felce, D. (1995) 'Measure for measure: how do measures of quality of life compare?', *British Journal of Learning Disabilities*, 23: 134–7.

Sinson, J.C. (1993) *Group Homes and Community Integration of Developmentally Disabled People. Micro-Institutionalisation?*. London: Jessica Kingsley.

Tyne, A. (1978) *Looking at Life in a Hospital, Hostel, Home or Unit*. London: Campaign for People with Mental Handicaps.

Weaver, T., Willcocks, D. and Kellaher, L. (1985) *The Business of Care: A Study of Private Residential Homes for Old People*. London: Polytechnic of North London.

Wilkinson, J. (1989) '"Being there": evaluating life quality from feelings and daily experience', in A. Brechin and J. Walmsley (eds), *Making Connections. Reflecting on the lives and experiences of people with learning difficulties*. London: Hodder and Stoughton.

Willcocks, D., Peace, S. and Kellaher, L. (1987) *Private Lives in Public Places*. London: Tavistock Publications.

Wolfensberger, W. (1972) *The Principle of Normalisation in Human Services*. Toronto: National Institute of Mental Retardation.

Youll, P.J. and McCourt-Perring, C. (1993) *Raising Voices: Ensuring Quality in Residential Care*. London: HMSO.

2

DISCOVERING THE PRESENT IN STORIES ABOUT THE PAST

John Adams, Joanna Bornat and Mary Prickett

Reminiscence and life history work with frail older people has, over the last fifteen years or so in the UK, become well established and recognised as a basis for supportive interventions in care settings. Recall of the past, it is argued, leads to the rescue and recognition of past identity and achievements. Outcomes for patients include more individualised care and support, opportunities for empowerment and a sense of valued status. Workers engaged in providing care tend to develop more positive attitudes towards older people whose life histories they have come to know.

The writers have been keen advocates of the benefits of reminiscence and life history in working with older people contributing our own observations to debates over a number of years. In this chapter we revisit data from a project carried out on continuing care wards during which frail older women were encouraged to talk about their past lives. In such a setting, people experience dislocation from families, environment and personal possessions. Each of these ruptures contributes to dislocation from past lives and identities. While reminiscence workers have always seen reflection on the past as a means to understanding current preoccupations, we argue that a close scrutiny of what is being said has a further significance, the affirmation of present individuality and capacities. By focusing on the present as we revisited the transcripts of life history interviews, we became aware of a rich range of observations and astute comments on life in the current context: a hospital ward.

In this chapter we begin by reviewing reminiscence research, outline the project which led to interviews and transcripts and then go on to identify some examples of talk about the present drawn from interviews with a number of frail older women living on a continuing care ward.

We conclude with some observations and recommendations relevant to care work.

Reminiscence: the background

In a recently published collection of papers focusing on research methods and findings in reminiscence work, Christine Kovach describes her 'Autobiographical Memory Coding Tool' (Kovach, 1995). The AMCT uses content analysis to arrive at what Kovach describes as the 'symbolic content' of group and individual reminiscence sessions (Kovach, 1995; 106). She identifies five steps necessary to measure 'autobiographical memory interpretations' from transcribed data. Step two involves 'Deleting units that do not refer to the past' (1995: 107).

Setting aside the question of how to decide what is 'past' and what is 'not past', Kovach's recommendation appears to fly in the face of what has been observed of remembering: talk about the past invariably links to present preoccupations and environments (Buchanan and Middleton, 1993; Wallace, 1992; Coleman, 1986). Given this awareness, how typical is the approach suggested by Kovach? To explore this issue we take a brief excursion into the reminiscence literature.

The literature relating to reminiscence research and life history work is now well documented (Haight, 1991; Merriam, 1980; Bornat, 1989). From the first phase of assumptions as to benefits and rewards (Butler, 1963; Lewis, 1971) debates have moved on through attempts to measure outcomes, test methods and compare responses. Analyses of reminiscence have yielded taxonomies of process, form and content (Coleman, 1986; Merriam, 1989; Watt and Wong, 1991). Discussions of therapeutic value and process abound and are resourced with research and critical evaluation (Thornton and Brotchie, 1987; Bornat, 1994). Instrumental approaches to the use of biographical information generated through reminiscence focused interviews have been developed as a means to enhancing the quality of care and support for older people in a range of settings (Cook, 1984; Adams, 1989; Norris, 1989; Fielden, 1990; Burnside, 1990; Lowenthal and Marrazzo, 1990; McKenzie, 1991; O'Donovan, 1993, Dant and Gully, 1994).

There is thus a wealth of evidence, much of which is soundly based in detailed research and observation, yet there still appear to us to be assumptions which require closer examination. The initial development of reminiscence and life history work drew heavily on psychologically based models of fulfilment, life stage role and therapeutic reward (Erikson, 1963; Butler, 1963). More recently, researchers from a number of different disciplines have begun to consider the social context of remembering (Boden and Bielby, 1983; Wallace, 1992; Moody, 1988; Buchanan and Middleton, 1993). Such accounts draw attention to the function which reminiscence and biographical remembering plays in the lives of older people, and some emphasise the particular tasks which face older people living in institutional settings. Thus for example, Holland and Rabbitt emphasise the effect of the use of memory in residential care, suggesting that early life events tend to be rehearsed more often under the encouragement of staff and other residents. This was in contrast with a matched group of older people living in the community (1991: 36–37). Similarly Wallace emphasises the 'social rewards of being a good storyteller' in residential settings (1992: 124).

Recent writing on the issue of dementia care has focused on the importance of encouraging talk about the past and of listening. As Faith Gibson explains: 'We need to be prepared, as best we can, to share the world of the person with dementia. Engaging in mutual reminiscence is one way of sharing this world. It conveys a sense of common humanity' (Gibson, 1997: 135). Similarly, John Killick stresses the importance of listening to accounts of the past. He advocates 'Pro-Active Care' as a means to understanding the concerns and anxieties which the person with dementia has about the present (Killick, 1997).

The need to focus on the person in their present context is a recent development in reminiscence work and is allied to approaches which focus on the whole person. The approach which Kovach recommends appears to go against this trend. At the time of our research we were interested to find out what part awareness of individual biographies played in continuing care settings, using naturalistic methods such as observation and interviewing. We were also aware that in most research the older people taking part tended to be relatively unimpaired, physically or cognitively. Our aim was to observe patients and staff involved in nursing settings and to devise methods which might provide the frail older people living on the wards with opportunities to communicate accounts of themselves at earlier points in their lives.

The project

The research project took place on two continuing care wards situated in different NHS hospitals within the same health authority. Both hospitals were previously workhouses and remembered as such by many of the older patients living there. The wards on which the women we interviewed lived were all-female wards of Nightingale design, and a mixed-sex ward divided into bays. The method chosen for this study was action research using the 'technical collaborative' approach, in which the researchers test a specific intervention in the practice setting (Holter and Schwartz-Barcott, 1993). This meant that we, as researchers, brought our own theoretical framework to the setting, and, with the help of practitioners who worked there, attempted to implement an innovation in clinical practice. The knowledge gained in this way was then to be fed back into the refinement of the theoretical basis of the intervention and into the identification of unforeseen problems associated with its implementation.

Once we had obtained the necessary consents to begin the study, baseline measurements were undertaken of the patients on the two wards which were the focus of the study. These were the abbreviated mental test of cognition (Hodkinson, 1972) and the Selfcare (D) rating scale for depression (Black et al., 1990). Barthel scores, which indicate the ability to perform activities of daily living, were calculated from information supplied by the nursing staff (Collin et al., 1988). These tests were undertaken in order to establish some of the characteristics of the patient sample:

Ward A (the ward where six of our case study women lived) accommodated 30 continuing care patients whose mean Barthel score was 3.97 out of a possible 20. Ten patients consented to undertake the cognition test (7 patients' scores indicated impairment) and 8 patients agreed to complete the Selfcare (D) (3 had scores suggesting depression).

Ward B (where two of our case study women lived) was located in a different hospital in the same locality, the ward had 24 beds of which 7 were for continuing care patients. These 7 patients were included in our study and their mean Barthel score was 5.57. Six patients consented to undertake the cognition test (4 patients' scores indicated impairment) and the Selfcare (D) test (none had a score suggesting depression).

We approached those continuing care patients who were capable of giving consent, to ask if they would be willing to take part in a tape-recorded interview about their lives before admission to the hospital. Nine interviews were conducted on Ward A, and four on Ward B, using an informal interview technique which aimed to allow respondents to convey their own concerns and priorities when invited to talk about their lives. In addition, two interviews were conducted with the relatives of patients who were unable to be interviewed themselves due to physical or psychological impairment. The interviews were then transcribed and a copy of the tape and transcription was given to each patient or relative who had taken part. Additional stages in the research process included participant observation of nurse-patient interaction as well as the completion of brief evaluative questionnaires by nurses.

Our original 'technical collaborative' research design had included the nurses. Our aim had been to develop a method of life story book development which was simple, not costly and which did not require a heavy time commitment. Our efforts met with resistance. Nurses were, with only one exception, always 'too busy' to take part even on a partnership basis with one of the research team. At the time, this was undoubtedly a set-back to our research plan. We discuss the implications of the nurses' responses later in this chapter. Revising our approach we decided to proceed by demonstrating the process ourselves. Using the biographical information contained in the interview transcripts as a basis, we assembled a life story book, using a cheap but attractively designed scrapbook, for 11 of the patients. Further discussion of issues raised in the taped interviews followed before the final content of the books was fixed. In some cases, personal photographs were produced and these were copied for inclusion. The local history collection of the public library provided much useful illustrative material; for images of other parts of the country, tourist information offices proved to be helpful. For some of the books a 'life line' which set the life story of the individual in the context of the major historical events in a simple graphical form was constructed, and for these and for some others where there was sufficient information about a particular life, a genogram was constructed.

Revisiting the transcripts

Our initial interest in taping life histories and encouraging reminiscence lay in the contribution we felt this would make to care provision and practice on the two wards where we were researching. This focus was subsequently discussed in relation to care planning with frail older people (Adams et al., 1996). In analysing the transcripts it became clear that having invited patients to tape-record their life stories we were also giving them the opportunity to comment on the situation in which they found themselves. Though the past featured as a significant reference point for the women we listened to, their accounts were punctuated by and oriented towards the present and, in particular, their life in the care setting in which they were living.

We noted earlier that researchers interested in reminiscence have recently begun to pay more attention to the ways in which accounts of past experience tend to be presented in terms of current preoccupations and contexts. This was an understanding which we also shared. However, in reviewing the reminiscence literature and in our work as trainers in reminiscence work, we had an additional set of concerns. While a focus on the past person is indeed an invaluable support to the maintenance of identity and individualisation in care settings and a major contribution to the delivery of good quality care, it may have the effect of distracting attention away from the present person. Examples of good practice in reminiscence work refer almost exclusively to childhood and experiences from periods in people's lives when they were fit, independent and active members of society (for example, Murphy, 1994). While this may be an important antidote to the tendency to deny personhood (Kitwood and Bredin, 1992) in dementia care, an emphasis on the person in the past may have the effect of distracting attention away from the person in the present. Moreover, an over-exclusive attention to the past may even lead to carers downplaying and ignoring comments and observations relating to the present. It may also, as we observed earlier, lead to the exclusion from joint activities of those least able to provide coherent or well-constructed narrations of their past lives.

We revisited our tapes with a focus on what people were saying about their present lives. As far as presenting the data here is concerned, this means that we have selected for analysis those parts of the transcribed interviews which focus on life on the wards and how people felt about this. In doing this we feel that we are able to identify a number of different ways, even where there was some degree of confusion in speech and talk, in which patients were making astute observations and sometimes indicating compensatory strategies for dealing with the situation in which they were living. The four aspects of talk about the present which we identify below relate to role expectation, adjustment, observation and reflection.

Role expectation

The ambivalence that has always surrounded life on a continuing care ward does not provide the patient or the interviewer with clear ground-rules as to how their respective roles should be played. The settings with the two rows of beds down each side of the Nightingale ward and the staff of nurses in clinical uniforms convey a strong message about active treatment of problems caused by disordered physiology and the hope of improvement and discharge. The roles which are customary for a conversation at the bedside revolve around the patient, submissive under the watchful eye of the nursing staff, recounting progress with the physical aspects of care and the interviewer recording the details of that treatment. The ward philosophies, on the other hand, emphasise that these settings are to be considered as the older person's home.

In a domestic setting, taking part in an interview creates the expectation that the interviewee will act as a hostess and that the interviewer will be able to range widely across many aspects of the life story. The interview tapes contain examples of both kinds of role expectations being played out. Many of the women were well aware of their physical problems which meant that they were required to live on a hospital ward. For Mrs A, the problem lay in her joints:

> That's why I'm here, because I'm absolutely riddled with arthritis – the rheumatoid that deforms you and the other one, the osteo, that creeps (up) on you. But you see there isn't the pain with that so you don't know you've got it, but you know you've got it (when) you find you land up like this.

Mrs B was troubled with leg ulcers which would not heal:

> Well, of course these ulcers, they itch at the side. They've tried everything – Sister's tried everything.

The difference between an acute hospital ward and continuing care was remarked on by Mrs C:

> I mean I know this is still hospital, but it's not the same as being in the ordinary hospital. I mean you get up when you're better I know, but I mean this is your home and this is where you gotta make it, and what you make of it is your effort and if it don't suit you then that's it.

One approach to the problem of making sense of the situation of being interviewed while resident on a continuing care ward was demonstrated by Mrs A when she briefly took on the role of a hostess who was entertaining the interviewer to tea in a hotel. The arrival of a member of the domestic staff distributing afternoon tea facilitated this switch:

> *Domestic*: Cup of tea?
> *Mrs A*: Yes please. What is on that plate, love?
> *Domestic*: Fruit cake.
> *Mrs A*: Fruit cake? Could I look at a piece before I decide to have it? Are you giving this lady a cup of tea?
> *Domestic*: Yes, if she wants one.

Despite this brief exchange which places Mrs A as the demanding customer, a comment made shortly afterwards reverts the scenario to that of a patient who is worried about what the nurses will think of her independence:

> I daren't say anything – I'm only going to pick the fruit out. Would you like to take (the plate)?

It seems from the transcripts that Mrs A is occupying a number of roles in turn: the grateful recipient, the victim and the host. Meanwhile Mrs C is clear about the contribution which she feels she needs to make if the ward is to begin to feel like home. It's her own 'effort' that will count. She sees patients as having a role to play in constructing an environment in which to survive.

Adjustment

Living on a continuing care ward for many patients must inevitably involve being reminded of the losses which brought them there and an awareness of the low status which society now awards them. For Mrs D, admission to the ward involved coming to terms with the fact that she would never be able to travel abroad to visit her relatives:

> I got scores of in-laws in America – I keep in touch with them. I don't suppose I'll ever see them again. While I'm here I try to make the best of a bad job. Staff (in this hospital) help all they can, so I do get all the help.

Some patients were well aware of the stigma which still attaches to such places. Mrs C had taken drastic steps to control the damage she felt which this information might cause:

> They don't know where I am, (her twin daughters aged 60) and I don't want them to know because she would come in here and she would just sling her weight about, and she'd say, is this the best hole or corner you could creep in?

> So I've told my niece not to tell them where I am. I don't want them to know, because I know her, and whatever trouble she makes, I've got to live in it. Haven't I?

This kind of tough-minded approach to her situation also characterised Mrs C's views about the losses she had experienced in being admitted to the ward:

> You can't be with the dead, you've just got to make a life – make the best of what you've got. I'm afraid it's the way I'll always be. That's why I don't like those moaning all the while in here. We've got nothing to moan about really. We know it's not home, we're well aware of that; you can't do the same, but when you can't look after yourself what have you got to do? There's not much you can do, is there? I mean I'm satisfied with it. I'd still like to own me own home, but me niece has give it up and that's it.

In addition to losing family and home, Mrs D was also required to live with the knowledge that her illness had destroyed the fine voice which had once been a source of great pride:

> I used my voice for lots of things, now I can't use it at all. Taught elocution – went in for competitions – won silver cups – now it's ironic I can't speak properly.

As each patient on the ward had to face their own quota of disappointments and losses, it is perhaps surprising that the wish to end life was not expressed more frequently. In fact the subject was mentioned on just one occasion. Mrs A was the only one of our informants to raise the issue and it was in the context of the embarrassment her condition caused for other people, rather than her own wish to die:

> So that's the story of me life, and this is it. And when I'm like this I've said to them – well, I've asked the doctor two or three times, I've said, You've got an injection and you know you could just give me a . . .

> You know, there's been a doctor and a nurse attending you, and there's something wrong that my bowels don't work properly, and I've asked them and I said I just want a little shot with those – like they do – inject you and I'd just go off to sleep like that and I wouldn't wake up anymore.

But they said, We're not allowed to do that.

So that was that.

Why have you asked for them to do that then?

Because if I have these sicknesses and that and they have to – well it's very unpleasant, I know – I feel so ill that I know I'm unpleasant because instead of whatever ought to happen to me, coming and going through the bowels, it comes up this way and shoots all over the place.

It was also Mrs A who chose to begin her life history interview in what was for her a typically aphoristic fashion:

Do you want to tell me what your name is?

It's on my husband's grave.

Perhaps this was her oblique way of dealing with her own finitude. She and her co-patients are only too aware of the fact that on a continuing care ward nothing about a person's physical condition or future can be concealed from others. Living and dying are public events.

The one certainty in this kind of environment is that the occupancy of a bed will be ended only by death in a public place (see chapter 3). Flimsy curtains do little to disguise the stark reality, as Mrs B recalled:

She wouldn't eat and she wouldn't drink. Course the doctor, same one as I've got . . . The doctor said, 'She won't last.' And her daughter sat with her while she died. Well of course the curtains all went round – they do when anything like that happens. They took her out and she was buried in K–.

Observation

A constant theme which dominates much of the literature about all kinds of residential settings for older people is the need to facilitate communication between residents. Yet our interviews revealed no great wish to be sociable either with other residents or with the nursing staff. In fact the characteristic stance was one of the shrewd and detached observer who noted human weaknesses and errors, but did not descend from this lofty vantage point to engage in conversation. Mrs C defended her position in terms of other people's inability to communicate:

Yes, I'm always reading. Well, you can't make any conversation with any of these. You can't make conversation with her for a start.

Mrs B demonstrated the shrewd and superior outlook which recorded the follies of others yet did nothing to assist them:

At night time she says, 'When is it supper time?'.

I said, 'What do you want – your soup?'

So she said, 'Yes'.

And she were real silly, silly. She asked for some sandwiches and she had a cup of soup and then her tea. (She) got mixed up and I remember she didn't eat all she had. So in the night she called out and she wanted something to eat. So they went and brought it her, and I thought, Well, that's what made her hungry. But I won't say. But she's watching my mouth while I'm talking to you. She doesn't like it because she can't hear it.

One patient, Mrs E, expressed a strong preference for having her bed as it had been, in a mixed bay of men and women, rather than in its present position in a bay of women alone:

Down there . . . they were really nice, and I came up here. This anyhow were only four women, the others were all men down there. These are all women – I don't like it here. I like the other basement. They're all nice really.

The work of the nurses also came in for critical scrutiny from Mrs B:

Course you don't say that now – people with ulcerated legs, they smell – we can't help it. But now they're getting dressings that take the smell away. But you see, there's a lot of difference in the nurses . . . one does it one way and one another, you see.

Lack of control over the activities of living which life in a hospital ward alongside others who have competing priorities was remarked on by Mrs F:

I've been having a go at all the nurses this morning. Not that one – all the other nurses. All got an answer for me. Wanted to get up this morning, and I was waiting to get out of bed and in the end one of the Italian nurses come and dressed me. She said, 'Nina, do you want to be dressed?'

And I said, 'Want to dress? I don't want to stop here all blooming day.'

Observations on ward life, including comments about preferences as to companions or particular nurses, as with the other quotations which we have included here, are interspersed amongst memories from past life. The identities presented in these parallel narratives of present times are of women who are surviving by retaining a strong sense of self in the face of an institutionalising adversity and who are seeking ways to balance desires for individual privacy against the logic of collective care.

If any kind of balance is achieved it may be hard-earned as an old hand like Mrs C observes:

> That woman across there sitting in the window, she come from downstairs, from rehab and she said, 'what time do you go to bed?' and she said, 'I get them to come and put me to bed at half past nine'. I thought, well, you'll be lucky, you can ask if you can stop up awhile then, but don't you demand it, cos they can say, 'no, you're not going to'. I mean . . . we sit here and watch the telly, but if they said we couldn't watch it, that'd be the end, no good grumbling, you just have to go.

Reflection

The one dimension of life which is present in abundance on a continuing care ward is time to reflect on past and present and to ponder on changes in circumstances. For example, as Mrs A explains, there is time to recreate pleasures enjoyed before admission to hospital:

> I can't get up and go. I can't get up and walk. I go outside – there's a tree out there with blossom on, like I had in my garden, but that's all white blossom on there. And they let me go out and sit under there, in this (wheelchair) – push me out there and leave me . . . I'm used to being a lot at home, so you see in here and all this noise . . . When I'm well enough I ask to go downstairs and then if people come by you they just say, 'Hello, nice day' or something like that and you can be quiet.

Paying attention to the type of preference expressed by Mrs A is now accepted as well-established good practice in reminiscence and life history work with people with dementia (Gibson, 1991; Murphy, 1994; Killick, 1997). Care plans which record individual lifestyles and choices are also helpful in supporting individuals whose speech and behaviour might otherwise appear to be unexplainable or, even, bizarre. In our experience recording life histories presented an opportunity to validate the past life and particularly the present experience of the individual in the face of multiple losses which have to be faced. When life has to be lived in a communal setting, it seems that an autobiography becomes still more important in affirming identity, as Mrs G claims:

> They all seem as if they have had much more interesting lives, but they haven't got more in them than I have in mine – none of them! And I don't know what they did, no.

When a life history becomes so important in countering the threats to individual identity, it is crucial to have continuing faith in its accuracy:

> Oh, I forget easy what's happening from one day to the other, but what I remember is right, you know. (Mrs H)

Mrs A's comment encapsulated the central purpose of our study into the uses which can be made of biographical accounts in a continuing care ward for older people:

> I perhaps have been telling you lies, and yet it all seems true. I don't know and yet it's funny – if it's true, why don't they know up here about me?

Time and an opportunity to reflect on a life seemed to raise issues for the women who talked to us. Highlighting their biographies leads to comparisons between lives, leads to questions about the fallibility of memory and finally raises the question of whether the staff actually know who they are caring for at all, an implicit contrast between the medical and the personal in terms of biography.

Conclusions

Revisiting our life history interviews with a focus on what is being said about present lives, has led us to emphasise the importance of taking into consideration the full account being offered. By selecting out references to the present we have excluded details of individual life histories. This was deliberate. With its focus on an often distant past, those of us involved in reminiscence work with older people are in danger of ignoring: the astute and often emotive observations which frail older people may be making about their present lives; and the *present* person. To be in receipt of continuing care is possibly the most low-status experience in the average individual's life. Reminiscence helps to correct assumptions as to both physical and mental impairment, retrieving identities which demonstrate earlier competence, capability and activity. However, if we are to be in a position to deliver sensitive and appropriate care, we need to value the person in the present with all their disabilities and restrictions.

Despite the resistance we encountered during the early stages of our research, nurses on the ward did finally express some enthusiasm for what we were doing. The life story books prepared for 11 of the patients were produced for visitors, and student nurses who subsequently spent time on the ward were given an account of the project by their established colleagues as part of the narrative of the ward's history. Working with the nurses as we carried out observations and interviews, it was clear that they were keen to hear more about the lives of the patients they were working with and that they had a good understanding of the relevance of the aims of the project. If they were not able to take advantage of our presence on the ward as we went about our research, then this had much to do with their situation in the nursing and hospital hierarchy. They were mainly untrained and working on continuing care wards. These multiple negative statuses contributed to a defensive attachment to a job which seems to have been perceived mainly in terms of its contribution to the labour involved in care. However, from comments which we collected from nurses at the end of the project, it was clear that they felt that they had gained from the experience, if only at second-hand. Most felt that they knew their patients better and that this was an important aspect to care. As one nurse said: 'It's important to know. There's not a lot of dignity left'.

Revisiting our data has demonstrated to us that physically and mentally frail older people have much to say about their present situations and that listening to what they are saying in the context of talking about the past provides a medium for self-expression and the communication of feelings and perceptions. It suggests an additional and significant role for reminiscence work as a vehicle for open-ended reflection and comment. By taking our tape-recorders onto the wards and working with patients and relatives on the construction of life story books, we were providing opportunities for communication on a wide range of topics. In this way, life history work legitimises talk for people who might otherwise not be listened to or whose feelings about themselves and their care setting may go unheard. What they have to say may not always be welcome or indeed completely coherent. It may be critical, emotional and from the perspective of outsiders to ward and nursing care cultures, it may even seem trivial. We must not fall into the temptation of giving priority to the past over the present either by deliberate 'deletion' (Kovach, 1995) or by our own subjective preference for accounts of what used to be. Revisiting our data re-emphasised for us the importance for practice and for research of acknowledging the present person, with all her feelings, emotions and capabilities in her present context of care.

References

Adams, J. (1989) 'Anamnesis in dementia: restoring a personal history', *Oral History*, 17 (2): 62–3.

Adams, J., Bornat, J. and Prickett, M. (1996) '"You wouldn't be interested in my life, I've done nothing": care planning and life history work with frail older women', in J. Phillips and B. Penhale (eds), *Reviewing Care Management for Older People*. London: Jessica Kingsley.

Black, J., Knight, P. and Belford, H. (1990) 'The use of selfcare (D) rating scale for depression in elderly continuing care patients – a pilot study', *Care of the Elderly*, 2 (3): 119–21.

Boden, D. and Bielby, D. (1983) 'The past as resource: a conversational analysis of elderly talk', *Human Development*, 26: 208–19.

Bornat, J. (1989) 'Reminiscence as a social movement: reminiscence and older people', *Oral History*, 17 (2): 16–24.

Bornat, J. (1994) (ed.) *Reminiscence Reviewed: Perspectives, Evaluations, Achievements*. Buckingham: Open University Press.

Buchanan, K. and Middleton D. (1993) 'Reminiscence reviewed: a discourse analytic perspective' in J. Bornat (ed.), *Reminiscence Reviewed: Perspectives, Evaluations, Achievements*. Buckingham: Open University Press.

Burnside, I. (1990) 'Reminiscence: an independent nursing intervention in the aged', *Issues in Mental Health Nursing*, 11: 38–48.

Butler, R.N. (1963) 'The life review: an interpretation of reminiscence in the aged', *Psychiatry*, 26: 65–73.

Collin C., Wade, Davies, D.T. and Horne, V. (1988) 'The Barthel ADL Index: a reliability study', *International Disability Studies*, 10: 61–3.

Coleman, P. (1986) *Ageing and Reminiscence Processes*. Chichester: Wiley.

Cook, J.R. (1984) 'Reminiscing: how it can help confused nursing home residents', *Social Casework*, 65 (2): 90–3.

Dant, T. and Gully, V. (1994) *Co-ordinating Care at Home*. London: Harper Collins.

Erikson, E.H. (1963) *Childhood and Society*. New York: Norton.

Fielden, M. (1990) 'Reminiscence as a therapeutic intervention with sheltered housing residents: a comparative study', *British Journal of Social Work*, 20: 21–44.

Gibson, F. (1991) *The lost ones: recovering the past to help their present*. Stirling: Dementia Services Development Centre.

Gibson, F. (1997) 'Owning the past in dementia care: creative engagement with others in the present', in M. Marshall (ed.), *State of the Art in Dementia Care*. London: Centre for Policy on Ageing.

Haight, B. (1991) 'Reminiscence: the state of the art as a basis for practice', *International Journal of Aging and Human Development*, 33 (10): 1–32.

Hodkinson, H.M. (1972) 'Evaluation of a mental test score for assessment of mental impairment in the elderly', *Age and Ageing*, 1: 233–8.

Holland, C. and Rabbitt, P. (1991) 'Ageing memory: use versus impairment', *British Journal of Psychology*, 82: 29–38.

Holter, I.M. and Schwartz-Barcott, D. (1993) 'Action research: what is it? How has it been used and how can it be used in nursing?', *Journal of Advanced Nursing*, 18: 298–304.

Killick, J. (1997) 'Listening and life history work', in M. Allott and M. Robb (eds), *Understanding Health and Social Care: A Reader*. London: Sage.

Kitwood, T. and Bredin, K. (1992) 'Towards a theory of dementia care: personhood and well-being', *Ageing and Society*, 12 (3): 269–87.

Kovach, C.R. (1995) 'A qualitative look at reminiscing: using the autobiographical memory coding tool', in B.K. Haight and J.D. Webster (eds), *The Art and Science of Reminiscing: Theory, Research, Methods and Applications*. London: Taylor and Francis.

Lewis, C.N. (1971) 'Reminiscing and self-concept in old age', *Journal of Gerontology*, 26: 240–2.

Lowenthal, R.I. and Marrazzo, R.A. (1990) 'Milestoning: evoking memories for resocializing through group reminiscence', *The Gerontologist*, 30 (2): 269–72.

McKenzie, S. (1991) 'A positive force', *Nursing the Elderly*, 3 (3): 22–4.

Merriam, S.B. (1980) 'The concept and function of reminiscence: a review of research', *The Gerontologist*, 20: 604–9.

Merriam, S.B. (1989) 'The structure of simple reminiscence' *The Gerontologist*, 29 (6): 761–7.

Moody, H.R. (1988) 'Twenty-five years of the life review: where did we come from? Where are we going?', *Journal of Gerontological Social Work*, 12 (2/4): 7–21.

Murphy, C.J. (1994) *'It Started with a Sea-shell' Life Story Work and People with Dementia*. Stirling: Dementia Services Development Centre.

Norris, A. (1989) 'Clinic or client? a psychologist's case for reminiscence', *Oral History*, 17 (2): 26–9.

O'Donovan, S. (1993) 'The memory lingers on', *Elderly Care*, 5 (1): 27–31.

Thornton, J. and Brotchie, J. (1987) 'Reminiscence: a critical review of the empirical literature', *British Journal of Clinical Psychology*, 26: 93–111.

Wallace, B.J. (1992) 'Reconsidering the life review: the social construction of talk about the past', *The Gerontologist*, 21 (1): 120–5.

Watt, L.M. and Wong, P.T.P. (1991) 'A taxonomy of reminiscence and therapeutic implications', *Journal of Gerontological Social Work*, 16 (1/2): 37–57.

3

TERMINAL CARE OR TERMINAL CARELESSNESS

Jeanne Katz

From reading newspapers and watching television, one might assume that the fate of dying people has, in recent years, become 'everybody's business'. Photographs of weeping relatives, terminally-ill children, distraught survivors of accidents appear on television screens and are plastered over the front pages of the newspapers, broadsheets as well as tabloids. But is it not so, that the items that are newsworthy reflect a very selective slice of the experiences of most dying people? An example of this was the way the media followed the case of Child B, Jamie Bowen, who in 1995 was refused a bone marrow transplant by her local health authority, Cambridge. According to her father and some medical opinion, a transplant might have saved her from leukaemia, which has historically aroused considerable sentiment, borne out by the relative ease of raising funding for leukaemia research in comparison with the difficulties of raising money for the treatment or care of older people with malignancies or non-malignant conditions. Public and media concern for Jamie's predicament created the environment in which an anonymous donor put up the money for her treatment in the private sector (Entwistle, 1996). This arguably extended her life for up to a year, although there is still some debate about the impact that the treatment had on the quality of the remaining months that Jamie lived and whether the expenditure would have been justified within the NHS, given Jamie's very poor chances of survival (Thornton, 1997).

Many stories reported in the media concern individuals with their own particularly heart-rending stories who have died or are dying following a traumatic (newsworthy) accident or a particular type of ailment, one which has aroused the attention of the public. But, in western societies, people die from a variety of causes, for example, from immune system failures, such as AIDS, or as a result of drug addiction.

Most people die in old age from cardiovascular problems and, less frequently, from malignancies. We know in some detail about the care provided for the 'privileged few' who receive technologically advanced treatments in medical 'centres of excellence' and those who are recipients of hospice and palliative care. (Chapter 7 raises the problems of caring for those deteriorating and dying as a result of chronic cardiac conditions or the complications arising from rheumatoid arthritis.) But what about the 'silent majority' who are dying from a range of acute or chronic conditions from which they will never recover, such as the less prestigious kinds of cancer, chronic obstructive airways disease or pneumonia?

This chapter explores the ways in which the care of dying people has changed in the UK and other western societies over the past 40 years, and in particular examines the contention voiced frequently in both the medical and lay press that the plight of dying people has improved considerably. There are several overall issues to be considered: the first relates to the evidence, or lack of evidence, that the care of *most* dying people has improved in the UK since the introduction of palliative medicine and hospice care; the second relates to whether the re-integration of care in the community has in itself changed the complexion of terminal care.

In the early part of the twentieth century the social organisation of death underwent radical changes. Hitherto death was regarded as a common occurrence, and all people regardless of age frequently confronted death in a variety of settings but most particularly in the domestic environment. As hospital care became commonplace, fewer terminally ill people were being nursed in their own homes; indeed, many contagious diseases were now no longer seen as life threatening as they responded to antibiotics and other pharmaceutical preparations. Dying as well as being born at home ceased to be routine occurrences, and death became primarily associated with old age rather than likely to occur at any stage of life. Dying people were no longer cared for in their own homes, nor was death observed by different generations and by the extended family. These changes in the care of dying people should be seen in the context of the great social and economic changes taking place in western society, with people living longer in smaller family units and increasing numbers living alone away from support of family and friends – indicative of a much more mobile and individualistic society (see Chapter 8 for a more extended discussion of social change).

The medicalisation of death

Progressively since the end of the First World War death and dying have become medicalised, insofar as they have been seen as requiring the intervention of health professionals in insititutional settings. Hence the person's home environment was no longer seen as the appropriate venue for birth and death. As a result of medical advances, health professionals' goal to cure became a realistic objective, and the alleviation of pain and the palliation of symptoms were not viewed as legitimate goals in themselves. Curative endeavours became associated with research, laboratory medicine and clinical trials, all of which required a tertiary hospital/medical-school base. Acutely and terminally-ill people were admitted to hospitals and became patient numbers (e.g. 'bed no. four with ca. breast') and clinical trial numbers. Ordinary people ceded control over their dying and that of their relatives to the health workers who by using euphemistic and technical terms isolated them further.

The impact of this change on dying people, their relatives and those professionals looking after them was not realised for some time. The implications for people dying in institutions where the focus was on cure rather than care were first studied in the US in the 1960s by Sudnow (1967) and by Glaser and Strauss (1965, 1968). They came to a number of interesting conclusions: for instance, a discrepancy between the ways in which health workers interacted with patients likely to survive compared to those who were expected to die. Dying patients had minimal contact with health workers and in some situations suffered real physical as well as emotional neglect. The extent to which this was true depended to some extent on the kind of institution in which dying patients were hospitalised (public or private, teaching or non-teaching). Health workers were also found to assess dying people according to a number of socially constructed characteristics – for example, his or her position in the family, age, occupation, social background and perceived moral character. This attitude was particularly apparent when choices were made about resuscitation of patients in accident and emergency units – those with the lowest social value were least likely to be rescuscitated.

Further studies of the interactions between health workers and dying people were undertaken in a variety of hospital locations in the UK in the 1970s and later (McIntosh, 1977; Bond, 1982; Field, 1989; Davey, 1993). These studies contended that much 'care' meted out in hospitals to dying people was tantamount to neglect. Health workers subscribed to the medical goal of cure and perceived dying as a failure. Therefore, they protected themselves from the distress of failure by planning communication with dying people so that minimal discussion about dying would occur. In addition, people who were expected to die were placed alone in side wards so that death could occur relatively unnoticed by others on the ward.

The implications for health workers of caring for dying people was the focus of some of these studies. It was suggested that one of the reasons why health workers marginalised dying people was to protect themselves from emotional distress. Working with dying people was found to have an impact not only on the health workers themselves and the dying people for whom they were responsible but also on workers' inter-personal relationships with their colleagues as well as their families and friends. Menzies (1959) and subsequently others (Baider and Porath, 1981; Wilkinson, 1991) demonstrated that nurses working with people with cancer or with dying patients had higher levels of sickness and absenteeism as well as a higher incidence of reporting late for work than nurses working with people likely to recover from an illness.

Many explanations have been offered about why some health workers (primarily in traditional hospital settings) find caring for dying people stressful. Melanie Klein and other psychoanalysts (Judd, 1993) saw the reasons as emanating from early childhood experiences. Other explana-tions focus on how health workers deal with the care/cure conflict, one of the central ideological issues in providing curative health care. In addition to their own fears of death, physicians are thus viewed as experiencing stress in facing the failure of their ministrations – the discrepancy between their aim to cure people and the expected reality (death). These conflicts are shared by nurses subscribing to the tradi-tional medical ideology which emphasises cure rather than care. Benoliel (1983) and others noted that nurses in these settings experienced acute distress because unlike their medical colleagues, they still had considerable contact with dying patients (even though they limited this as much as feasible). In settings where death is viewed as a failure, communication with dying people and their relatives is thus seen to be a source of stress for health workers.

Palliative and terminal care

In many areas of the UK the scenario painted above remained typical of hospital care for dying people throughout the middle and latter parts of the twentieth century. The extent to which these practices are sustained depends on a variety of factors relating to the provision of care by the National Health Service and by local hospice and palliative care services.

The hospice movement, pioneered in the 1960s by Dame Cecily Saunders with the establishment of St Christopher's Hospice in Sydenham, Kent emerged out of an awareness that the modern medical establishment, particularly hospital medicine, was not addressing the range of needs of dying people. From its inception, the goal of the hospice movement was to provide a model which addressed the care needs of people dying in pain from cancer.

> The experience of apparently intractable pain, fear of dying and the growing prominence of cancer were part of a public mood of anxiety about death with which the aspirations of the hospices resonated. (Field and James, 1993)

There were a number of socio-economic factors which contributed to the development of the movement including:

- demographic changes in terms of life expectancy;
- the increasing number of dependent older people living alone with no family carers;
- changing public opinion.

The hospice movement fostered a reconceptualisation of the care of dying people and contributed to a social reconstruction of the terms 'dying' and terminal illness – in other words, it is not necessarily the proximity of death which labels someone as dying, but the *definition* of the person as near to death. Thus, even those who are very close to death but not labelled as such might not be defined as terminally ill nor treated (in all senses of the word) as such. It is, therefore, relevant to look at the rhetoric of care as espoused by the hospice and palliative care movements in the UK and the USA and how they challenged the assumptions previously prevalent in the medical dominance of the care of dying people.

Notions about the term 'hospice' differ among organisations and countries, as do the services and facilities provided (Clark, 1993). In the UK a hospice usually refers to a place with an inpatient facility for dying people, admitted on the basis of a clear end-point in sight. This facility may also incorporate a number of additional features – for example, day care or respite care services, and usually, but not always, a domiciliary team functioning out of the building. Palliative care teams, and more often Macmillan nurses, work out of a number of settings, providing advice and expertise for other professionals working with dying people in hospitals, residential care and in the community.

The hospice movement grew out of grassroots activities, with many local groups fundraising and clamouring for this type of local facility; and consequently there was little planning reflecting population/age distribution or concern about the paucity of services or duplication. In areas where there were few voluntary facilities (most hospice buildings were financed through donations) and there was a clear need, some units (called 'continuing care units') were funded by the National Health Service and established, usually in partnership with a charity which put up the money for the bricks and mortar.

Who do hospices care for?

The hospice and related palliative care movements subscribe to a policy which selects individuals for care on the basis of a *time-limited* dying trajectory. Hence palliative care in its 'accepted form' excludes those who do not fit into a clearly defined dying mode such as those dying slowly from congestive heart or lung failure. There are obvious contra-dictions in this approach: one which states that all people should be entitled to a pain-free death, yet imposes a range of conditions that dying people have to meet, and most importantly a clear end point by which stage their care will have terminated.

The hospice movement was predicated on the assumption that contemporary modes of caring for dying people both in their own homes and in hospitals were unacceptable. Despite dramatic advances in medical technology, diagnostic tools and pharmacology, little attention had been given to the relief of symptoms – especially pain – with most of the research directed at cure. However, some of the curative 'cocktails' had proven palliative effects in terms of relieving symptoms, and even these had been largely ignored by physicians intent on cure rather than alleviation of distress. The combination of grassroots support for the hospice movement and research into pain control contributed to the acknowledgement by the medical establishment that traditional medicine was not addressing all the needs of dying people and that pain control in particular needed to be brought within conventional medicine. The focus on pain should encompass emotional, spiritual and social issues. In 1988 a sub-specialty in palliative medicine was established within the Royal College of Physicians.

In the late 1980s, palliative *care* as a more generalised health movement emerged to parallel the development of palliative *medicine* to meet the needs of a much wider group of people in different kinds of pain, and not necessarily terminally ill. The intention was to apply some of the tools of palliative medicine, including complementary therapies, especially those focusing on symptom control and pain relief. But so far, there is little research evidence to suggest that a wider net has been cast, and it is questionable whether more people are indeed benefiting from the advances in pain relief and symptom control techniques and/ or have access to the skills offered by palliative care teams or Macmillan nurses.

Some might argue that the hospice movement is a replacement for the original hospice concept where religious orders provided shelter to travellers and tended to their religious needs. This may explain the relatively low take-up of hospice services by those from religious minorities in the UK (NCHSPCS Occasional Paper, 1995).

Philosophy and practice: new ways of thinking

In parallel with changing concepts of caring for dying people initiated by the palliative care and hospice movements came changes in nursing philosophy and practice. In the 1970s there was the introduction of the nursing process and a reconceptualisation of the role of nurses as separate from, yet complementary to, their medical colleagues. Since then a number of studies have been made to ascertain the impact of these changes on people dying in different settings, particularly in hospitals, and to compare different kinds of wards representing different medical models (e.g. Field, 1989; Vachon, 1987; Katz, 1989; and Siddell et al., 1997). In the model of care rather than cure, medical and nursing staff acknowledge that treating 'aggressively' till the end is not appropriate in all cases, and at a certain stage they recognise that heroic (usually chemotherapy or radiotherapy) treatment will not halt the progression of disease, although in some cases it might have a palliative effect. As a replacement for a curative stance, another model of care is adopted which emphasises easing of symptoms and pain relief.

Several studies have explored nurses' reconceptualisation of the process of caring for dying people (Katz, 1989, 1996; Field, 1989; Wilkinson, 1991): exploring first whether the switch to a caring model is in itself a source of stress (Quint, 1967; Vachon and Pakes, 1984; Vachon, 1987); and second, whether carers use blocking tactics to prevent patients from discussing their concerns (Wilkinson, 1991). This concept implies that stress is related to staffing levels (Katz, 1989, 1996) and whether nurses feel able to practise 'good nursing'. The nurses studied in the 1980s and 1990s maintain that nursing dying people fulfils their criteria of good nursing. In Katz's study (1989) of nurses of all ranks caring for dying people on a cancer ward, the nurses held particular beliefs which related to their identity as nurses and their aim to provide 'total nursing care' for their patients. Their world view was related to whether they could provide patients with optimal nursing care which in the case of dying people they called *tender loving care*. This entailed more than simply changing dressings and doing practical tasks for patients, by incorporating the dying person and his/her family into the decision-making and enabling dying people to influence their mode and place of death to some extent.

Indeed, caring for dying people enabled nurses in this study to provide what they saw as good nursing. This implied that all the patients' needs, whether emotional, psychological, physical, technical or spiritual, could be addressed. Caring for dying people enabled nurses to provide an excellent *nursing service*, rather than being adjuncts to their medical colleagues. This became an area that nurses carved out for themselves as separate from their medical colleagues: they cure, we care. Providing good care meant paying attention to details:

> We learned a lot of detailed things like caring for patients, giving them bed baths, having time to do things like that, simple things, like cleaning their dentures or washing their faces and hands.

Good quality care means careful assessment of the dying person's problems and providing appropriate nursing solutions – this has distinct similarities with the palliative care approach which makes the dying person's concerns and needs as central and requiring attention. Nurses in this study (Katz, 1989) focused on problems as articulated by the patients themselves, in contrast to the traditional ward where management problems were constructed by the medical and nursing staff. Talking to dying people was seen as the route to establishing their concerns. One nurse put it like this:

> I like to be able to talk to patients, I don't think you can really assess their needs unless you can sit down and talk to them – in some wards you just have not got the chance to do that – you may have 10 or 11 patients that want hoist baths, so when do you get the chance to talk to them – that's not nursing to me. I mean that's not nursing the way I like it, I like to be able to get to know patients, and perhaps understand them a bit more.

Having elicited their problems from the dying people themselves, student nurses presented them in the daily ward report where senior nurses probed and prompted the allocated nurse until they were satisfied that the student nurse had elicited the patient's real concerns and had understood the rationale for the medical and nursing decisions taken. Nurses saw themselves as the dying person's advocate, there to help them resolve the problems that bothered them most:

> We (nurses on the ward) don't see that the patient's main problem is his lymphoma – his main problem is whatever he is complaining about – could be dysphagia – the fact that he cannot swallow because he's having radiotherapy.

Good nursing care, as portrayed by nurses in this study (Katz, 1996), included flexible responses to changes in the dying person's physical condition as well as to their spiritual, emotional and social needs. This approach sometimes brought nurses into conflict with medical staff on issues such as notifying relatives about the imminence of death and increasing doses of analgesia. Most importantly, dying patients were not perceived as a nursing failure but as a challenge which enabled nurses to demonstrate their skills, exemplified in the way they assessed the needs of patients who had difficulty communicating their concerns.

Nurses in the study conducted during the 1980s were not familiar with the principles and practice of palliative care. Nevertheless, the perspective that they adopted, which emerged primarily from the concepts of total nursing care, mirrors those of palliative care, particularly the key feature of keeping the dying person's needs central at all times (NCHSPCS guidelines, 1995). Knowing patients as people enables nurses to feel strongly about patients' rights to information and the necessity of respecting their individuality and privacy at all times, whether alive or dead. Nurses thus found it offensive when other hospital workers did not share the view that a patient was a person with a history – for example, they reported that the porters' casual treatment of deceased patients was quite unacceptable to them.

Applying 'good nursing' to other settings

As noted in Chapters 7 and 8, the increasing numbers of older people in British society and their greater longevity means that more older people are dying in nursing and residential homes in the UK.

Despite the large numbers of deaths in old people's homes, few studies have analysed the care provided for terminally-ill residents (Counsel and Care, 1995). However, a large national study recently explored (Sidell et al., 1997) the perspectives of all participants in this care. Findings suggest that very few nursing and residential homes are familiar with the principles of palliative care. Indeed, most managers of homes see hospice care as appropriate to younger people dying of cancer and irrelevant to the population they serve. Some homes do not consider their role as caring for people till death and focus rather on the rehabilitative or warehousing models (see Chapter 8) and transfer any dying resident into the hospital sector. Nevertheless, substantial numbers of nursing and residential home heads believe that their residents are there till they die and that they should have the same right to die 'at home' as people living in their own domestic settings.

Many managers of residential and nursing homes conceptualised good care for dying residents in a similar way to the descriptions by nurses in the 1980s study described above. Heads of homes maintained that they strove to give dying residents good nursing care or tender loving care. However, careworkers in residential and nursing homes in the mid-1990s focused on relieving physical pain, rather than on holistic care.

Careworkers in residential homes are generally untrained, specifically in nursing matters. They have little knowledge about pain assessment and symptom control, nor are they familiar with the types of advice, support and practical help that they could gain from the input of a Macmillan nurse or a district nurse with knowledge or experience of palliative care. Although a number of managers of nursing homes as well as residential homes for older people are aware in general of the services provided in domestic settings by Macmillan nurses – and several had personal experience of this – most assumed that palliative care was appropriate only for younger people dying of cancer and had not considered that palliative care techniques could be useful in the settings in which they worked. Equally importantly, few heads of homes or care staff had considered that certain aspects of palliative care including pain control could be extended to and applied to residents dying from chronic ailments, such as cardiac or respiratory failure, and that access to this type of care might reduce the necessity to hospitalise patients in their last hours.

In those homes where residents were routinely sent to hospital to die, the careworkers conceptualised their roles rather differently, and some even acknowledged that they were not providing a 'till death do us part' service. Findings have indicated that levels of care for older people dying in residential and nursing homes are extremely variable and tend to depend on local conditions, sometimes driven by economic considerations (Sidell et al., 1997).

Conclusion

This chapter has briefly explored the similarities in perceptions of what constitutes good terminal care from the perspectives of workers not familiar with the principles and practices of palliative care. It is apparent that there may well be an argument for incorporating elements of palliative care into a much wider range of settings than currently available and at the most minimal level provide nationwide guidelines to indicate at what point outside advice should be sought, be it from a GP, district nurse or Macmillan nurse. Palliative care which focuses on different aspects of individual need could be available to most dying people regardless of whether they are in their own homes or in residential care. Applying these principles might enable more older people to play a greater role in their own care and affect an improvement in the quality of care they receive currently.

Part of the explanation about why it has taken so long for palliative care to be seen as potentially appropriate for all types of terminal illness lies in defining someone as terminally ill. Palliative and hospice care were developed using people with cancer as the model – where it was possible to chart disease process along a time trajectory. It is more difficult to ascertain when someone with chronic obstructive airways disease is dying, yet knowledge about pain relief is such that it should not matter if the person may die tomorrow or next year, that person should still receive analgesia appropriate to their suffering.

We can only ensure that the quality of caring for dying people is good if there is recognition of the needs of the dying person regardless of whether that person or their relatives are able to communicate those needs in words. Despite the fact that the studies reported in this chapter demonstrate good practice, at the turn of the millennium services for dying people are still patchy and unpredictable; and the care for many dying people is still unacceptably poor with inadequate pain relief and support services. Yet still so much publicity, effort and finance is being focused on the hospice and palliative care world which may do its job well – but too little for too few. Good palliative care needs to be available to a wider population than those for whom it is currently accessible, those with access to a specialist team. The knock-on effect of nationwide access to palliative care services in its broadest sense will, it is hoped, facilitate the maintenance of care for dying people in their own environments and consequently reduce the number of dying people admitted to hospital. This should release more resources for caring for dying people in all settings as well as improve the quality of living while dying.

References

Baider, L. and Porath, S. (1981) 'Uncovering fear: group experience of nursing in a cancer ward', *International Journal of Nursing Studies*, 18: 47–52.

Benoliel, J.Q. (1983) 'The historical development of cancer nursing in the US', *Cancer Nursing*, 6 (4): 261–8.

Bond, S. (1982) 'Communications in cancer nursing', in M.C. Cahoon (ed.), *Recent advances in cancer nursing.* London: Churchill Livingstone.

Clark, D. (ed.) (1993) *The Future for Palliative Care.* Buckingham: Open University Press.

Counsel and Care (1995) *Last Rights.* London: Counsel and Care.

Davey, B. (1993) 'The nurses' dilemmas, truth telling or big white lies', in D. Dickenson and M. Johnson (eds), *Death, Dying and Bereavement.* London: Sage.

Entwistle, V.A., Watt, I.S., Bradbury, R. and Pehl, L.J. (1996) 'Media coverage of the Child B case', *British Medical Journal*, 312: 1587–91.

Field, D. (1989) *Nursing the Dying.* London: Routledge.

Field, D. and James, N. (1993) 'Where and how people die', in D. Clark (ed.), *Death and Dying: Future Issues in Policy and Practice.* Buckingham: Open University Press.

Glaser, B. and Strauss, A. (1965) *Awareness of Dying.* Chicago: Aldine Publishing Company.

Glaser, B. and Strauss, A. (1968) *Time for Dying.* Chicago: Aldine Publishing Company.

Hockey, J. (1990) *Experiences of Death: An Anthropological Account.* Edinburgh: Edinburgh University Press.

Judd, D. (1993) 'Communicating with dying children', in D. Dickenson and M. Johnson (eds), *Death, Dying and Bereavement.* London: Sage.

Katz, J.T.S. (1989) 'Context and care: nurses' accounts of stress and support on a cancer ward', Unpublished Ph.D. thesis, University of Warwick.

Katz, J.T.S. (1996) 'Nurses' perceptions of stress when working with dying patients on a cancer ward', in G. Howarth and P. Jupp (eds), *Contemporary Issues in the Sociology of Death, Dying and Disposal.* London: Macmillan.

Menzies, I.E.P (1959) 'The functioning of social systems as a defence against anxiety: A report on a study of the nursing service of a general hospital', *Human Relations*, 13: 95–121.

McIntosh, J. (1977) *Communication and Awareness on a Cancer Ward.* London: Croom Helm.

National Council for Hospice and Specialist Palliative Care Services (1995) *Specialist Pallaitve Care: A statement of definitions.* London: NCHSPCS.

Quint, J.C. (1967) *Nurse and the Dying Patient.* New York: Macmillan.

Sidell, M., Katz, J.T.S. and Komaromy, C. (1997) 'Death and dying in residential and nursing homes for older people: examining the case for palliative care', Report for Department of Health.

Sudnow, D. (1967) *Passing on: The Social Organization of Dying.* New Jersey: Prentice Hall.

Thornton, S. (1997) 'The Child B case – reflections of a chief executive', *British Medical Journal*, 314: 1838–9.

Vachon, M.L.S. and Pakes, E. (1984) 'Staff stress in the care of the critically ill and dying child', in H. Wass and C. Corr (eds), *Childhood and Death*. New York: Hemisphere.

Vachon, M.L.S. (1987) *Occupational Stress in Caring for the Chronically Ill, the Dying and the Bereaved*. New York: Hemisphere.

Wilkinson, S. (1991) 'Factors which influence how nurses communicate with cancer patients', *Journal of Advanced Nursing*, 16: 677–88.

4

YOUNG CARERS

Stan Tucker and Penny Liddiard

A different story?

The lives of young people in society are frequently the subject of critical public gaze. Often the prime purpose of that gaze is to 'expose' those considered to be 'troubled' and 'troublesome'. In turn, research into the lives of young people tends to be dominated by perspectives that encourage health, social care and education professionals to respond to the needs of 'diseased', 'perverted', 'needy' and 'rebellious' youth (Griffin, 1993). In this chapter we tell a different kind of research story. It is a story based on findings that serve to emphasise the potentiality, creativity, tenacity and strength of young people. It is a story about the diverse and demanding experiences of young carers in the community.

In recent times the experiences of young carers have become the focus for increasing levels of public attention. In part this growing awareness has served to influence legislation (Carers [Recognition and Service] Act 1995) to the extent that the needs of young carers are now formally acknowledged within the public domain. However, as can be seen from the discussion to follow, a great deal of work has still to be done in relation to the promotion of the rights of young carers as potential users of public and voluntary welfare services.

The experience of caring for a sick, frail or disabled relative from an early age is not new – images of young carers abound in literature, for example Dickens's *Little Dorrit*. Yet despite the existence of historic as well as more recent evidence, the needs of young carers go largely unnoticed or unmet when resources for community care and support are apportioned (Aldridge and Becker, 1994). And in many instances, when there is a young person in the family who is willing to take on a caring role, it can often mean that support services are offered on a limited basis, or withdrawn completely (Aldridge and Becker, 1993: 37).

Research into the lives of young carers has largely been produced during the course of the 1990s, although it still remains difficult to estimate accurately the numbers of young carers nationally. Certain small-scale surveys have tried to estimate the number of young carers nationwide (Page, 1988; O'Neil, 1988). Such estimates suggest that there are somewhere in the region of 10,000 children under the age of 18 acting as primary carers in the UK – and many more who share the caring role with others. More recent estimates have moved the figure still further upwards, indicating that the number is potentially around 40,000 or even higher (Becker, 1995).

Much of the developing research interest can be directly related to the need to explore the outcomes of the NHS and Community Care Act (1990). Accordingly, a picture of the lives of young carers has been constructed which emphasises their lack of access to many of the social, personal and educational opportunities enjoyed by their peers. Indeed, young carers are frequently described as individuals who offer much needed care to parents and sibling family members at great personal cost (Meredith, 1991).

In many instances young carers take up their roles and responsibilities for the same reasons as their adult counterparts: family illness, 'closeness' to the person in need of care, or because there is nobody else to take on the task (see Pitkeathley, 1989). Yet societal reactions to young carers can vary considerably. Sometimes they are viewed as carers first and children and young people second (particularly when their contribution to care assists in holding the family unit together). At other times the defining feature of developmental immaturity is used to declare their activities as inappropriate 'for their age'. In all this we see a reflection of the historical ambiguity that has existed concerning the social, economic and political status of children and young people within the family. On occasions they are seen as adults 'in waiting' with the capacity to carry out their family responsibilities, whereas on other occasions a 'socialization mode' (de Mause, 1974: 52) is applied to family life which stresses the need for control, regulation, protection and the production of social conformity in young people. In reality, many families need and value the contribution of young carers, but have to place this alongside competing societal pressures concerning 'good' parenting practice. To have a young person caring for an adult or sibling family member can, on occasions, be viewed with suspicion and no small amount of uncertainty by some social care agencies.

Who cares?

In embarking on our research we set ourselves the task of capturing the diversity of young carers' lives. We wanted to see what happens when young people care, as well as how existing welfare support services are used (or not), or might be improved on, to meet the needs of the young people concerned. In all this, emphasis was placed on young people's rights and entitlements as service users and their ability to define and assert their expectations and ambitions. We accepted as fact that young people were caring and that whatever the rights and wrongs of such a situation, there was a need to understand the influence that caring had on their lives. By doing this we actively embraced a position advocated by Aldridge and Becker (1996: 61) that:

> as long as assessments and fully resourced support services are not available to all disabled parents at all times, children will continue to care.

In addition, it was considered important that the caring relationships involved were explored from the widest possible perspective within the family. There was a requirement not only to examine how young people were feeling about their caring roles, but also to explore how those being cared for, and other family members, saw the contribution of the young carer in the home. Here an attempt was made to counter the criticism that research into the lives of young carers deflects attention away from the needs of their disabled parents (see Keith and Morris, 1995). To put it at its simplest, caring by young people happens, will continue to happen, and in some cases young people, given the choice, might want to carry on with their caring roles (provided that appropriate forms of support are available). We concluded, therefore, that it was necessary to create a research agenda that concerned itself with examining and evaluating the physical, social and emotional contribution of young carers to family life. In doing so we accepted the fact that disabled and sick parents, like any other parents, perform their duties and responsibilities to the best of their ability. But we also felt that it was important to establish whether having a young carer in the family significantly alters the nature of family relationships.

So, which group of young people did we focus our attention on? The Carers National Association (CNA) describes young carers as those 'whose lives are restricted' because they are involved in looking after a disabled or sick relative (Heal, 1994). The CNA's definition of young carers includes children and young people who have the legal status of children i.e. are under the age of 18. However, for the purposes of our research, we chose to take account of those economic, social and political changes which have extended the transition to adulthood and the existence of a 'benefits regime' which leaves young people 'financially dependent upon the family until the age of 25' (Coles, 1997: 100). If young people are staying in the family home longer they are more likely to be called on to perform caring tasks. Thus, we aimed to examine the experiences of a group of children and young people who broadly fell into the 11 to 25 age group.

Background to the research

To explore the experiences of young carers we chose to examine two very different kinds of communities – Milton Keynes and Dudley/Wolverhampton. Milton Keynes is a rapidly growing new city that was characterised some 25 years after its initial construction, by having exceptionally high numbers of young people living in the locality. At the time of the research (1996–7), 25% of the population were aged 16 or under, with that figure rising to 38% if young people up to the age of 25 years were included. On the other hand, the Dudley/Wolverhampton area in the West Midlands represents a long-established industrialised community of around 800,000 people. The demographic profile of the area is somewhat different. In Dudley alone, for example, those aged 16 and under made up some 12% of the population, with the inclusion of those aged up to 25 years bringing that figure to 24% in total.

From the outset it was envisaged that contacting young carers would be a difficult and complex task. Previous research (Segal and Simpkins, 1993) had served to establish that young carers are often reluctant to reveal themselves. The reasons for this are complex but include a general unwillingness to be singled out as a young carer for fear of removal (or removal of the person being cared for) from the family home. In addition, many young people do not define what they do as caring, but in fact see it as being part of normal family life.

The preferred route of most research studies had been to make contact with young carers via those who carry out various kinds of professional family support roles – nurses, social workers, education welfare officers, and so on. However, consideration was given to the fact that making contact with carers via known health and social welfare personnel could pose particular problems. For example, introductions to young people might be focused on locations where 'best practice' was on view. Such a route might also bias the sample because many workers are unaware of the existence of young carers or, more typically, if they are, appear to ignore their needs.

For the purposes of our study a different approach was adopted. We attempted to engage with young people on neutral non-caring territories such as schools and youth groups. We contacted a variety of self-help community groups whose participants were directly involved in providing care to sick, frail or disabled relatives. We publicised the existence of the project in the local media. We liaised with national and local voluntary bodies who could potentially point us towards young people with caring responsibilities. This kind of extensive networking proved to be very time consuming, but it did allow us to locate a number of young people and their families who were receiving little or no support from public and voluntary sector welfare agencies.

By the end of the research period in November 1996 (Liddiard et al., 1997), some 40 interviews had been undertaken involving 16 female carers, 8 male carers, 8 adults being cared for, and 8 other adult family members. The age range of the young people interviewed was 10–21 years. Most were white: only one young woman carer came from an ethnic minority background. In all but one case the young people involved were caring for someone in their immediate home environment. The age ranges of those being cared for was 7–78 years, although the vast majority of caring situations involved parents and/or siblings. In over 80% of cases young carers had some responsibility for looking after brothers or sisters as well.

A focused interview format (Cohen and Manion, 1989) was used which enabled interviewers to explore issues of: the experience of caring; how caring impacts on family life; levels of support available; matters of personal and social development; and ambitions and hopes for the future, with both young carers and other family members. All participants agreed to have their interviews recorded on tape, and a verbal summary of the issues explored was presented and agreed at the end of each interview.

The old new problem of identification

Even though a great deal of time and trouble was taken to contact young carers in their own communities, the task of meeting with them still proved to be difficult. Often contact was hard to establish because of the involvement of a third party in the introduction process. Sometimes agencies and groups would pledge support only to 'run out of steam' and ideas when young carers did not readily reveal themselves. Schools, for their part, showed themselves capable of providing statistical data on the numbers of young people who might potentially have caring responsibilities, but often failed to convert that information into young people who wished to be interviewed.

Contact, when it was finally established, frequently involved a period of building up the confidence of the young person to take part in the interview. On the other hand, many of the adult family members approached proved only too willing to talk about their personal circumstances and the role of the young carer in the family. For some the interview offered an opportunity to 'tell it like it is'; to describe in detail what the implications of community care are for many people in society:

> What they do [young carers] saves the state millions of pounds a year. . . . If they weren't around then more would have to be done by those who are supposed to do the work. . . . The point is the youngsters involved take the pressure away. (Parent of young carer)

Key findings from the research

The experience of caring

It is important to recognise that caring takes many different forms within families. Sometimes the young person may find themselves acting as the sole carer (frequently for short periods), while at other times they perform secondary caring tasks which may involve looking after brothers and sisters. Indeed, in many instances young people have expectations and demands placed on them that they see stretching into the future:

> I'll be honest about it, I don't think about it [the future] because it scares me. I can see myself stuck at home for a long time. (Young carer)

The issue of dependency upon the young person, and how it might influence their later life chances, was raised by the majority of parents being cared for. A common recognition existed that the role of the young carer was invaluable in maintaining family life, and that their departure from the family home was likely to create difficulties:

> What Lesley does is invaluable, not just in terms of looking after me, but also for the day-to-day chores. . . . The future without her is bleak . . . will I depend on her too much by then? (Mother of young carer)

In many instances it is clear that caring skills are generally gained through an experiential process of learning by 'trial and error'. Young carers also have to cope with emergencies that require prompt and appropriate forms of action. For example, the young people involved variously encountered crises that necessitated a response to breathing difficulties, blocked or faulty medical equipment and in a number of instances supporting a parent who had fallen over and injured themselves.

An important point to stress is that caring does have connected to it responsibilities that frequently take precedence over social arrangements and activities. Working parents, in particular, need support available to fill those hours when they are away from the family home; young people have to 'fit in'; compromises are required and respite tends to come in the form of a few hours snatched here and there. Such factors also impact on schooling, even though, generally speaking, in our research, school work did not appear to suffer unduly from carrying out caring duties. However, we do note the findings of recent research by Dearden and Becker (1995) that some young carers are losing significant amounts of time in terms of their school attendance.

In reality, for some of the young people involved (nearly 50%), the beginning of the school day merely signalled the end of the first stage of caring responsibilities:

> I get my brothers up, make sure they are wearing their uniforms . . . make
> sure they've got their money . . . and I go to school leaving the house relatively
> tidy. (Young carer)

In addition there is often the need to return home speedily once school
has finished:

> You can't really stay for clubs and different activities, because you're needed
> at home. . . . Mum works at a supermarket at night so I have to get home to
> dish the tea up. (Young carer)

The ability of some young carers to cope with the pressure of school
work, reflects, in no small part, the levels of maturity and personal
organisation skills that many of them clearly have. Sometimes, however,
and it is easy to forget this, young carers do attend school in an
exhausted state – particularly when their caring duties have denied
them the opportunity of a restful night's sleep. In such instances the
existence of high quality pastoral support systems becomes all the more
important.

For the most part young carers appear reasonably happy (even if on
occasions reluctant) to take on caring roles. Yet it needs to be recognised
that quite deep feelings of anger and resentment can also develop. For
example, a number of the young people interviewed posed the question
'Why me?'. This is perhaps not an unexpected reaction and one that
reflects the experiences of adults in similar circumstances. Such anger
and frustration, however, appears to have a common root, for it frequently emanates from 'others not making the effort'.

While in most cases immediate family members offered support to
facilitate the task of caring, contact with extended family members was
far less significant in terms of the caring tasks being shared. Aunts and
uncles (as well as some grandparents) appeared reluctant to become
involved, and little support was given by brothers and sisters once they
had left the family home. Perhaps being 'out of the situation' brings with
it different expectations and priorities, even when a much younger
person may be left with wide ranging and complex caring tasks:

> We live quite close to my grandparents and my Mum's one of six children . . .
> I felt they could do so much more. They could come and see her or 'phone,
> but nobody did. Unless she went to them, she didn't see anyone. I resent them
> even now, my grandparents. Well I've got no time for them any more. (Young
> carer)

Gender differences and expectations

In almost all cases where the caring responsibility fell on a young
woman, they found themselves cast in the role of 'mother substitute'.
Furthermore, where the father was present within the family unit a clear

division of family-based responsibilities had been constructed. Fathers generally saw themselves as the 'bread winners' – even when they were unemployed – while their daughters were expected to perform the range of tasks that are frequently allocated to mothers: 'regulators of behaviour' (Brannen et al., 1994), providers of support and care, resolvers of problems and difficulties, day-to-day family management, and so on. One young woman summed up the situation for her thus:

> You're the girl; you're expected to help out and do the jobs mum does, just fill in even when you resent it . . . I'm being honest, I still think that way now sometimes when it gets on top of me. At the end of the day I'm there to help dad as much as possible whatever that means. (Young female carer)

And her father saw the situation in very similar ways:

> Becky's brilliant, she just took over from her mother in all kinds of ways, cooking, cleaning, shopping, all kinds of stuff like that . . . You couldn't ask a lad to do the same thing. Basically it comes more natural to a girl. (Father of young carer)

In many ways, the difficulties young women face reflect wider societal expectations placed on women to adopt caring roles. As Johnson argues in chapter 10, community care in many instances has 'really meant care by women'. Certainly the expectation exists in some families that not only will young women 'naturally' possess the skills and knowledge to carry out caring work but that they will also want to do it.

For boys, on the other hand, different pressures exist which are essentially concerned with the maintenance of patriarchal roles and relationships within the family unit (see Giddens, 1989). There is an expectation that they will act out the role of 'man of the house', discipline siblings and respond positively to crisis situations as they arise:

> The thing with leaving Pete in charge is that I can trust him to deal with things like I would . . . take control and sort things. . . . (Father of young carer)

The issue of the availability of free time was also one that a number of the young people interviewed focused on. However, here again, the experiences of young women were generally different to those of young men. Young women carers, for the most part, appear to have a restricted social life. Some struggle to find time to socialise with friends: 'I went out last night with a friend . . . I was something like fifteen minutes late and she was worried.' For one young woman free time had to be negotiated around her father's work commitments: 'when Dad gets up he's got about an hour to two hours before he goes out – so I go out'. While another young woman was only able to go out when an adult family member was present: 'I don't tend to go out in the evenings 'cos my Dad would be at work and the boys would be on their own.' Boys seem to have less pressure placed on them to respond in such a rigid way to family demands. And where there were instances of boys and girls living in the same family who might potentially share the caring role, it generally fell to the girl to provide the bulk of that care.

The dynamics of family life

In all this then, expectations concerning family roles and relationships can be transformed. This transformation manifests itself in a whole of host of ways. Yet in essence young people are expected or encouraged to take on some of the roles that would normally be seen as the preserve of a particular parent or adult family member. The changed dynamics and family relationships encountered, however, also have an impact on many of the adults involved. For example, some of the parents being cared for expressed the view that the relationship that existed between themselves and the young person, created a degree of confusion about their own role within the family:

> It's strange to be looked after by your daughter . . . it is reasonable to think that it should be the other way round. . . . It feels wrong when they have to make the decisions because you're feeling rough. (Mother of young carer)

When this happens parents can feel that they are not carrying out their responsibilities in a way that meets with wider societal expectations. In making this point we are not arguing that parents with disabilities, or those who are temporarily or permanently ill, do not care very deeply about the welfare of their children. However, some do experience a profound sense of guilt that they are actually denying their children opportunities to meet friends, join clubs, take part in school activities, and so on.

The demands of caring place an enormous strain on all those involved. For young carers that strain manifests itself in very particular ways: frustration with not being able to go out unless it is carefully planned; resentment directed at the person being cared for or other family members; feelings of being trapped; anxiety about leaving the cared for person alone even when attending school, etc. Furthermore, the point was consistently made by both young carers and their parents that respite care needs to be provided on a regular basis, and the provision of care should also be coupled with the opportunity for young people to take part in activities outside the family home.

It is also important to recognise that the sickness or disability of any family member can place a strain on that family's budget. Adults may not be able to work, or such work may have to be restricted to part-time hours. In some families it was obvious that very little money is available for leisure activities, and family holidays are frequently non-existent. Thus, the limited financial resources of many young carers have to be taken into consideration when any assessment is being made of their personal, social, educational or recreational needs.

Public recognition of the needs of young carers

One of the major messages revealed by the research is that the roles and responsibilities undertaken by young carers frequently go unrecognised by welfare professionals. Young people do not normally feature in the formal assessment processes carried out by social work personnel. Nursing staff fail to provide advice and information on how to carry out particular caring tasks, and the contribution of the young carer is frequently ignored in terms of its overall value in helping to sustain the family unit. This situation causes no small amount of frustration and anger in the young people involved:

> A nurse came once and that was it . . . She didn't even talk to me.

> You are ignored it's like you're not there. . . . Nobody has ever said thanks you are doing really well. . . . There is an assessment, but I can't remember anyone asking what I think . . . nobody wants to know what I want. (Young carers)

In addition, other agencies who might also provide support to young carers appear largely unaware of, or unresponsive to, their needs. For example, we were unable to locate in either of the geographic areas support activities involving either voluntary or statutory sector youth work personnel. Perhaps one of the primary reasons for this is because young carers are not easily identified. Certainly some investment in terms of time and resources would be needed to locate young carers. However, the informal nature of youth work approaches might very well lend themselves to the development of advice and information services, activity groups and counselling facilities – just some of the support resources that young carers said they would find useful.

In any discussion about public recognition there is a much wider debate to be had about the rights of children and young people as service users. For it is easy, on the one hand, to say that such caring arrangements are the 'private property' of the family; to see the welfare of young people as solely the responsibility of parents within a 'liberal-humanistic' perspective (Stainton Rogers et al., 1995) that minimises professional intervention in terms of those who are considered to be 'at risk' or have 'special needs'. And yet, on the other hand, we can sit and wait for the next public outcry that will necessarily follow the latest 'exposure' of the lives of young carers.

In all this we advocate a different level of response. A response that encapsulates the spirit and intention of the United Nations Convention on the Rights of the Child (1989) – where the child's opinion is valued (Article 12); where the 'best interests' of the child are always taken into consideration (Article 3); where 'non-discrimination' (Article 2) under-pins any assessment process, and due regard is given to the 'status' of the child or young person within the family when they are actively performing a caring role.

Thus, the research raises much wider issues concerning the par-ticipation of children and young people in decision-making. This group of young people find it difficult to assert their rights to equality of treatment and access to appropriate welfare support. Yet they are called on to make a major contribution to family life in terms of the caring duties they carry out. Perhaps it is the case, therefore, that welfare professionals, who are all the time required to prioritise the use of scarce resources in both the public and voluntary sectors, tend to ignore the needs and aspirations of those individuals and groups who do not fit neatly into the dominant discourses of the 'troubled' and 'troublesome' (see Griffin, 1993). However, the demands and expectations of young carers are unlikely to disappear, particularly when the thrust of social policy continues to be directed towards the maintenance of caring within the private domain of the family. At the very least young carers want a say in some of the key decision-making processes that can have a direct bearing on their lives and access to resources that might offer much needed support. Those who work with young people, or meet them within various caring contexts, need to respond to this important message.

References

Aldridge, J. and Becker, S. (1993) *Children Who Care: Inside the World of Young Carers*. Loughborough University: Young Carers Research Group.

Aldridge, J. and Becker, S. (1994) 'The price of caring', *Community Care*, 20 January: 18–19.

Aldridge, J. and Becker, S. (1996) 'Disability rights and the denial of young carers; the dangers of zero-sum arguments', *Critical Social Policy*, 16: 55–76.

Becker, S. (1995) 'Letter of the law', *Community Care*, 3 August: 17.

Brannen, J., Dodd, K., Oakley, A. and Storey, P. (1994) *Young People, Health and Family Life*. Buckingham: Open University Press.

Cohen, L. and Manion, L. (1989) *Research Methods in Education*, 3rd edn. London: Routledge.

Coles, B. (1997) 'Welfare services for young people', in J. Roche and S. Tucker (eds), *Youth in Society*. London: Sage.

Dearden, C. and Becker, S. (1995) *Young Carers: The Facts*. Sutton: Reed Business Publishing.

de Mause, L. (1974) 'The evolution of childhood', in L. de Mause (ed.), *The History of Childhood*. London: Souvenir Press.

Giddens, A. (1989) *Sociology*. Cambridge: Polity Press.

Griffin, C. (1993) *Representations of Youth: the Study of Adolescence in Britain and America*. Cambridge: Polity Press.

Heal, S. (1994) *An Introduction to the Issues in Respect of Young Carers*. London: Carers National Association.

Liddiard, P., Tatum, C. and Tucker, S. (1997) *Young Carers Research Project: Study of the Common Experiences of Young Carers in Two Different Communities*. Milton Keynes: The Open University.

Meredith, H. (1991) 'Young carers: the unacceptable face of community care', *Social Work and Social Science Review*, 3: 47–51.

Keith, L. and Morris, J. (1995) 'Easy targets: a disability rights perspective on the "young carers" debate', *Critical Social Policy*, Autumn: 36–57.

O'Neil, A. (1988) *Young Carers: The Thameside Research*. Thameside: Thameside Metropolitan Borough Council.

Page, R. (1988) *Report on the Initial Survey Investigating the Number of Young Carers in Sandwell Secondary Schools*. Sandwell: Sandwell Metropolitan Borough Council.

Pitkeathley, J. (1989) *It's My Duty, Isn't It? The Plight of Carers in Our Society*. London: Souvenir Press.

Segal, J. and Simkins, J. (1993) *My Mum Needs Me: Helping Children With Ill or Disabled Parents*. Harmondsworth: Penguin.

Stainton Rogers, R., Stainton Rogers, W., Domenech, M., Iniguez, L., Pujal, M. and Pujol, J. (1995) 'Understandings of childhood: a study on concept similarities and differences between England and Catalonia', *Intervencion Psisocial*, 12: 81–98.

5

CARE, SUPPORT, OR SOMETHING ELSE?

Jill Reynolds and Jan Walmsley

In this chapter we look at issues concerning care for adults with learning disabilities or with mental health problems. In the main, society is organised as if the need for care is exceptional, exclusive to the very young, the very old, or adults who experience short periods of illness. Hence, the dominant ideology of care in western society is derived from models of parenting young children (Hockey and James, 1993), whereas in contemporary community care, the blueprint for services, such as home care, or meals on wheels, have been those developed for older people who are numerically the largest group. Younger adults who need continuing support, because of long-term intellectual impairment or intermittent mental health difficulties, present rather different challenges, and examining how they relate to care throws up some controversial questions.

Care services have been challenged forcefully by (mainly physically) disabled people (see Chapter 6) as creating dependency and infantilising. Even the word 'care' is under attack from these quarters. What has not been systematically attempted is an analysis of care related to adults who, while often included under the broad 'disabled' banner (see Brown and Smith, 1992, for example), are not in the main physically impaired. This chapter seeks to fill that gap.

We address these questions under three broad headings:

- is care what people with mental health problems or learning disabilities need?
- what roles do families play?
- how can control and autonomy be promoted and sustained?

We start by addressing the question of whether people with mental health problems or learning disabilities need care.

Is it care that's needed?

> Let us state what disabled people do want by stating first what we don't want. WE DON'T WANT CARE! (Wood, 1991: 201)

This rather startling statement by a disabled writer shows that the notion of 'care' and 'carers' is not always acceptable to those who are depicted as on the receiving end (see Chapter 6). The attention paid by feminist researchers in the 1980s (see Introduction) to work carried out by unpaid women carers has received particular criticism from disabled writers (Morris, 1993). As Lloyd put it, 'The force of the feminist argument has been provided through the construction of the disabled person as a burden' (1992: 215). From this perspective care can come to be equated with control, as Wood suggests.

Since the 1970s feminists have argued for a recognition that care for dependent adults represents additional work for women in the family. Concern over the burden that this places on women led to a search for non-sexist alternatives to family care (Dalley, 1993; Finch, 1984; Ungerson, 1993). However, as well as work, care involves a relationship. Hilary Graham (1983) focuses on the two aspects of caring as it is commonly understood in western culture: caring *about* as well as caring *for* someone. She argues that women's identity is shaped by their involvement in caring, and that research on caring which shows the exploitation of women's labour tends to 'underplay the symbolic bonds which hold the caring relationship together' (p. 29). Graham warns of the dangers of separating out the 'labour' and 'love' aspects of caring since to do so is to give a reified picture of caring which may involve the loss of its most compelling qualities.

From a disability rights perspective, Jenny Morris argues that the whole notion of care and carers is premised upon the essential dependency and helplessness of older or disabled people, and fails to challenge 'the social and economic factors which disable people' (1993: 49). It is this assumption of helplessness and dependency that is being challenged by some disabled activists. If being cared for is synonymous with being dependent and without agency, then care itself must be suspect.

This chapter, however, is not specifically about physically disabled people. Its focus is people with learning disabilities and users of mental health services, people who are sometimes included in the broad category 'disabled' but whose situation, if they do not have additional physical impairments, is usually rather different from that of wheelchair users, blind or deaf people. How far do the critiques developed by disabled writers apply to people whose needs for support do not spring primarily from physical impairment?

While this is a diverse range, a common feature is that any personal care is less likely to be physical assistance than a more diffuse 'being responsible for' kind of relationship (Twigg and Atkin, 1994). 'Support' might seem a more suitable description here. When physical assistance with the tasks of daily living is not the main issue, it is less easy to identify sets of tasks which constitute the work undertaken by 'carers'. Lynch and McLaughlin (1995) distinguish 'love labour' from the aspects of care work which can be translated into paid work. By love labour they mean the emotional work that is primarily directed at creating bonds: 'the very real activities of looking out for, and looking after, the other; and that includes the management of the tensions and conflict which are an integral part of solidary relations' (1995: 259).

The kind of care offered by relatives of people with learning disabilities or mental health problems is usually quite diffuse, involving being available and responsible when they are needed, offering company, emotional support and often fighting for services. It can nevertheless be understood as labour, which is sometimes stressful and demanding of time. For instance, a parent of someone who attends a day centre may need to be on hand at different points in the day when transport picks up or sets down their son or daughter. Their time is structured in much the same way as that of parents (usually mothers) of young children is by the start and end of the school day. Some parents of adults with learning disabilities find themselves in captive roles, denied opportunities to develop the post-parenting lifestyle other parents take for granted (Todd and Shearn, 1996). The spouse of someone with a diagnosis of manic depression may have to spend hours on the telephone at times of crisis, trying to arrange for help or treatment. A survey by the National Schizophrenia Fellowship into carers' needs (Hogman and Pearson, 1995: 13) remarks that many carers' day-to-day lives are built around the person that they care for.

If support is what is needed, rather than care, then there is a need to challenge the ubiquitous use of the term 'carer' to refer to those who provide support to people with mental health problems and learning disabilities. Viewed in this context, it is inappropriate because it implies that care recipients are incapable and need looking after.

The uncritical use of the term carer fails to reflect ambiguities and inconsistencies in caring relationships themselves, where there may be a greater degree of reciprocity and symmetry than the simple carer/cared for dichotomy implies (Walmsley, 1994; Morris, 1995). People with learning disabilities and mental health service users are frequently 'carers' themselves. Indeed, those who are women may face particularly strong expectations that they will also provide care within the family. 'Eileen', for example, provided physical care for her 80-year-old father while retaining the label 'woman with learning difficulties' who attended local 'day care' (Walmsley, 1994). Women with children cannot avoid expectations that they should be 'good mothers', even though this is hard to fulfill when they are combating periods of distress and hospitalisation (see for example A.N., 1996).

When people with learning disabilities have the opportunity to represent themselves, they will emphasise, not their need for care, but their capacity to offer assistance to others:

> Again and again, self advocates would point out how they were making some kind of contribution to the community around them . . . helping others was a central issue. (Simons, 1992: 18)

Our argument so far is that caution is needed in thinking of people with learning disabilities and mental health problems as in need of care. The lead has been taken by disabled activists in challenging everyday notions of care, and in pointing out how the whole idea of being a care recipient implies dependency and helplessness. As Ann Kestenbaum put it:

> Care is being rejected by growing numbers of disabled people because it . . . relates their needs to a society which treats them with compassion, rather than to a society which respects their civil rights. (1996: 6)

We have suggested that the issues for people with mental health problems and learning disabilities are not identical to those for able-minded disabled adults, in particular that the 'labour' involved is less likely to be physical assistance, and more likely to be diffuse forms of emotional and practical support. But the disability rights perspective provides a refreshing antidote to images of those who receive care services, from family or paid workers, as passive ungendered objects.

What role for families?

If people with learning disabilities or mental health problems do need something which is not care, as it is conventionally conceived, but reliable and ongoing emotional and practical support, who should provide it? Often it is, as feminists point out, members of the family. The issue is partly one of resources. The contradictions in community care policy leave families in an invidious position: the policy espouses the rhetoric of providing the means for a life as independent as possible, while at the same time relying on families, friends and neighbours to provide services cheaply. Urged to care by pious exhortations which appeal to their moral sense, and frequently, their genuine love and concern, they are at the same time often excluded from key decisions, and, sometimes, resented by their dependent relatives. In a set of three-way relationships between so-called informal carers, service users, and paid service providers, there are endless possibilities for divide and rule. In families where a member is reliant on support, relationships are far from straightforward, for all concerned. David Jones's research (1996) on people who have a close family member suffering from severe mental health problems (usually involving a diagnosis of schizophrenia) found that the most central and common experience was of loss. The person the interviewees had known who had become ill had gone away: they had become like someone else. Many of the carers' views and experiences could be understood as an attempt to come to terms with the experience of discontinuity and loss. Research by Gareth Hill et al. (1996: 44) on people with manic depression living with their spouses or partners suggests that carers' self-esteem and self-confidence is very much dependent on their partners' mood state. One respondent reported:

> When my wife is depressed it obviously has an enormous effect on my life; my confidence is definitely reduced because I feel so inadequate, I'd go off the chart. When she feels good, I feel very positive.

Dependency on relatives can be trying for people when their relationship with their relatives is inextricable from their whole experience of mental distress. For instance, one young women who had been hospitalised several times, saw her initial crisis at eighteen years as closely related to parental disapproval of her boyfriend, pressure over A-levels, and the additional housework she undertook when her mother had back trouble. After a more recent hospitalisation as an adult she did not want to move back to her parents' home, but found that she was not offered alternative help, so had perforce to rely on them:

> And when I was discharged nothing happened, no community care whatsoever. No, not a soul came to see me here, to see how am I living, can I cook a meal, no I mean just let the family get on with it. . . . I couldn't even travel at first I was so phobic after the time in hospital. (Open University, 1997)

The close and caring relationships of people with mental health problems are subtly and intricately interwoven with the nature and effect of the particular form taken by the mental distress. Their needs for care or support may well be intermittent rather than continuing. The close involvement of families in caring when neither party has consciously chosen it may exacerbate rather than relieve distress.

However, it is not always a matter of unwilling relatives feeling morally obliged to care. Twigg and Atkin (1994: 110–12) found that consultant psychiatrists often had different views from the parents of offspring diagnosed as schizophrenic about the ability of their patients to live independently. The psychiatrists might be keen to see the person diagnosed schizophrenic establish an independent life, and while sympathetic to the problems of family carers, by and large they neglected issues of interdependence between their patients and other family members. There is a tradition in mental health services of seeing relatives as part of the social background of patients rather than as carers. Twigg and Atkin note that the psychiatrists in their study tended not to intervene overtly in the family relationship, but acted in a negative way, by not reinforcing the relationship, and by sometimes ignoring the views of carers.

Community psychiatric nurses (CPNs) did get involved with carers at times, but situations were limited to those of spouses who were depressed, and as such came within the remit of the CPN in their own right, rather than as a carer (Twigg and Atkin, 1994). In general it seems that close relatives often feel left out of discussions about diagnosis and prognosis of people with mental health problems, ill informed about how they can best help, and that they receive little attention to their own needs (see for example Gareth Hill et al., 1996; Hogman and Pearson, 1995; Shepherd et al., 1994).

The issues in learning disability are somewhat different. Historically the 'user' voice in campaigning for change in learning disability provision has been the voice of parents, speaking through powerful organisations like Mencap (founded in 1946) and Enable (in Scotland). Until People First was established in London in 1984 there was no organised voice for the direct users, people with learning disabilities (Downer and Walmsley, 1996). The result has been that at least until the 1990s it was the voice of parents which was heard, and it was parents who were consulted about the welfare of their sons and daughters, if consultations took place at all (Grant, 1996). Even the possibility that there was a potential conflict of interests took time to be recognised. As one parent commented about the All-Wales Strategy for the Development of Services for Mentally Handicapped People:

> It's the needs of the person with a learning disability that are important and the needs of the parents may be quite different. The Strategy is really providing for something the parents don't want. It's going to take a long time. (quoted in Grant, 1996: 131)

In an exploration of the relationships adults with learning disabilities have with their parents, Walmsley (1996: 326) cites research which indicates that 'living with your family well into chronological adulthood did not foster increased autonomy, and limited potential for assuming the trappings of adult life'. The results of her own research suggest that relationships with parents can be grouped into three broad areas: supportive, dependent, and conflict-ridden. Respondents tended to describe supportive relationships with parents only when the parents in question were absent, dead or distant (due to the respondent having moved away). Far more commonly in co-residential situations, relationships were characterised as dependent or conflict-ridden, and she concludes by arguing for service inputs which 'do not lock [families] into continuing co-residence for better or worse' (p. 339).

However service providers and parents frequently disagree over questions of risk. The following examples, quoted in a publication in favour of retaining segregated 'village communities', give a flavour of the sorts of conflicts that arise when service providers push for living options which promote autonomy against the wishes of families:

> A young man was moved from a campus hospital to a small house. In the name of 'freedom' and 'risk-taking' he was allowed out unaccompanied, although he lacked traffic sense. He was killed on the road within a few weeks.

> A man was moved, against the wishes of his mother, to a house 'in the community' although she emphasised his habitual drinking of all kinds of liquids. Within a short period he was in hospital, acutely ill, having drunk cleaning fluid. (Cox and Pearson, 1995: 6)

While these are quotations used for a particular purpose, to challenge the policy of closing long-stay hospitals in favour of community provision, they are illustrative that parents and service providers can have very different views of what is best for adults with learning disabilities. When the people for whom care is intended are unable to speak for themselves, through impairment, or simply because they have never had the opportunity to express their own opinions, professionals and parents have considerable scope for disagreement over what is best.

The Carers (Recognition and Services) Act, 1995, may bring about some improvement here in drawing attention to carers' needs. The Act provides for individual assessment by local authorities of carers' own needs. However, many family members who support people with learning disabilities and people with mental health problems could find themselves excluded from consideration. For inclusion, they need to be 'providing or intending to provide substantial amounts of care on a regular basis'. 'Care' is not defined in the Act, but the practice guide (DoH, 1995) directs attention to the 'heavily involved carer' and acknowledges that their typology, because of its emphasis on tasks, can be criticised for its potential exclusion of carers of people with chronic mental health problems, such as schizophrenia. A further hurdle for such people is that one of the triggers for them to receive an assessment is that the user is being assessed. If the potential service user refuses an assessment, then his or her relatives have no right to request an assessment for themselves. Yet it is often the issue of getting appropriate help for the person in need in the first place which presents families with problems.

There are clearly problems in the drive to recognise the work done by family members as carers for dependent relatives, as we have outlined above. The identification of unpaid carers in legislation such as the Carers (Recognition and Services) Act, 1995 may represent an advance in terms of acknowledging, and making some resources available to support family carers, but it may well not reflect the wishes of either party in the care relationship.

It appears that families and other loved ones are, on the one hand, expected to cope and continue, while, on the other, they are often not included in discussions about what kind of care or support is needed by the person whom they are concerned about. A rhetorical emphasis on the rights of service users is sometimes used as an excuse for exclusion of families and for efforts to establish individuals in independent life-styles. At other times, often in quite difficult circumstances, close family members are expected to provide the kind of instrumental caring it would be expensive to provide by other means.

It seems appropriate to end this part of our discussion by returning to the labour and love components of care discussed above in the context of feminist analyses. Gillian Pascall summed up the issue for families in this quotation:

> Caring is not just a labour which women are looking for someone else to perform. It involves both a relationship and a dependent whose fates are of the utmost consequence. Any attempts to restructure caring will have to take these issues seriously. (Pascall, 1985: 101)

The final part of the chapter discusses questions of how control and autonomy for the adult user of learning disability or mental health services can be promoted without excluding those individuals who are frequently their best and most reliable advocates, their families.

Promoting control and autonomy

A desire for greater control over their lives has been expressed by enough self-advocates to suggest that it is a desirable goal for many with intellectual impairments or mental health problems. Describing himself as a mental health system survivor, Mike Lawson states crisply:

> I want the choice when I want to be cared for and when I want to be left alone, like any other human being would. (Open University, 1993)

Peter Campbell, another survivor, argues for a change in the character of services:

> Like most people, we want to be in control of the significant aspects of our lives. One aspect of this is to have greater control over our own care and treatment. I believe that a creative caring relationship demands a greater degree of equality between the giver and receiver of care and treatment. (Campbell, 1993)

People with learning disabilities also argue for increased choice in the kinds of support on offer. One self-advocacy group put it like this:

> We are weary of the term 'community care' because it implies we need caring for rather than supporting us to live our lives in the community. (Northamptonshire People First, 1993)

In making these arguments, they are paying attention to those facets of care which involve labour. Choices can possibly be made about services, but not, on the whole, about relatives. If relatives feel obliged to offer care, or their sons and daughters or spouses feel obliged to accept it, the emotional dimension of care in its positive aspects can be distorted.

Those disabled writers who reject 'care' and 'carers' as terms appropriate for services directed at adults have taken the lead in arguing for services to be arranged in such a way as to maximise the user's autonomy and control. This involves separating the labour elements of care from the love elements.

Jenny Morris demands the right for disabled people 'to live in a non-disabling environment with the kind of personal assistance that we would choose' (1993: 162). Underlying the argument that assistance from paid employees directly employed by the disabled person is preferable to 'care' is that being cared for and being looked after leave the recipient powerless and dependent. If, as Hockey and James (1993) suggest, care is a means by which powerful groups – able-bodied adults – maintain their dominant position in society, then the carer can use this inherent power as a way of controlling and managing behaviour which deviates from the norm. If the disabled person becomes the 'employer' of personal assistants, this changes the power dynamics.

Ann Macfarlane (1993) describes an example of this sort of arrangement. In a pilot project agreed with social services in Kingston-upon-Thames, she and Jane Campbell, both professional business-women with disabilities, were able to arrange their own system of obtaining personal support. They developed job descriptions and interviewed applicants for posts of personal assistants who would be responsible for a variety of tasks including bathing, dressing, toileting, hair care, cooking, shopping, maintaining wheelchairs and so on. Macfarlane describes the project as taking her from 'a state which "imprisoned" to one which "liberated"'. Morris emphasises that 'caring for' in a 'caring about' relationship can only work when there is real choice based on real alternatives. People do not necessarily want to receive physical assistance from someone they care about, and, like McFarlane and Campbell, may prefer to accept this kind of help from a paid employee with whom they do not have an existing personal relationship.

The model of Direct Payments to disabled people to employ their own personal assistants is a major campaigning goal of the Independent

Living Movement on behalf of all adults who need assistance in daily living. Jenny Morris argues that the aims are:

> as relevant to those with intellectual impairments, to older people (including those with conditions such as Alzheimer's disease), and to those who are survivors of the mental health system, as they are to the stereotype of the fit, young male paraplegic. (Morris, 1995: 74)

However, most thought has gone into the ways in which the labour elements of care can be taken on by a personal assistant. Far less consideration has been given to the ways in which what we have described as a diffuse range of support roles can be delegated to an employee by someone whose very need for assistance is prompted, not by physical impairment, but by mental impairment or mental distress. The personal assistance model is adapted from the commercial world. It is bosses and managers who have personal assistants, and the notion appears to be based on two assumptions. First, that care can be divided up easily into physical labour or love; and second, that the employer of personal assistants has the capacity to manage the work of another person. It may be significant that Campbell and Mcfarlane describe themselves as businesswomen, experience which probably did give them the requisite experience and skills to be successful employers. The model espoused by the Independent Living Movement will need some adaptation if it is to successfully translate to the circumstances of people who are less advantaged.

It is perhaps for these reasons that strategies for independent living with personal assistance are less developed in relation to people with learning disabilities and people with mental health problems. There are examples in Canada of individualised funding for people in these client groups which allows them to purchase support services with the help, if necessary, of a broker (Brandon, 1991: 158–9), but we are not aware of examples in the UK as yet.

The Independent Living Movement aspires to Direct Payment to personal assistants as an ideal which will offer disabled people control over their lives. There is an implication that this excludes families from the labour involved in care, freeing all, perhaps to pursue family relationships which are about ties of affection rather than ties of obligation. It is not yet clear how this model might affect family involvement where people with learning disabilities or mental health service users are concerned.

There may be a danger that in emphasising choice self-advocates also appear to be rejecting the more positive and relational aspects of care: care as love. In Chapter 12 Brechin suggests that a 'working alliance' is a useful concept in considering quality of care. If a Direct Payments model is to be adopted by people with learning disabilities and people with mental health problems, it will be important that family carers are included in discussions about how it will work, and are helped to sustain a working alliance over its operation. Operationalising choice for people who are not used to making choices is always a difficult matter, and it will require a delicate balance for families to be included in planning for Direct Payments without undermining the wishes of the service users. On the other hand, if families are insufficiently involved in such processes, there is a danger that those people with more severe impairment who are less likely to make their voices heard may fail to get the special help that they genuinely need.

There will need to be considerably more work done with disabled people and people involved in their care or support in order to discover how Direct Payments can be used in ways that promote autonomy and control without fracturing emotional bonds. In the meantime there are a number of emerging approaches which appear to offer some possibilities for greater control by the person with learning disabilities or a mental health service user and which bridge some of the gaps between rhetoric and reality in terms of employment of personal assistants. Approaches which acknowledge the stake which the immediate circle have in moves towards increasing choice and control for the service user may have something to offer the development of the Direct Payments model.

We have highlighted some conflicts in the aspirations of service users and those involved in their support or care, but there are also a number of areas of need on which they are likely to agree. For instance, surveys of mental health service users and their carers invariably find that priorities include better access to professional support, information and education about the condition concerned, improved service co-ordination and communication from professionals and more opportunity to learn personal coping strategies (Gareth Hill et al., 1996; Hogman and Pearson, 1995; Shepherd et al., 1994). We consider here two approaches which can help improve service co-ordination and communication: *circles of support* and *crisis cards*. The former have been used with people with learning disabilities and with mental health service users, while the latter are more likely to be relevant to someone whose needs are intermittent and may take the form of a crisis.

The idea of a circle of support is to help to create a social network. The circle is a group of people who come together and meet regularly to offer support and advice to the individual. It is a way of sharing concerns and plans for the future with someone who needs extra help in their life. The circle members will spend time listening to the person and their family, getting to know them well. They will then help the person to discuss and explore things they want to achieve, by gathering information, making enquiries, writing letters, and generally fighting for the resources the person needs to reach her goals. The circle is intended to enable the person to escape dependence solely upon her family, or on paid service providers (Open University, 1996).

The approach may be most acceptable when someone has quite chronic and severe needs, and is a way of giving support to families without undermining the need of the individual being supported to choose and direct what help they receive. However, Igor Spreizer (1996), describes how, in Slovenia, a support team was formed to help him avoid going into hospital for a manic episode. The team consisted of members of his user group, friends and family. They agreed with him some rules about how he and his family would deal with the crisis: for instance, how much medication he would take, what time he would be in bed. His psychiatrist supported the arrangement by reducing the amounts of medication each week.

Circles of support have the potential to assist someone in managing a Direct Payments package. They could help to arrange interviews and supervise personal assistants, manage budgets, and generally act as advocates for the person who is the central focus.

A second strategy is crisis cards. These can be carried by mental health service users to ensure that their needs are met should they be unable to communicate their requirements directly at a time of crisis. They were launched by the International Self-Advocacy Alliance at the Survivors Speak Out annual general meeting in 1989. The user should complete the card at a time when they are not in crisis. What they specify is entirely up to them. The card has space for a nominee to be contacted in a 'mental health emergency', points that should be taken into account, actions which should be taken, and for any further comments. If the card is acted on, it could avoid problems of being given medication which disagrees with the service user, or of the next of kin being automatically contacted rather than the preferred nominee of the user.

The implication of crisis cards is that service users are put in control of the circumstances which attend an emergency. If relatives are the preferred point of contact, then they can be certain this is the wish of the person with mental health problems, and not a residual assumption on the part of others that they *should* offer their help and care. The service user can decide on different levels of involvement for people in their lives, provided they negotiate this with the persons concerned.

While neither of these approaches gives the equivalent degree of control over the personal assistance package that Direct Payments claim, what is promising about both is that they acknowledge the place of the care and support that those closely involved in service users' lives are already offering, while extending possibilities for additional forms of help. They are both tools which can be instigated by service users for themselves, although without recognition from relevant professionals their effectiveness would be considerably reduced. When individuals and their families have conflicting views about what is required, these are approaches that can help open up a debate, and may enable different perspectives to be listened to and respected in whatever arrangements are made.

It remains the case that finding ways to promote control and autonomy by people with learning disabilities and people with mental health problems is less well advanced than is the case with people whose needs for assistance are primarily physical. When the needs are for diffuse forms of support rather than direct physical care, families cannot be relieved easily from a continuing role; and our argument is that to exclude families from the process of extending support would often be against everyone's interests.

Conclusion

Disability rights activists are asking for opportunities for service users to be in control of the care they receive, through a model in which they can purchase personal assistance. However, it is difficult to be insistent about what should happen where personal relationships, involving people's feelings and emotions, are concerned. It would be challenging for people with learning disabilities or with mental health problems to separate out from the context of their close personal relationships, which may well involve considerable interdependency, those aspects of their care which can be seen as a commodity to be purchased. There are examples of approaches which involve service users in having more control over the kinds of help they wish to receive, while offering opportunities to close friends and family carers to take part in discussions and negotiations. If a Direct Payments model is to be successfully adopted and extended to people with a wide range of disabilities, it will be important to learn from such approaches and build in consultation which is inclusive of those people who are already involved in their care or support.

References

A.N. (1996) 'Paying the penalty', in J. Read and J. Reynolds (eds), *Speaking our Minds: an Anthology of Personal Experiences of Mental Distress and its Consequences*. Basingstoke: Macmillan.

Brown, H. and Smith, H. (1992) *Normalisation: A Reader for the Nineties*. London: Routledge.

Brandon, D. (1991) *Innovation Without Change? Consumer Power in Psychiatric Services*. Basingstoke: Macmillan.

Campbell, P. (1993) 'What more do users want?', paper given at the All-Wales Community Mental Health Conference. Unpublished paper.

Cox, C. and Pearson, M. (1995) *Made to Care: the Case for Residential and Village Communities for People with a Mental Handicap*. London: Rannock Trust.

Downer, J. and Walmsley, J. (1996) 'Shouting the loudest?: self-advocacy, power and diversity', in P. Ramcharan, G. Roberts, G. Grant and J. Borland (eds), *Empowerment in Everyday Life: Learning Disability*. London: Jessica Kingsley.

Dalley, G. (1993) 'The principles of collective care', in J. Bornat, C. Pereira, D.

Pilgrim and F. Williams (eds), *Community Care: a Reader*. Basingstoke: Macmillan.

Department of Health (1995) *Carers (Recognition and Services) Act 1995: Policy Guidance and Practice Guide*. Wetherby: Department of Health.

Finch, J. (1984) 'Community care: developing non-sexist alternatives', *Critical Social Policy*, 9 (4): 7–18.

Gareth Hill, R., Hardy, P. and Shepherd, G. (1996) *Perspectives on Manic Depression: a Survey of the Manic Depression Fellowship*. London: The Sainsbury Centre for Mental Health.

Graham, H. (1983) 'Caring, a labour of love', in J. Finch and D. Groves (eds), *A Labour of Love: Women, Work and Caring*. London: Routledge and Kegan Paul.

Grant, G. (1996) 'Consulting to involve or consulting to empower?', in P. Ramcharan, G. Roberts, G. Grant and J. Borland (eds), *Empowerment in Everyday Life: Learning Disability*. London: Jessica Kingsley.

Hockey, J. and James, A. (1993) *Growing Up and Growing Old: Ageing and Dependency in the Life Course*. London: Sage.

Hogman, G. and Pearson, G. (1995) *The Silent Partners: The Needs and Experiences of People who Provide Informal Care to People with a Severe Mental Illness*. Kingston upon Thames: National Schizophrenia Fellowship.

Jones, D.W. (1996) 'Families and the experience of mental distress', in T. Heller, J. Reynolds, R. Gomm, R. Muston and S. Pattison (eds), *Mental Health Matters: a Reader*. Basingstoke: Macmillan.

Kestenbaum, A. (1996) *Independent Living: A Review*. York: Joseph Rowntree Foundation.

Lloyd, M. (1992) 'Does she boil eggs? Towards a feminist model of disability', *Disability, Handicap and Society*, 7 (3): 207–21.

Lynch, K. and McLaughlin, E. (1995) 'Caring labour and love labour', in R. Clancy, S. Drudy, K. Lynch and L. O'Dowd (eds), *Irish Society: Sociological Perspectives*. Dublin: Institute of Public Administration in association with the SAI.

Macfarlane, A. (1993) 'The right to make choices', in J. Bornat, C. Pereira, D. Pilgrim and F. Williams (eds), *Community Care: a Reader*. Basingstoke: Macmillan.

Morris, J. (1993) *Community Care or Independent Living?* York: Joseph Rowntree Foundation.

Morris, J. (1993) '"Us" and "Them"? Feminist research and community care', in J. Bornat, C. Pereira, D. Pilgrim and F. Williams (eds), *Community Care: a Reader*. Basingstoke: Macmillan.

Morris, J. (1995) 'Creating a space for absent voices: disabled women's experiences of receiving assistance with daily living activities', *Feminist Review*, 51: 68–93.

Northamptonshire People First (1993) 'Response to the Draft Community Care Plan for Northamptonshire', unpublished paper.

Open University (1993) *Community Care*. Milton Keynes: Open University.

Open University (1996) *Learning Disability: Working as Equal People*. Milton Keynes: Open University.

Open University (1997) *Mental Health and Distress: Perspectives and Practice* (K257), Milton Keynes: Open University.

Pascall, G, (1985) *Social Policy: A Feminist Analysis*. London: Tavistock.

Shepherd, G., Murray, A., Muijen, M. (1994) *Relative Values: The Differing Views of*

Users, Family Carers and Professionals on Services for People with Schizophrenia in the Community. London: The Sainsbury Centre for Mental Health.

Simons, K. (1992) *Sticking up for Yourself: Self Advocacy and People with Learning Difficulties*. York: Joseph Rowntree Foundation.

Spreizer, I. (1996) 'Recovery at home', in J. Read and J. Reynolds (eds), *Speaking our Minds: an Anthology of Personal Experiences of Mental Distress and its Consequences*. Basingstoke: Macmillan.

Todd, S. and Shearn, J. (1996) 'Struggles with time: the careers of parents with adult sons and daughters with learning disabilities', *Disability and Society*, 11 (3): 379–402.

Twigg, J. and Atkin, K. (1994) *Carers Perceived: Policy and Practice in Informal Care*. Buckingham: Open University Press.

Ungerson, C. (1993) 'Caring and citizenship: a complex relationship', in J. Bornat, C. Pereira, D. Pilgrim and F. Williams (eds), *Community Care: a Reader*. Basingstoke: Macmillan.

Walmsley, J. (1994) *Gender, Caring and Learning Disability*, unpublished Ph.D. thesis, Milton Keynes: Open University.

Walmsley, J. (1996) 'Doing what Mum wants me to do: looking at family relationships from the point of view of adults with intellectual disabilities', *Journal of Applied Research in Intellectual Disabilities (JARID)*, 9 (4): 324–41.

Wood, R. (1991) 'Care of disabled people', in G. Dalley (ed.), *Disability and Social Policy*. London: Policy Studies Institute.

6

NORMALITY AND DISABLING CARE

John Swain and Sally French

In the name of care

Care is a multi-faceted concept suggesting concern and consideration for others. Caring for others and being cared for in return is important, indeed essential, for most of us. We feel happier and more fulfilled when others care about how we feel and what we achieve. Care can be expressed in many ways, by giving practical assistance, advice, emotional support, social support, physical intimacy and prayer. In many caring relationships, caring is reciprocal and may serve to strengthen the relationship by increasing rewards, between, say, close relatives or friends. It is not always two-way, particularly as we may care about people we have never met, or those who have yet to be born. Even when reciprocity of care may not always be present, however, for example when caring for young children or a spouse with advanced Alzheimer's disease, experiences of providing and receiving care can still be valued. Caring is ostensibly, then, a process of meeting people's needs and concern for the welfare of others.

Such dominant positive views of care have been increasingly challenged, and the most radical critiques have come from people perceived to be at the receiving end of care. Many disabled people feel stifled and oppressed by the care which they receive. From their viewpoint, they have little or no control over who provides it or the amount that they are given (Oliver, 1996). Marcfarlane writes, 'Many disabled people will define the care they have received as being oppressive, often of a custodial nature and provided in a controlled way' (1996: 13). Rather than being 'cared about', disabled people frequently find that others are taking responsibility for them, over-protecting them, placing them in a dependent role, controlling them and thwarting their autonomy. Jenny Morris argues that, '. . . where someone does not have control over the help which they need, their human and their civil rights suffer', and that

'. . . the use of words like "carers" and "caring" contribute to a refusal to confront the reality of being made dependent, of being made powerless' (1993: 152).

Caring within loving relationships can also lead to restriction, exploitation and oppression on both sides, especially if too much pressure is placed upon one individual to provide the physical, social and emotional support the other person needs. Parker, talking about caring within marriage, notes:

> They reported increased bad temper (from both sides of the relationship), the strain of being together too much, and the very substantial effects that impairment had had on their physical relationship. . . . Even in relationships where there was a great deal of affection, when the carer was providing a substantial amount of physical care, strain in the marriage was likely. (1993: 97)

Existing literature has concentrated on the analysis of the oppression of caring at the societal level and, in particular, the enforced dependency of disabled people in the structural and power relations of care. Dependency is not the inevitable consequence of impairment, but is created by the social, economic and political system in which disabled people live (Oliver, 1993a). In this chapter, we address the oppressive nature of seemingly humanitarian acts of caring, and the denial of control by disabled people, focusing on the personal and interpersonal levels of understandings. Our central thesis is that, at this level of analysis, the oppressive nature of care lies in its judgemental basis, and, in particular, that the dominant ideology of 'normality-abnormality' is a pervasive factor in determining conceptions of care and the nature of caring relationships. Care is not inherently oppressive. It is oppressive, however, when it incorporates a mould for the 'cared for' as a person, for behaviour, for appearance, and for lifestyle. The concept of normality and its role within the oppression of disabled people has been analysed in the literature from sociological and political perspectives (Abberley, 1993). In this chapter we shall explore its manifestations within the more immediate experiences of disabled people in relation to care.

The chapter develops through the following stages:

- *Foundations of oppressive care* – the pervasive nature of the dominant 'normality-abnormality' ideology in the interpersonal perceptions and judgements of care.
- *Measuring up to normality* – the application of such perceptions and judgements to disabled people.
- *To be or not to be normal* – the predetermination of disabled people's identities.
- *Human relations of oppressive care* – the predetermination of relationships and processes of care.

- *The recognition and celebration of difference* – the rejection of the ideology by the Disabled People's Movement and the redefinition of discourse in terms of differences between individuals and groups of people.

As mentioned above, we recognise that care can be oppressive for those who provide as well as those who receive it. Furthermore, those who are 'cared for' are frequently carers themselves (Morris, 1993; Walmsley, 1993), and people labelled 'carers' rarely view themselves as such. Our particular focus here, however, is the experiences of disabled people at the receiving end of care.

To illustrate our discussion of these general issues, we concentrate on the experiences of visually disabled people. We interviewed two groups of visually disabled people, seven who attended a special school with a residential unit, and six who attended a special unit within a mainstream school; three of these young people were also interviewed with members of their families. In addition, we interviewed eight visually disabled adults, including three married couples. We also used interview data, collected in 1989, from a group of 45 visually disabled physiotherapists. All the interviews were open-ended and covered a wide range of topics, experiences, views and feelings. We have attempted to explore the complex interrelationship between the concepts of normality and care drawing on these interviews and examining the literature relating to disability.

Foundations of oppressive care

At the personal and interpersonal levels of understanding, the denial of control by people who are 'cared for' is articulated though preconceived judgements of people, problems and solutions. The main basis for such judgements when applied to the care of disabled people is notions of 'normality' and 'abnormality'. These are not unitary concepts, but they are diffuse and diverse and pervade thinking and understanding in relation to disability in countless ways. Below we trace the nature of such judgements, and their particular application to disabled people. We also argue, however, that this ideology is crucial to the general-value basis of personal and interpersonal perception in our culture.

The development of the concept of the norm or average in European culture can be traced, as Davis (1995) does, to the early nineteenth century and is associated with, for instance, the introduction and application of statistics in social research. Closely interwoven with this changing ideology of interpersonal judgement were changes in the social construction of disability. Davis writes:

the very concept of normalcy by which most people (by definition) shape their existence is in fact inexorably linked to the concept of disability, or rather, the concept of disability is a function of a concept of normalcy. Normalcy and disability are part of the same system. (1995: 2)

He analyses 'the notion of normalcy that makes the idea of disability (as well as ideas of race, class and gender) possible' (1995: 159). Judgements of disabled people are, in western society at least, in accordance with *normative criteria*, whereby we decide whether a behaviour or situation is normal or abnormal by comparing it with the behaviour and situation of the majority. Thus a visually disabled person would be deemed abnormal simply as measured against the sighted majority, and a special school regarded as abnormal simply because most schools are main-stream – indeed, they are often referred to as 'normal' schools.

The dominance of the ideology of normality-abnormality is such that is is difficult to think of areas of contemporary life in which it is not brought to bear. Its importance in understanding the social construction of disability lies not simply with the dominance of this ideology, how-ever, but also with its inherent value basis. Social judgements of nor-mality or abnormality have an inherent value judgement of 'desirable' or 'undesirable', 'good' or 'bad' and so on, given credibility and power by association with the claims of statistics to neutrality and objectivity. Thus, normality and abnormality are seen as social facts rather than interpersonal value judgements. Drake writes:

the concept of 'normality', far from describing some natural or preordained state of affairs, instead represents an acknowledgement of the values which have come to dominate in a particular community at any given time. (1996: 147)

The value basis of the ideology of normality is predominantly negative on the side of abnormality. Abnormality may, for example, be judged by considering the contribution the person, or group of people, can make to society, that is, perceptions of their physical and social worth. Disabled people are often thought to be incapable of contributing meaningfully to the community by, for example, becoming parents or engaging in paid employment.

Being judged abnormal because of physical attributes is not peculiar to disabled people. Judgements of 'abnormality-normality' permeate all interpersonal perception in western culture. For instance, as Hahn writes:

For decades non-disabled viewers have been bombarded with almost unattainable media images of physical 'perfection' that most of them could never possibly approximate. (1990: 215)

Thus people who are judged too fat, too short or otherwise 'aesthetically unattractive' may be in a similar position to disabled people. They may develop anorexia nervosa or undergo lipo-surgery, breast enlargement or reduction, or various procedures to mask the inevitable manifestations of ageing. The willingness to undergo such procedures illustrates the enormous distress that possessing the 'wrong' kind of body can bring.

These 'ideal' physical attributes are culturally determined and are thus subject to change. It is no longer as fashionable as it once was, for example, to become very suntanned, as it is now known that exposure to the sun ages the skin and increases the risk of skin cancer. In the past, and within particular cultures, some impairments have been regarded as particularly desirable. The tiny deformed feet of women in China, due to binding from infancy, were a source of erotic pleasure to men, and the chances of finding a marriage partner were greatly reduced for women whose feet had not been bound. Similarly it was considered 'feminine' for upper-class Victorian women to be weak and subject to swooning and hysteria. This physical and psychological 'frailty' was supposedly associated with attributes like sensitivity and perceptiveness as well as a need to be 'cared for' and dominated by men. This image was reinforced by the tight-fitting clothing and the sedentary lifestyles the women were compelled to lead.

Measuring up to normality

When applied to disabled people and conceptions of disability, judgements of abnormality-normality are insidious and pervasive. Such judgements are applied to all aspects of physical appearance, behaviour, and to the whole person.

Normality can be applied to particular behaviours; when a visually disabled person holds a book very close to his or her face, squints, or fails to make eye contact, these behaviours are frequently deemed to be abnormal. They are outside most people's experience and are not generally understood, but may, nonetheless, be judged abnormal even if the reasons for the behaviour are known. Looking abnormal may be enough to stimulate an intervention even though the behaviour may be functional. In the 1950s, when visual aids were being developed, many visually disabled children received them even though they could see to read print unaided if the book was held very close to their eyes. The main motivation seemed to be to prevent the child acquiring a poor posture and to allow a greater reading distance. French, one of the chapter authors, talking of telescopic lenses, recalls:

I remembered being photographed wearing the lenses by an American man whom I perceived to be very important. First of all he made me knit while wearing them, with the knitting held right down on my lap. This was easy, as I could in any case knit without looking. He was unduly excited and enthusiastic and told me how much the lenses were helping. I knew he was wrong. Then he asked me to read, but this changed his mood completely; he became tense, and before taking the photograph he pushed the book, which was a couple of inches from my face, quite roughly to my knees. Although I know he had cheated and that what he had done was wrong, I still felt culpable for his displeasure and aware that I had failed an important test. (1993: 71)

Physical attributes, like nystagmus and albinism, may also be deemed abnormal and may arouse curiosity, staring and comments. Below is an extract from a group interview where two young men are discussing people's reactions to albinism and their own feelings about this:

James: I have people coming up to me in the street and touching my hair.
Robert: I hate it, when I was at the checkout right, this person, a lady goes 'Oh you've got gorgeous hair'. She touched my head, it was really embarrassing.
James: We went to Spain and there were these girls who asked me to cut my hair so they could have some of it. A lot of the girls try to dye it. For girls it's all right because they might bleach their hair anyway, but if we did it people would think we were really stupid.

In many ways the reactions of the non-disabled people were complimentary. From the boys' viewpoint, however, these judgements were patronising and disliked for highlighting difference.

With diseases such as diabetes and glaucoma it can be tremendously reassuring to learn that measures – of blood sugar and eye pressure – are within the 'normal' range. But even with physiological measurements of this kind, the concept of 'normality' is problematic. Many people with 'abnormal' physiological measurements, of, for example, heart rate and blood pressure, experience no signs or symptoms of illness or disease. Indeed, the potential for preventative medicine to 'create' illness and disease, by causing people to believe they are ill, is well documented (Coleman, 1988).

The whole person may be viewed as abnormal rather than just the impairment itself. People with learning difficulties, for example, were, until the 1930s, regarded as a serious threat to society mainly in terms of their supposed excessive sexual urges and reproductive capacity. They were removed from society under the guise of 'care'. Blind people, on the other hand, are sometimes credited with psychic gifts. A blind physiotherapist, talking of his patients, said:

I've had a few who reckon they can feel the strength ebbing into them from me . . . I'm unaware how I do that, it's obviously irrational. (French, 1990: 3)

Closely associated with the tendency to view the whole person as abnormal, is the tendency to attribute all of a person's failings to his or her impairment. As a blind physiotherapist said:

> If people with sight have an accident, well, it's an accident; but if you have an accident when you can't see, it's because you can't see and that is a big problem.

Social judgements are a form of stereotyping beliefs that disabled people are all the same. A blind physiotherapist, talking about his work, explained:

> One of the problems of being blind is that you are labelled, labelled with the previous person who has been around. I found this once when someone had been there who wasn't very good, and then I had to work very hard to produce my own reputation. They think you are all the same which is a great shame.

To be or not to be normal

Much has been written about the psychological, social and political consequences of denying disability (see Sutherland, 1981; Morris, 1993; French, 1993); and yet, given the strength of the 'normality-abnormality' ideology which prevails, denial of disability can be regarded, not as psychopathological, but as a rational response to a particular situation. This can lead visually disabled people, especially young people, to deny their disabilities or to try to 'pass' as normal. For at least one young person we interviewed, Michael, his whole body language expressed denial of belonging within the unit of visually disabled pupils. Like others within the unit, and some of the visually disabled adults we interviewed, he also talked about 'passing' as sighted:

> *Michael*: I'm not that bad, so not that many people know from my friends so . . . some do but they never say owt.
> *Interviewer*: So it matters whether they know or not? . . .
> *Michael*: They don't say owt, but I don't want them to know.

The pupils at the special school also talked about 'passing' as sighted when outside the school:

> *Simon*: You just don't tell them.
> *Greg*: But they're going to ask why you've got glasses on, so what are you going to say?
> *Pam (teacher)*: But loads of people wear glasses who are not partially sighted, I do.

> *Interviewer*: But if you don't tell people, don't you sometimes find that a little bit of a strain? Don't you find that you have to struggle a bit if people don't know?
> *James*: The problem is when you tell them what school you go to.
> *Simon and Greg*: Yeah, yeah.
> *Richard*: I'm not worried about telling them where it is, I'm worried about telling them what it is. I tell them it's a private school.
> *Interviewer*: So you don't like to tell them that you go to a special school'
> *Everyone*: No, no.

'Passing' for these young people involved both denial of disability and denial of the lifestyles they lead because of disability, for example attendance at a special school. In this interaction, the teacher played her part in encouraging denial, with her reference to the common experience of wearing glasses.

An example of 'passing' which emerged particularly clearly in our interviews with visually disabled adults referred to situations in which they were assumed to be sighted, such as when they used the telephone. George, a totally blind amateur radio enthusiast, said that one of the reasons why he enjoys this hobby is that people do not know he is blind. The situation can get very awkward, as sometimes he talks to the same person on many occasions and is wrongly assumed to be able to see and to do sighted tasks like driving a car. George does not disabuse them which leads him into some fairly elaborate deceptions. On occasions people have wanted to meet him, and at that point he always terminates the relationship. One of the reasons George finds the hobby so rewarding is that people do not know he is blind and therefore treat him 'normally'.

Although denial of disability was not unusual among visually disabled adults, it was most clearly expressed by the young visually disabled and blind people who attended the 'integrated' unit within the mainstream school. Denial of disability took many forms involving both the assertion of normality and the denial of abnormality. Perhaps the most dominant expression of denial were repeated assertions by the young people that they were normal. One of them, Helen, said 'They treat you the same because you're a normal person, but all you've got is a visual impairment'.

Her message is, to a certain extent, an assertion of normality. It is complicated, however, by its reflection on other people's behaviour; normality is not simply a judgement by people about themselves, but a reflection of how they are treated by others. Identity, in terms of the 'normal-abnormal' concept, is thus formed against the criteria and responses of non-disabled people and reflects the assertion of 'liberal' professionals, such as the head of the unit, that disabled people are 'people first'. This could be seen in the head of the unit's dismissal of labels as an issue. Though the unit was called the Visually Handicapped

Unit, he claimed that terminology was not an issue for himself or the young visually disabled people within the unit.

The paradoxical nature of the pressures put upon visually disabled people emerged in a number of ways in the interviews and were referred to by Alan, a visually disabled man we interviewed, as 'a vicious circle'. Visually disabled people were expected to aspire to normality through either the achievement of ordinary tasks:

> Helen: And when I go to college I'm going to travel on a British Rail train by myself.

or extra-ordinary tasks:

> Helen: And seeing as I cannot drive on a road I want to drive in a field . . . just for a laugh. And I want to jump out of a helicopter as well.

However, though Alan told us 'You are expected to behave as a sighted person', the paradox is that the denial of abnormality remains the interpretation of non-disabled people. The ordinary and extra-ordinary are invariably interpreted as 'striving for normality', or a pathological denial of abnormality, rather than emerging from the person's individual motivations, aspirations and goals. Evans, cited by Morris, points out that a common assumption non-disabled people make about disabled people is:

> That we go about the daily necessities or pursue an interest because it is a challenge through which we can prove ourselves capable. (Morris, 1991: 19)

The vicious circle can become locked when disabled and non-disabled people are in competition with each other. A visually disabled physiotherapist explained:

> The problem is, if you start introducing exemptions, you will introduce more barriers and people won't be as ready to employ a partially sighted person if they feel they won't be able to do 'on call' and this and that. . . . It creates more of a barrier and more of a stigma . . . it's politically dangerous.

Although disabled people are expected to be 'normal', a further complication arises when their achievement of 'normality' becomes threatening to non-disabled people. Alan told us:

> Even if you achieve certain things. . . . All they saw was that you were a bloody nuisance because you were successful. They resented my success, but they didn't see what price you pay to get there in personal terms.

And a blind physiotherapist said:

> Often there is an air of 'I feel very proud of this profession, and I do very
> complicated things, so how on earth can someone without sight do it too?' It
> deflates their ego . . . it's an imperious attitude, a sense of jealousy. I found it
> when I was a superintendent and someone said to me 'This is an easy job, the
> department runs itself.'

Human relations of oppressive care

Having explored the nature of the normal-abnormal ideology and its
manifestations in judgements of disabled people, we turn now to its
consequences within the human relations of caring. The oppressive
nature of caring lies, in this analysis, in the predetermination of identities of 'cared for' and 'carers', and their relationships. As Davis states,
'The concept of a norm, unlike that of an ideal, implies that the majority
of the population must or should somehow be part of the norm' (1995:
29). Judgements of normality and abnormality underlie the oppressive
nature of the human relations of caring, and determine the meaning of
'caring'.

Two major themes run through critiques of care by disabled people:
the questions of control and need. Social judgements of abnormality are
crucial to both the denial of control of the caring process by disabled
people and conceptions of caring as meeting the needs of the cared-for.
The need for care is prejudged against the norm in terms of presumed
inability, incompetence, personal inadequacy, dependency and so on.
The process of oppressive caring is, thus, conceived in relation to the
needs of the cared-for, as defined by the carer. Many forms of oppressive care are subtle and insidious, but the ideology also underpins
directly abusive interventions under the flag of so-called 'care':

> Surgical intervention and physical rehabilitation, whatever its costs in terms of
> the pain and suffering of disabled individuals, is always justified and
> justifiable – the ideology of normality rules. (Oliver, 1996: 37)

Oppressive care, seen in this light, can take many forms. The dominance
of the ideology of normality is, as argued above, pre-eminent in shaping
the aims of care – that is, the achievement of normality, or as near as
possible, for the disabled person. Drake writes:

> The reaction to citizens who do not conform to 'normality' is to seek to change
> them through punitive treatment, rehabilitation or amelioration. (1996: 148)

Visually disabled physiotherapists, for example, were taught to behave
in particular ways so as to be acceptable to their profession and to

reduce the supposed negative effects of disability upon it. French explains:

> We were taught to use special equipment that we did not need and were encouraged to 'feel' rather than 'peer' because feeling, it was thought, was aesthetically more pleasing, especially when dealing with the poor unsuspecting public. There was great concern about the way we looked in our professional roles, white canes were not allowed inside hospitals where we practised clinically, even by totally blind students, and guide dogs were completely banned. It appeared that the blind students were expected to be superhuman, whereas the partially sighted students were expected to be blind. Any attempt to defy or challenge these rules were very firmly quashed so, in the interests of 'getting through', we outwardly denied the reality of our disabilities and complied. (1993: 74)

It is interesting that the preferred image for visually disabled people was blindness rather than that of 'deficient sighted people'. Normality can be a Catch 22 for disabled people: to be aspired to but, by the aspiring, never achieved. This incessant and unquestioning search for the Holy Grail of normality is also clearly evident in attempts to teach visually disabled children to look at people when they speak and to use 'appropriate' (normal) non-verbal communications.

Another common experience for disabled people, for instance, is what might be called care which is 'overdone'. Normality is a value judgement which is not just applied to impairment but to people as a whole and their lifestyles. Even with strangers, despite the transitory nature of the relationships, disabled people experience this form of oppression (Keith, 1996). When the person being cared for is young and disabled, care which is overdone is often thought of as overprotective. The following example comes from research into the experiences of young people with arthritis.

> Many parents seemed unwittingly to extend the period of childhood without being aware of the consequences of their actions or by being convinced that their total involvement in, and in some cases, domination of, the young person's life was necessary. (Straughair and Fawcitt, 1992: 30).

Dependence is not, as is so commonly assumed, a personal quality shared by disabled people, but a quality of oppressive care relationships.

Finally, under the impetus of normality, care can also be withheld. Visually disabled people, for instance, can find that the provision of equipment is thought to normalise (in the form of independence) and can lead to the deprivation of human help and false expectations of 'coping normally'.

To recognise and celebrate difference

In this chapter we have attempted to analyse the pressures placed upon disabled people to achieve normality and/or to accept abnormality, particularly within the context of interventions aimed at care for disabled people. Central to our analysis of intervention is that care is founded upon, justified, and practised through pre-determined, non-disabled ideologies of normality and abnormality.

The 'normality-abnormality' ideology is defined and maintained by non-disabled people, their interests and their power. Arguments based on shared humanity and the essential normality of disabled people – for example 'we are all people first' or 'to be able-bodied is only a temporary state') – only serve to reaffirm the 'normality-abnormality' philosophy. The acceptance of abnormality, through arguments based on needs and 'special' needs, again reaffirms and reinforces this way of thinking.

The main strategies of the Disabled People's Movement are well documented and include the promotion and establishment of a social model of disability and, at least in this country, the struggle for anti-discrimination legislation (Oliver 1990, Barnes 1991, Davis 1993). This is not an assertion of normality, or a denial of abnormality, but a rejection of the whole 'normality-abnormality' ideology through which disabled people's lives are determined by non-disabled norms (Corbett, 1996).

Radical change must encompass a rejection of these ideas and their dominance within policy and intervention. In redirecting discourse towards policy and practice, which not only recognises but celebrates difference, the Disabled People's Movement aims to shift the power base for decision making away from professionals and towards disabled people themselves. In doing so the movement sets itself against all the cultural, social, institutional and psychological forces which have constructed and maintained the 'normality-abnormality' ideology for so long.

The struggles of disabled people and their supporters are difficult enough when the focus is easily defined and relatively neutral in terms of ideology, for example changing the name of The Spastics Society to SCOPE. However, the general assertion of normality or denial of abnormality, as argued here, is highly diffuse, pervasive and imbued with culturally humanistic values which have implications for the identity of non-disabled, as well as disabled people.

The insistence by a non-disabled person that 'you are not disabled', for example, is for disabled people, as oppressive as attitudes more usually identified as prejudicial – that is, disability defined as abnormal. This is because denial of disability is a denial of a central aspect of the disabled person's identity. The struggle to shift the discourse from normality, and denial of abnormality, towards difference and diversity is a struggle against deeply held values and understandings which can threaten the very identity of non-disabled people. As we argue else-where (Swain and French, 1997), being disabled need not be a tragedy for disabled people, but may, on the contrary, enhance life or provide a lifestyle of equal satisfaction and worth. This perception of disability, which arises from the writings of disabled people themselves, challenges deeply held, negative assumptions about impairment and disability.

Cultures which are more tolerant and which even celebrate differ-ences between people and groups are more likely to be responsive to changes for which the Disabled People's Movement is struggling. This is illustrated, in a small way, by Louise's experience at Oxford University in the 1950s:

> I didn't realise this at the time but I think it was a very tolerant society to be in because people accepted oddities about each other, people would dress outrageously and that was accepted and it was only when your parents came up that anyone commented. In a way disability fitted into that because people accepted you for what you were.

As well as the overtly political activities in which disabled people are engaged to change the meaning of disability and secure civil rights, the disability arts movement is also challenging perceptions of disability from notions of tragedy to the celebration of difference. Disability arts have the power to communicate the distinctive history, skills, customs, experiences and concerns of disabled people, which many believe constitute a distinctive lifestyle and culture. Most gatherings of disabled people, such as demonstrations, include disabled artists who express the experience of disability from their own perspective, providing alterna-tive positive, and often openly heretical, ways of viewing disability and society.

The notion of 'disability culture' can be deeply threatening to non-disabled people, as well as disabled people who have achieved assimi-lation in the 'normal' world. This is because it challenges the cultural representations of disability and gives disabled people as much worth and value as other members of society. As Oliver (1990) states, 'cultural expressions of the Disabled People's Movement provide a challenge to the stigmatisation of difference in its insistence that disability is a cause for celebration.'

The ideology of normality and disabling care

To summarise, the starting point of our analysis was disabled people's experience of care as disabling. We have argued that the controlling, oppressive and restrictive nature of disabling care is underpinned by the normality-abnormality ideology. This dominant value basis has particular pertinence to disabled people since it is key to the meaning of disability in our society. The World Health Organisation's international classification, for instance, explicitly uses either the term 'abnormality' or 'normal' in its definitions of 'impairment', 'disability' and 'handicap' (Crow, 1996).

The dominance of the ideology of normality-abnormality is immediately apparent in the professional terminology of caring, such as 'special needs' and, most obviously, 'normalisation'. It permeates the whole basis of caring from the eugenics movement to needs-led assessments. Judgements of normality-abnormality justify the power relations of caring and underlie various issues: decisions about the need for caring; criteria for assessing disabled people; the pressures for change faced by disabled people; and the criteria for evaluating the effectiveness of care. Indeed, the whole medical model of disability is deeply rooted within this ideology.

The reconstruction of care requires a shift in the underlying values from the 'normality-abnormality' ideology towards the recognition, acceptance and celebration of difference. It needs the reformulation of policies and practices away from the non-disabled 'normality-abnormality' ideology towards policies and practices that recognise differences between people and which provide support and services as a resource and a right. This is not to say that disabled people do not want 'care' (though many reject the use of a term so closely associated with oppression). Disabled people would welcome care on their own terms, through the control of the reformulation of the policies and practices of care.

References

Abberley, P. (1993) 'Disabled people and normality', in J. Swain, V. Finkelstein, S. French and M. Oliver (eds), *Disabling Society – Enabling Environments*. London: Sage.

Barnes, C. (1991) *Disabled People in Britain and Discrimination: a Case for Anti-Discrimination Legislation*. London: Hurst and Co. in association with the British Council of Organisations of Disabled People.

Coleman, V. (1988) *The Health Scandal*. London: Sidgwick and Jackson Ltd.

Corbett, J. (1996) *Bad-Mouthing: The Language of Special Needs*. London: Falmer Press.

Crow, L. (1996) 'Including all of our lives: renewing the social model of disability', in C. Barnes and G. Mercer (eds), *Exploring the Divide: Illness and Disability*. Leeds: The Disability Press.

Davis, K. (1993) 'On the movement', in J. Swain, V. Finkelstein, S. French and M. Oliver (eds), *Disabling Society – Enabling Environments*. London: Sage.

Davis, L. (1995) *Enforcing Normalcy: Disability, Deafness, and the Body*. London: Verso.

Drake, R.F. (1996) 'A critique of the role of the traditional charities', in L. Barton (ed.), *Disability and Society: Emerging Issues and Insights*. Harlow: Longman.

French, S. (1990) 'The advantages of visual impairment: some physiotherapists' views', *The New Beacon*, 74, 872: 1–6.

French, S. (1993) 'Can you see the rainbow? The roots of denial', in J. Swain, V. Finkelstein, S. French and M. Oliver (eds), *Disabling Society – Enabling Environments*. London: Sage.

Hahn, H. (1990) 'Can disability be beautiful?', in M. Nagler (ed.), *Perspectives on Disability*. Palo Alto, CA: University of Southern California Press.

Keith, L. (1996) 'Encounters with strangers: the public's responses to disabled women and how this affects our sense of self', in J. Morris (ed.), *Encounters with Strangers: Feminism and Disability*. London: The Women's Press.

Macfarlane, A. (1996) 'Aspects of intervention: consultation, care, help and support', in G. Hales (ed.), *Beyond Disability: Towards an Enabling Society*. London: Sage.

Morris, J. (1991) *Pride Against Prejudice*. London: The Women's Press.

Morris, J. (1993) *Independent Lives?: Community Care and Disabled People*. London: Macmillan.

Oliver, M. (1990) *The Politics of Disablement*. London: Macmillan.

Oliver, M. (1993) 'Disability and dependency: a creation of industrial societies', in J. Swain, V. Finkelstein, S. French and M. Oliver (eds), *Disabling Society – Enabling Environments*. London: Sage.

Oliver, M. (1996) *Understanding Disability: From Theory to Practice*. Basingstoke: Macmillan.

Parker, G. (1993) *With this Body: Caring and Disability in Marriage*. Buckingham: Open University Press.

Staughair, S. and Fawcitt, S. (1992) *The Road Towards Independence: the Experience of Young People with Arthritis in the 1990s*. London: Arthritis Care.

Sutherland, A.T. (1981) *Disabled We Stand*. London: Souvenir Press.

Swain, J. and French, S. (1997) 'Whose tragedy?', *Therapy Weekly*, 24, 13: 7.

Swain, J., Finkelstein, V., French, S. and Oliver, M. (eds) (1993) *Disabling Society – Enabling Environments*. London: Sage.

Walmsley, J. (1993) 'Contradictions in caring; reciprocity and interdependence', *Disability, Handicap and Society*, 8 (2): 129–41.

7

TREATMENT OR TENDER LOVING CARE

Moyra Sidell

Chronic illness by definition defies the expectation of cure. Although not necessarily life-threatening, chronic illness can impose long-term suffering and hardship. The relief of that suffering has not been a high priority for allopathic medicine. Medical effort has, with good reason, been more zealous in searching out and effecting treatment and cure rather than providing relief. No one would deny that a cure for arthritis would be more than welcome; but in the absence of such a cure, and until such a time as a cure might be found, there is an equally important function for the health services, it could be argued, and that is to bring relief from some very unpleasant and life-diminishing symptoms.

This chapter focuses on the distinction between caring and curing in relation to chronic illness. I am using the term treatment as the harbinger of cure and 'tender loving care' (TLC) as care given to bring comfort and relief from unpleasant and often debilitating symptoms. I argue that we should be prepared to look outside of orthodox medicine to find ways of helping and supporting people with chronic illness.

Treating chronic illness: the response of orthodox medicine

Chronic illness such as arthritis, strokes or Parkinson's disease afflict a sizeable proportion of the population. Older people, especially older women, are overrepresented (OPCS, 1983).

Orthodox medicine does provide effective treatments for some illnesses. Joint replacements bring a new lease of life to sufferers of osteoarthritis, and L-dopa counters the debilitating effects of Parkinson's disease. But apart from anti-inflammatory drugs and painkillers, sufferers from back pain and other musculo-skeletal conditions find very little comfort in the present health care system. Indeed, many people with chronic illness feel that the health care system fails them (Bakx, 1991; Furnham, 1993).

Biomedicine is still influential in western societies, with health seen as the absence of diagnosed disease. This view of health is both sanctioned and supported by the health care system. Biomedical explanations relate to the physical body, and health is explained in terms of biology. It is a mechanistic view which concentrates on the structure of the body, its anatomy, and the way it works, its physiology. This functional view of health sees the human being as a complex organism which can be best understood by breaking it into isolated parts, each with a 'normal' way of working. Disease can then be narrowed down to the malfunction of a particular part of the body. Medical treatment focuses on the diseased part, and the tendency is to concentrate on discrete parts or organs and to pay less attention to the whole or the interaction of the parts.

By far the most powerful, and some would argue the most successful, model of providing health care is the biomedical model. The NHS in Britain is based on this model and has had considerable results in increasing longevity and eradicating disease. The primary goal of bio-medicine is to treat and cure disease. The disease has first to be detected in order to apply the appropriate treatment. This is done by an appro-priately qualified medical practitioner who records the signs and symp-toms. Although doctors are now more inclined to listen to the patient's own feelings and versions of their condition, traditionally this approach has been less regarded than more 'objective' ones such as a physical examination or clinical tests – e.g. a blood test or an X-ray. Nicky Hart summarised the distinctive features of current medical practice as follows:

1. A dominant concern with the organic appearances of disease combined with a tendency to ignore, if not dismiss, the link between mind and body, between physical and mental well-being. . . .
2. An orientation towards cure, towards the manipulation of organic symptoms with the intention of effecting their disappearance if at all possible. . . .
3. A perception of disease as an autonomous and potentially manageable entity which threatens personal health in temporary or episodic fashion. . . .
4. A focus on the isolated individual as the site of disease and the appro-priate object of treatment.
5. A belief that the most appropriate place for treatment is a medical environment, the consulting room or the hospital, not the environment where symptoms arise. (Hart, 1985: 11–12)

Most doctors and research scientists still believe that the way our bodies work can be understood within a biological framework and that a cause and therefore a treatment can be found for all disorders, even mental disorders. Chronic illness represents a failure in this system, and this can leave people with chronic illness feeling less than satisfied with the treatment they receive. The case of Elsie Durant indicates some of these frustrations. This case study is based on a tape-recorded interview which was conducted with Elsie and the quotations are taken from the transcript.

Living with a chronic illness: Elsie Durant's experience

Elsie Durant was a 75-year-old widow who lived alone in a comfortable detached house in an affluent suburb of Norwich. At the time of the interview, she was a very unhappy woman mainly because for the last three and a half years she had suffered from a rather baffling array of musculo-skeletal problems.

Elsie looked after her husband who suffered from dementia which gradually got worse over a period of six years. For the last three years of his life he had needed full-time care and was incontinent. She had looked after him at home with some help from her married daughter. She had had to lift him quite a lot and she attributed some of her back problem to that; but although most of her troubles began at about the time he died, she herself did not connect them directly.

It was just before he died that her daughter noticed that Elsie had lost some height, and that, as well as the backache, prompted Elsie to go to her GP. She had various tests and was told she had osteoporosis and was put on oral natural oestrogen. She had been taking this for about a year and a half when her doctor decided to change her prescription from oral oestrogen to oestrogen patches which are stuck on to the lower part of the body and changed twice weekly. The oestrogen is absorbed through the skin. After only a couple of weeks of using the patches she had problems with her right leg – it was sore and stiff from the hip downwards. She went back to the doctor and told him about the leg and that she did not like the oestrogen patches. Whereupon he stopped the oestrogen altogether, saying she didn't need it and that her leg trouble was probably phlebitis. She was absolutely sure this was not the case. About two months later Elsie woke one morning and found that all her joints had seized up, she could hardly move. She was sent to the hospital as an outpatient for tests and was told that she had a virus which attacks the joints. She was put on steroids and told that for some people the virus goes in about six months but that it can go on for a year, even two, and that some people end up in a wheelchair. She had been taking the steroids for about a year, and the hospital was gradually reducing them; but although she had regained much of her movement she said, 'those steroids have nearly killed me'. She explained:

> My shoulder has always been bad because I can't put pressure on it. My fingers are all swollen and stiff, that's not going. I can't put a watch on because it seems to make the bones feel sore. And my wrists are getting

thinner. I've got pressure on my back and this hip. I have to use a stick, I can't go out without a stick because my back is unsteady. When I've done a bit of walking it feels like a bit of jelly . . . the only answer is pain-killers which I don't like taking because it's no good masking something, and they also upset the system.

Elsie felt very bitter because before all this started she had been very active and a keen gardener. She did all the housework and shopping as well as looking after her husband before he died. She felt that her afflictions had affected her whole life:

I'm afraid to go out, I've not had a holiday for three and a half years. I've got another daughter in Bury St Edmunds and I could go on the coach and stay there for a week or so, but I'm afraid to go anywhere. I'm afraid to do it because I'm not like normal people, being able to rush around and carry bags and things like that. I get frightened, if you know what I mean, of being on my own and not being able to join with whatever is going on.

She felt totally confused by her condition and did not know whether it was the effect of the steroids, the virus or osteoporosis which were causing her pain and stiffness. And the same problem she had with her back and the pressure on her right hip was still there. Elsie had lost all confidence in doctors and felt that they never listened to what she had to say. Every time she went to the hospital she says:

He takes a blood test, and apparently in the blood test it tells them whether this complaint is getting better or not. So every time I go, as far as I can see, he just says 'How are you? I think you'd better have another blood test'. So I've had a blood test every time I've gone, and they are going by the blood test and nothing else. And you can't say to him about your back because he's not interested, he's treating me for this complaint which he says is this virus. It gets so frustrating.

She believed that her own GP saw her as something of a nuisance and that his attitude was that the hospital were doing everything they could for her and she just wasn't satisfied.

My own doctor looks blank at me sometimes when I try to explain it to him. I'd rather them turn round and say to me, 'Well look, you've got this, this, and this, we can help you with that, we can't help you with that'. Nobody says to you, 'We can't do anything, we can only relieve it; at least you want relief'. But you don't seem to get anybody who understands you want relief.

Elsie Durant's illness had completely taken her over. She was just about managing with the help of her daughter, but she knew she was not coping at all well with it. What she said she would really appreciate was some genuine attempt to relieve her symptoms and for her situation as a whole to be assessed rather than focusing on the disease or virus. She was willing to accept that she had some condition which was not amenable to treatment and cure, but for her that should not be the end of the story. She wanted to explore other ways of making her life more tolerable.

The problem for a GP lies in the nature of the health problems presented by people like Elsie. The highly symptomatic but 'incurable' illnesses which many bring to their GPs presents them with a dilemma. GPs have little in their armoury with which to deal with these conditions. When faced with a person seeking relief from the chronic pain of arthritis, they have only painkillers and anti-inflammatory drugs to offer.

Competing paradigms: rethinking chronic illness

The tendency to focus on the disease rather than the whole person – which Elsie experienced in her dealings with the medical profession – has been termed 'the pathogenic paradigm' by Aaron Antonovsky (1984). He claims that all our models of health are dominated by this paradigm. Antonovsky points out some of the consequences of this domination. 'We have come to think dichotomously about people, classifying them as either healthy or diseased' (1984: 115). Those categorised as 'healthy' are normal, those categorised as non-healthy or diseased are deviant. He also claims that we have come to think of specific diseases such as 'cancer' or 'heart disease' instead of being in a state of dis-ease. We have become obsessed with morphology instead of theory and practice in relation to generalised dis-ease and its prevention. We look for specific causes for these specific diseases in order that the causes can be eradicated instead of accepting that 'pathogens are endemic in human existence' (1984: 115). Antonovsky believes that we need to explore the capacity of human beings for coping with pathogens. Elsie's ability or inability to cope with her pain and distress was not explored, and no atttempt was made to find ways to help her with this pain and distress. Treating the 'complaint' or 'virus' seemed to be the only concern of the hospital doctors. The pathogenic paradigm deludes us into thinking that if we can eliminate 'disease' we will have health. This 'mirage of health' (Dubos, 1961) has been the driving force behind the 'technological fix' and 'magic bullet' attitude to eradicating disease.

Health and disease have become polarised and mutually exclusive. If you have a disease you are unhealthy; if you are healthy, you cannot have a disease. Antonovsky claims that instead of assuming that the normal state of the human organism is one of homoeostasis, balance and equilibrium, it makes more sense to acknowledge that the 'normal state of affairs for the human organism is one of entropy, of disorder, and of disruption of homoeostasis' (1984: 116). He suggests that none of us can be categorised as either healthy or diseased but that we all can be located somewhere along a continuum which he calls 'health–ease–dis-ease'. He explains:

> we are all somewhere between the imaginary poles of total wellness and total illness. Even the fully robust, energetic, symptom-free, richly functioning person has the mark of mortality: he or she wears glasses, has moments of depression, comes down with flu, and may well have as yet nondetectable malignant cells. Even the terminal patient's brain and emotions may be fully functional. (Antonovsky, 1984: 116)

Within this model there is always scope for people to move towards the health end of the continuum. If the dis-ease of people with chronic illness can be relieved, they will feel better and move towards ease and health.

Antonovsky is anxious that this reorientation towards health does not minimise the achievements of medical science, nor would he wish to impede the progress of technological change. Rather, his purpose is to redress an imbalance inherent in the way we view health, not to abandon the struggle against disease but to widen the armoury and explore other ways of achieving health and in relation to chronic illness to bring relief from symptoms and provide 'tender loving care' for the whole person.

A holistic approach: a role for complementary therapies?

The tendency of biomedicine to focus on parts of the individual rather than the whole has been recognised by some in the medical profession, and many practitioners are adopting a more 'holistic' approach. This has been most marked in the case of nursing where a whole-person approach has radically changed nursing practice. But 'holism' has also been predominantly the philosophy and rationale behind 'non-orthodox' medicine, sometimes known as alternative or complementary therapy. Some forms of alternative therapies such as acupuncture and osteopathy are now becoming more acceptable to orthodox medicine, but many practitioners of orthodox medicine in Britain have been deeply suspicious of practitioners of alternative therapy. Much of this suspicion is based on what, in biomedical terms, would be seen as a lack of 'hard' evidence of the benefits of these therapies. Alternative practitioners counter this argument by pointing out that biomedicine is imposing its own method of scientific proof on alternative therapy which is wholly inappropriate because the goals of orthodox and non-orthodox medicine are different. Non-orthodox medicine is also concerned to cure where possible, while providing relief from unpleasant symptoms and taking a whole person approach are equally sought after goals. Fulder (1988) has outlined some basic features of alternative therapies. These are:

- A full constitutional and biographical history of the individual is taken and treatment is geared to restoring imbalances, defects and destructive patterns by exploring why they have arisen.
- Barriers between considering the mind, body and spirit are broken down; and everything is thought relevant in treatment including attitude, outlook, energy level and posture, as well as lifestyle.
- Therapy is based on a broad definition of health which includes complete physical and mental well-being.
- Alternative therapies are well suited to treating chronic, psychogenic and organic diseases which require a degree of individual resistance.

What would this approach have to offer people with chronic illness if it were freely available? Broadly, alternative therapies offer relief from symptoms such as pain and stiffness which was what Elsie found most wanting in her orthodox medical treatment. They also offer an understanding of the effect on health of emotional burdens. To heal rather than to cure is the aim which is particularly relevant to degenerative conditions such as arthritis. Unlike biomedicine which mainly seeks to cure, complementary therapy does not lead to the sense of hopelessness and failure which characterised Elsie's experience. For people suffering from chronic and potentially disabling conditions, alternative therapies could have much to offer. Findings from a recent survey of the perceived efficacy of complementary and orthodox medicine (Vincent et al., 1995) showed that complementary therapies were thought to be most effective in relation to chronic conditions but that orthodox medicine was preferred in the case of life-threatening conditions.

Competing frameworks of care

In the UK the dominant form of health care is orthodox western medicine. Even the terms orthodox and non-orthodox imply that they represent two incompatible and competing systems of care. Easing therapies such as massage and acupuncture have not generally been available on the NHS, and the whole range of non-orthodox medicine has developed independently and with a degree of mutual hostility. Exponents of western medicine remain deeply sceptical about the benefits to be had from alternative therapies and want proof of their efficacy before endorsing their use. As noted earlier, alternative therapies do not operate within a scientific paradigm and resent being judged by these standards. Many therapies operate with different expectations. They may not be seeking 'cures' but attempting to bring relief from symptoms which is very much what many people, especially those suffering from chronic illness, are seeking when they consult their doctors. Research studies about users of alternative medicine suggests that most people sought help because of the failure of biomedicine to effect a cure or because they were dissatisfied with their doctor. What they valued most was the 'holistic' approach which considered the 'personal context of illness', and they liked the more equal and informed relationship with their therapist (Sharma, 1990).

Although alternative therapies are sometimes known as complementary, there are very few examples where allopathic and complementary therapies truly complement each other in the British health care system. Yet this approach is much more common in other parts of Europe where the distinction between orthodox and non-orthodox medicine is less rigidly drawn. In France and Germany both are available under the standard health insurance schemes (Ooijendijk et al., 1981). And the European Community is seeking to regulate the practice and training of practitioners in non-orthodox therapies which would help allay the anxieties which arise from the uncontrolled proliferation of these practices (Lewith and Aldridge, 1991).

One successful attempt to integrate orthodox and non-orthodox medicine is the Marylebone Health Centre in London. This is an NHS health centre run by Dr Patrick Pietroni where NHS doctors work in conjunction with a range of complementary therapists providing acupuncture, massage, osteopathy and healing to all its patients – free of charge. Another very strong advocate of complementary therapies is Helen Passant, who in the 1980s worked as a sister on what used to be an old style 'geriatric' ward at the NHS Churchill Hospital in Oxford. She taught herself, and in turn trained her nurses in aromatherapy, massage and herbalism, and she explored a wide range of diets and healing therapies in her efforts to improve the health and well-being of her older patients, many of whom had lived with chronic illness for many years. She described her work:

> I began to look outside conventional methods of care – at complementary therapies which would enhance our nursing. . . . I began to massage my patients, using herbal oils and I taught my staff to do likewise. We also began to use essential oils to enhance the effect of massage and discovered that we were able to reduce conventional sedative drugs to a minimum. We used the oils intuitively. Lavender and rose geranium were used for patients suffering from dementia; cedarwood for mood swings and chest problems; cardamom for memory; lavender for headache and muscular pain. (Passant, 1990: 27)

The introduction of complementary therapies into the routine in a residential home for older people in Richmond, Surrey, proved very beneficial. A six-month pilot project was set up jointly by Age Concern and the Kingston and Richmond Health Authority and monitored and evaluated by Dr Sidney Jones at Birkbeck College. The main therapies offered were aromatherapy massage, reflexology, therapeutic hand massage, Reiki (a Japanese form of laying hands on particular problem sites) and relaxation sessions. The pilot project ran from October 1994 to March 1995, and the main effects recorded were:

- The exercise class improved dexterity and agility, and groups seemed happier and livelier after their class.
- Some found it easier to sleep after the relaxation class, others were able to release pain and tension and generally gained new confidence.
- Therapeutic hand massage resulted in a general improvement in the mood of people after the sessions.
- The benefits of Reiki included pain relief and a general sense of well-being. During a Reiki session one woman with severe hearing problems for over 40 years heard sounds that she had never heard before.
- Reflexology proved useful in treating localised conditions of the feet and legs. It also helped to treat fluid retention and enabled greater mobility.
- Deep relaxation was achieved by using aromatherapy. Benefits recorded included pain relief, leg ulcer improvement, calming restlessness, peace of mind and an overall sense of well-being for clients.

Although there are a growing number of examples of complementary therapies being integrated with orthodox care, in the main non-orthodox therapies remain outside of the NHS and therefore only available in the private sector for those who are able to pay. This raises anxieties about the exploitation of vulnerable people in a system which can lack regulation and supervision. Expense apart, many people are put off from seeking help from non-orthodox medicine precisely because it is 'outside' the orthodoxy of biomedicine. People may be afraid to tell their GP that they go to a shiatsu masseur because it could seem like a rejection of what the doctor has to offer. There is no reason why someone with arthritis should not avail themselves of a range of therapies, taking anti-inflammatory drugs from their GP as well as shiatsu massage and herbal remedies from non-orthodox practitioners. For people with chronic illness who are managing and coping with their symptoms for a long period of time, the opening up of a diversty of therapies can, under the right conditions, be of great benefit.

Patrick Pietroni, the GP who instigated the integration of some non-orthodox therapies into the Marylebone Health Centre, has identified some of the reasons why the UK medical establishment has found it difficult to accept non-orthodox therapies. One reason he discusses is the vastly different forms of therapy which come under the umbrella terms of 'alternative' 'complementary' and non-orthodox therapies. In fact, their only unifying feature is that they are outside of orthodox medical practice. As Pietroni points out:

> Some of the methods that fall into these categories require four years full-time training akin to undergraduate medical school, while others can be learnt and applied after a few weekend seminars. It is inappropriate and does reasoned debate an injustice to lump all these categories together under one definition and respond with a prejudiced or enthusiastic stance. (Pietroni, 1992: 564)

He goes on to point out some of the difficulties experienced at the Marylebone Health Centre between general practitioners and complementary practitioners (p. 566);

- The variety of clinical models informing the different practitioners, which led to different assumptions about outcome.
- The nature of the referral process and the power issues implied by the general practitioner acting as the only gatekeeper.
- Organisational conflicts that arise out of the appropriate allocation of resources (rooms, funds, secretarial help, etc).
- Empowerment of patients and the subsequent disempowerment of practitioners.

Many alternative practitioners might feel that their professional autonomy would be threatened if they were to operate within an NHS primary health care team under its present form. Pietroni advocates a change to the traditional model of primary health care where the GP acts as contract holder and gatekeeper. He proposes a multi-professional model of practice where all clinicians and senior administrative staff jointly own the premises, where decisions are made by a practice management group which would comprise the multi-professional team. Medical accountability would be corporate and not individual, and patients would be registered with the 'practice', not an individual GP. In this system a patient might make an appointment directly to see the acupuncturist rather than first being referred by the GP.

Conclusion

Orthodox medicine has failed many people with chronic illness whose symptoms resist treatment and cure. This gap in our health care system could be filled by the judicious use of certain non-orthodox therapies. It is not within the scope of this chapter to differentiate between the array of non-orthodox therapies on offer but to argue for neither a prejudiced nor an overenthusiastic response to their adoption within the NHS. This would make them more widely and freely available and also open to regulation and accountability. Increasing the armoury of easing therapies would bring much needed relief to many sufferers of chronic illness.

References

Antonovsky, A. (1984) 'The sense of coherence as a determinant of health', in J.P. Matarazzo (ed.), *Behavioural Health*. New York: Wiley.

Bakx, K. (1991) 'The "eclipse" of folk medicine in western society', *Sociology of Health and Illness*, 13: 17–34.

Dubos, R. (1961) *Mirage of Health*. New York: Andor Books.

Fulder, S. (1988) *The Handbook of Complementary Medicine*, 2nd edn. Oxford: Oxford University Press.

Furnham, A. (1993) 'Attitudes to alternative medicine; a study of the perception of those studying orthodox medicine', *Complementary Therapies in Medicine*, 1: 120–126.

Hart, N. (1985) *The Sociology of Health and Medicine*. Ormskirk: Causeway Books.

Lewith, G. and Aldridge, D. (eds) (1991) *Complementary Medicine and the European Community*. Saffron Walden: The C.W. Daniel Company Limited.

Ooijendijk, W.T.M., Mackenback, J.P. and Limberger, H.H.B. (1981) *What is Better? An Investigation into the Use of, and Satisfaction with, Complementary and Official Medicine in the Netherlands*. London: Threshold.

Office of Population Censuses and Surveys (OPCS) (1993) *General Household Survey, 1991*. London: OPCS.

Passant H (1990) 'A holistic approach in the ward', *Nursing Times* 86, 24 January: 26–8.

Pietroni, P. (1992) 'Beyond the boundaries: relationship between general practice and complementary medicine', *British Medical Journal*, 305: 564–6.

Sharma, U. (1990) 'Using alternative therapies: marginal, medical and cultural concerns', in P. Abbott and G. Payne (eds), *New Directions in the Sociology of Health*. London: Falmer Press. pp. 127–39.

Sidell, M. (1995) *Health in Old Age: Myth, Mystery and Management*. Buckingham: Open University Press.

Vincent, C., Furnham, A. and Willsmore, M. (1995) 'The perceived efficacy of complementary and orthodox medicine in complementary and general practice patients', *Health Education Research*, 10 (4): 395–405.

8

CARING IN PLACE

Sheila M. Peace

Community care is said to:

> enable people to live as normal a life as possible in their own homes or in a
> homely environment in the community. (para 1.8, *Caring for People*, 1989)

Most informal caring relationships take place within contexts which are
shaped by family histories, shared experiences, attachments and emotional commitments. They are commonly affectional relationships, but in
most cases also highly instrumental, requiring practical tasks to be
undertaken in order to meet daily needs. While 'caring about' someone
may exist unbounded, 'caring for' someone demands a setting, a
physical space to embody caring tasks which is most commonly the
domestic home in 'ordinary' housing. Yet for some people at different
stages of their lives and for different periods of time, care and daily
living become in some ways formalised, facilitated or organised by paid
carers and carried out in a range of settings. The more common
experiences are short stays in hospital or the childs' experience of a
nursery class or day school; the less common, but perhaps more
intensely felt, involve long periods of time away from home.

This chapter seeks to examine further what caring in place really
means. The rhetoric of community care has at its heart a basic philosophical principle that 'receiving care at home is infinitely better than in
institutions'. While family living based in the 'home', and termed
domestic, is put forward as a model for other care settings, our imagi-
nations around institutional care have been fed on a diet of abuse and
oppressive regimes such that:

> community-based domestic settings = family = good
> and
> group care settings = institutional = bad.

Place	Care	Time	Example
Domestic	Unpaid Paid	Continuous	Care in own home
Domestic	Unpaid Paid	Continuous	Care in informal carer's home
Domestic	Paid	Continuous	Foster care Abbeyfield House Small residential homes for adults
Domestic	Paid	Daily, intermittent	Childminding Respite care
Non-domestic	Paid	Daily	Day care – hospital, centre, community hall, residential home
Non-domestic	Paid	Intermittent	Respite care in residential care home
Non-domestic	Paid Unpaid	Continuous	Hostels, purpose-built group homes
Non-domestic	Paid	Continuous	Residential care home, nursing home, hospital

Figure 8.1 *Places for care*

The stark comparison between 'home' and 'institution' has been made many times. In the field of disability it has been central to debates about 'ordinary living' environments and 'special needs' housing (King's Fund Centre, 1980; Towell, 1988; BCODP, 1996). In the care of older people critiques of residential care have been set alongside the need for greater support to families and the development of alternative environments such as sheltered housing (Townsend, 1962; 1986). More specifically, Willcocks et al. (1987) have considered how the model of the domestic home has been used within the design and organisation of care settings for older people; Higgins (1989) has discussed the use of the rhetoric of home within our understanding of institutions; Allen (1989) has identified who crosses the boundaries of the home in terms of the role of kin and non-kin; Arber and Ginn (1991) have begun to explore the context of caring; Dalley (1996) has sought an alternative justification for collective living outside of the family, and Twigg (1997) has considered the boundaries of formal and informal care within the home.

The range of people (paid/unpaid carers), places (domestic/non-domestic) and times (daily, intermittent, continuous) involved in caring relationships is complex (see Figure 8.1). For some these demand constant short-term transitions in place, for others long-term, more permanent changes. For example: many older people continue to stay at home while a range of formal carers – home care, meals on wheels, community nurses – move in and out in order to offer support; in other situations the adult or child in need of care moves to the home of the carer such as in childminding, fostering or respite care schemes; some people find that daily or periodic day care may meet their needs for company, meals, help with personal hygiene and/or to provide respite for informal carers; while still others experience a more permanent move to situations where accommodation and care are more closely intertwined – hostels, group homes, residential care and nursing homes.

This discussion recognises the complexities which lie at the boundaries of caring places – between individualised and group care, paid and unpaid care in public and private spaces. It focuses on the similarities and differences between them and in so doing aims to shed some new light on why these boundaries can sometimes be so difficult to cross, while at other times they are easily abused. It seeks to build on the work of earlier authors mentioned above by bringing together the people and the places and recognising the importance of time and space. This analysis is carried out primarily in relation to the experiences of older people who, in the main, have not spent their lives as recipients of paid care and who commonly come to consider their need for accommodation and care services after a lifetime of living in their own homes and managing their own affairs. To begin, there is a need to establish some of the basic features of domestic and non-domestic settings and who lives where.

Domestic settings as care environments

As noted above, while some people may receive care services in their own homes, others receive services in the home of the carer(s). So what do we know about the domestic setting that we so often call 'home'? In our western culture home has become the embodiment of family life and in particular the normative ideal of the nuclear family – 'two plus two children'. As a physical environment the home has traditionally been seen as a 'woman's place' where domestic work is undertaken. Housework, the nurturing of children, the care of family members and the pursuit of leisure are all activities which go on within the home. Formerly (and now less frequently) a place of reproduction,[1] it has now become a centre of consumption and caring. While there is a history of paid home-working, with the home as a place of production, currently this is not its dominant function though patterns of home-working are changing.

The home has also been defined as a private sphere rather than a public one, and this has been reflected in the form in which domestic housing has evolved. The feminist architectural group Matrix (1984) in their analysis of English housing point to the ways in which over time domestic spaces have reflected changing ideas about family life based on middle-class values as perceived by predominantly male designers. In particular, housing has been increasingly designed for the nuclear, rather than the extended, family; and the development of, and access to, modern conveniences and new technology have increased the self-sufficiency of the family unit:

> The most striking theme of the plans is the privatisation of family life. Accommodation for each household became self-contained as a family unit. While very little privacy is provided for the individual within the family, families as a whole were increasingly expected to be private from each other. The dominant household form – almost the only one that has been designed for – is that of the nuclear family. Yet there have been subtle shifts in relationships within households which vary from decade to decade and from class to class. (Matrix, 1984: 55)

One of the most important factors highlighted here is the fundamental importance that *privacy* has for many people living within family homes in Britain today. This concept which is often equated with (although not synonymous with) *private space* is concerned with the individual's ability to control what they reveal of themselves to others and demands that individuals have access to solitude (separation from other people) and anonymity (being within a group but apart from it) (Ittelson et al., 1974; Willcocks et al., 1987). The sense of control which privacy represents can be seen to contribute to a sense of independence, autonomy and individuality, although this may vary between members of a household and be culturally specific.[2] In the quote set out above privacy operates at the level of the family or the household rather than the individual. Individuals within the family or household may have unequal access to private space; some, like the busy housewife, may find little privacy (Holland, 1996). However, during the latter half of the twentieth century children have come to experience (and expect) more privacy in the home, especially teenagers (Matrix, 1984). The need for 'a bedroom of one's own' which is a bounded, personalised space is now well-established in middle-class families and reinforced where there are children of different sexes. It is an aspect of the built environment which has found support within non-domestic residential care environments.

The concept of privacy beyond its spatial dimensions also encompasses issues of *choice* and *accountability*. The choices people make about what they can and cannot do within their own homes remains for most unproblematic. While legislation may have developed which acknowledges the rights of children, women and people from different ethnic groups, familiar traditions around the rights of households still remain. In relation to the physical environment of the home people can be advised on good practice in terms of, say, food hygiene and fire safety but the environmental health officer and the fire officer do not call except if lives have been put in danger. While it is common knowledge that the right to change the design of a building may need planning permission, the rights of different people to access within the domestic home depend upon the circumstances. Those seeking access need authority – from the gasman who has a right to read the meter, to the police officer with a warrant to search; to social services staff who have rights to follow up suspected cases of child or adult abuse, to the estranged marriage partner prevented from access through a court order. To some extent then the privacy of the home can be protected, although this has to be set alongside the protection of the individual.

People are accountable for their actions within their own homes and yet lives remain relatively private. The home as a place of informal care provided to family members is not a regulated setting, but if used as a place of paid care it may be subject to regulation and inspection. For example, under the Children Act 1989 registered childminders are subject to annual inspection and there are strict regulations regarding fire and health safety. Since the Registered Homes (Amendment) Act 1991, small residential homes for adults with fewer than four places have had to be registered with the local authority; and while not mandatory, many inspection units do carry out annual visits (Holland and Peace, 1997). However, at the present time anomalies exist and small homes for children remain unregulated. Such homes are commonly domestic settings – a majority, the family home run by the owners. In all of these circumstances the home as a *place of un-paid care* has become the home as a *place of paid care work*. In some cases these two functions are carried on simultaneously. The domestic home is more accountable to public scrutiny and yet the sense of ownership and attachment to place remains.

In the examples given here identification with place through ownership and attachment is more firmly centred with the carer(s) than the cared-for(s). Where the family allows itself to take into its home the care of non-family members, then the demarcation of domestic space as public and private (family and non-family) is important in maintaining this identification (the childminder's children have their own rooms to retreat to). For the non-family member, moving to non-familiar territory can mean a loss of self-identification with place. The changing nature of home and home-life has meant that it has come to mean something more than just a habitat, a form of shelter, it is a part of our psychological environment and impacts upon well-being (Sixsmith and Sixsmith, 1990; Altman and Low, 1992; Gurney and Means, 1993). Talk to people of home and they talk about security, safety, permanency, a private place where they can 'be themselves', of possessions, decoration, creativity, intimacy, control. The home can become a repository of objects, possessions and associated memories which provide continuity between past and present. This is the language of *attachment to place* and of a major investment in people's lives (Altman and Low, 1992). But while most people tend to express positive views about their home, the experience of home can be both positive and negative. Some may talk of isolation, fear, conflict, insecurity, abuse, loneliness and physical environments which no longer meet needs. Feelings about home are complex and often contradictory such that a poor physical environment may also be a secure environment or a much-loved home a place of abuse. These are factors which some people find themselves setting alongside an alternative of homelessness itself, or in the case of many older people, the option of re-locating late in life.

In the maintenance of well-being, much attention has been paid to the attachment to significant people and continuity in relationships, particularly within childhood but also across the lifespan (Bowlby, 1969; Jerrome, 1996). In later life, when the likelihood of losing significant others becomes most common, attachment to place, as an alternative source of well-being, should be considered seriously. Arber and Ginn (1991: 140–2) highlight four factors which reinforce the importance of familiarity of place when considering contexts of care: the association of place with the maintenance of roles throughout life – argued as particularly important to older women; the concealment of frailty and the maintenance of competency within a familiar place; the importance of privacy in relation to intimate care, and the need for older people to maintain their independence and not to feel a burden on others. The changing nature of households and housing tenure in the late twentieth century make these considerations more, not less, pertinent.

Homes, Households and Caring

The Matrix quote from the 1980s alludes to 'subtle shifts' in households which have become far more overt in the mid-1990s. It is not just, 'what is home?', but also, 'who lives within the home?'. A household is defined in a different way from the family; for one thing, the occupants may or may not be related by blood, marriage or ties of affection. The 1991 Census has this definition:

> A *household* is defined as one person living alone or a group of persons (not necessarily related) living at the same address with common housekeeping – that is sharing at least one meal a day or sharing a living room or sitting room. (HMSO, 1992: 2, para 4.3)

So, to be a household of more than one person, there is an element of sharing of meals and space. A 'communal establishment' is defined as somewhere where communal catering is provided and includes hotels, boarding houses, hospitals and homes (HMSO, 1992). Here 'communal catering' implies an organisational structure over and above 'common housekeeping'.

The twentieth century has seen dramatic changes in the nature of households. In 1961 there were 16.2 million households in Britain, while in 1994 there were 23.1 million. This rise has been due to a wide range of factors but of greatest importance has been the growth in one-person households amongst the older age groups (particularly older women in their 80s) and younger men in their 20s; the relative decline of married couples with 1–2 dependent children, and the growth of households of lone parents with dependent children (see Haskey, 1996). What these figures begin to tell us is that households have become smaller and more diverse and so too will be the types of homes established, pre-dominantly within existing housing stock. Not surprisingly, older people have occupied some of the older housing stock in need of greatest repair, yet recent surveys show an improvement in their housing conditions (Department of Environment, 1993). While there has been some targeting of new housing at the one-person household, particularly with the development of sheltered housing schemes for older people to rent and buy (see Peace and Johnson, 1997), the last 20 years have been a rather stagnant period for new housing, and the family home still remains dominant.

For older people, particularly older women, living alone in their own home at the end of life is a common experience. Also common among today's older generations is the experience of owner-occupation, as over half of all retired people now own their own home outright (Office for National Statistics, 1997). Yet at an earlier stage of their lives many will almost certainly have rented property and have shared accommodation with other family and non-family members[3] (Holland, 1996a; Peace and Johnson, 1997). It is argued that an investment in private capital allows people to develop control over their own personal territory and a form of ontological security (Saunders, 1990), although issues concerning ownership and security remain subject to debate (Gurney and Means, 1993). What is perhaps more important is that the experience of privatised family life now includes long periods of living either alone or as a couple. This, together with the investment in home as a place of consumption, has in some ways made our lives more individualised. Attachment to home goes hand in hand therefore with greater individualisation. But the private home is also seen as a financial asset which may be both inherited by subsequent generations and/or, more commonly now, used to support the funding of accommodation and care in later life. In this sense housing is a form of consumption in itself, as well as the embodiment of care.

How may these changes in the nature of households and investment in the home affect people's views on how and where care may be received? Arber and Ginn's (1991) explorations of older people's preferences for how and where they receive community-based care and from whom reflect the importance of remaining in your own home. In their estimation staying in one's own home and being cared for by someone who does not live there is preferred to moving in with an informal carer. This maintains a pattern of independent living between adult generations which is long established within British culture and reinforced by the more complex patterns of kinship with family members often living distant from each other (Wall, 1984). Self-care or spouse care are the preferred options for most older people; and there is evidence that if people are not living with a spouse and they have care needs, then they increasingly prefer the support of formal carers, which adds to a picture of self-sufficiency (Ackers and Abbott, 1996; Phillipson, 1990). It is the combination of independent living, manageable space and availability of care that makes sheltered housing attractive to some older people, although it is also argued that these needs could be met without the development of age-segregated housing through greater investment in small housing units and a greater variety of home-based services (Women's Design Service, 1991; Peace, 1993). Given the differences in life expectancy between men and women, and the fact that older women have a greater incidence of chronic long-term health problems than men, it is not surprising that women form the major recipients of formal services in old age (Arber and Ginn, 1991). It is also women who are more likely to experience the change of environment which results in living in residential care or nursing homes (Arber and Ginn, 1991). Changes in places may therefore occur when people are at their most vulnerable to attacks upon their self-identity – so what can the non-domestic setting offer them?

Non-domestic settings as care environments

As shown in Figure 8.1 there are a range of non-domestic settings which offer care services on either a daily, intermittent or long-term basis. Here the focus is predominantly on those settings which offer 24-hour care and accommodation for older people: sheltered housing, residential care homes and nursing homes, settings which at the end of the twentieth century are begininng to share some common features. But first, as with domestic settings, there is a history grounded in institutional care. There seems to be an inherent contradiction in the juxtaposition of institution and care. Much of the ill-feeling is due to the way in which institutions, from the early workhouses and asylums, have been used to *control* as well as care, to protect and isolate the general public from those deemed to be a danger to it – the feckless, the mad, the poor, the old, and the infirm (Peace et al., 1997). Operating in the public arena, these institutions were (and some would argue still are) as much about maintaining social control and the cohesion of society as they were about the care and day-to-day lives of those who lived and worked within them. In this way they were not seen as giving people a choice over where and how they might receive accommodation and care – that was seen as the province of the family and the home.

Daily living in institutional settings was often seen as a reflection of this wider purpose. In the 1950s, 1960s and 1970s the function of such institutions was gradually unravelled. Studies within mental hospitals (Barton, 1959; Morris, 1969; Miller and Gwynne, 1972) and old people's homes (Townsend, 1962) revealed the features of 'institutionalisation' perhaps most commonly associated with the work of Irving Goffman whose book *Asylums* (1961) included the essay on 'the characteristics of "total" institutions' which identified the following four underlying features:

- *Batch living* – where people are treated as a homogenous group without the opportunity for personal choice. Activity is taken *en masse*. Rules and regulations dominate and residents are watched over by staff.
- *Binary management* – where the two worlds of residents and staff are seen to be totally separate, with staff wielding power over residents through maintaining distance between them.
- *The inmate role* – where people who come to live in institutions are stripped of their former roles, made to break with the past, lose their personal identity and become an inmate.
- *The institutional perspective* – over time the inmate may come to accept the loss of self and the power of the institution

Goffman does not suggest that these characteristics always occur in institutional settings but that they can occur and are related to each other. They are most likely to occur in what he considered 'closed' institutions – those least open to the influence of the wider community and society.

The four characteristics given above have been utilised by researchers in a wide range of settings (e.g. King et al., 1971) where they have commonly been translated into concerns for: the public nature of life in care; choice over daily living activities; the relationships between paid workers and residents, and the maintenance of individual autonomy and well-being within group living. These ideas still provide fruitful areas for exploring change within care settings and for contrasting domestic and non-domestic settings. But first, there is a need to consider the wider context in which settings which provide accommodation and care for older people have developed over the past 20 years, for, as with many other care services, it is the market economy through the independent sector which now drives the provision of care environments and the places for care.

Changes in ownership, changes in environment?

In 1981, there were 220,300 places for older people and chronically sick and disabled people in residential care homes – 62% were provided and run by local authorities, 20% by voluntary organisations and 18% by the private sector. By 1994, 55% of homes were run by the private sector, 28% by local authorities and 17% by voluntary organisations (Laing, 1995). In addition, by the early 1990s growth in nursing home provision was beginning to outstrip that of residential care (Laing, 1996). Such figures highlight the major changes in providers of care settings: but the concern here is not with the privatisation of or 'perverse incentive' towards residential care of the 1980s which is well-documented (Audit Commission, 1985, 1986), nor the consequent push towards community care, rather it is with the changing nature of the residential environment seen alongside developments in both sheltered housing and nursing homes.

During the post-war period new buildings gradually replaced old hospital stock, the development of the local authority residential home saw fluctuations in *size* – with recommendations for 30-bedded and 60-bedded homes (Peace, 1986), and changes in *design*: the 1973 Building Note introduced the idea of 'family' groups/units in larger homes both in 'new build' and adapted settings (Willcocks et al., 1987). Emphasis also began to be placed on the wishes of older people for greater privacy through having a single room rather than the sharing of double or multiple bedrooms which were common in the early 1980s (Peace et al., 1982; Willcocks et al., 1987). The balance of public to private space within homes therefore began to shift in favour of greater privacy.

The coming of the residential home as a small business in the 1980s saw another change in the type of environment which was more akin to the long-standing history of the private nursing home (Davis, 1987). Proprietors, commonly husband-and-wife teams, utilised large detached domestic houses as homes, often adding modern extensions as bedroom wings in order to accommodate more single bedrooms (Weaver, Willcocks and Kellaher, 1985). Laing reports that in the year to mid-1994 'the average new private (non-corporate) residential registration was 16 beds, [whereas] the average new nursing home registration was 36 beds' (Laing, 1995, PA222). The use of large domestic settings has continued, but in addition the corporate sector has entered the industry and at this end of the spectrum there are a wider variety of purpose-built facilities. The range of amenities available within homes has grown – for example, there has been an increase in ensuite rooms (Laing, 1996), but such amenities come at a financial cost; and finding an environment which provides desired accommodation with flexible levels of care is still the province of a minority within a minority. Finally, in terms of the physical environment there is growing recognition of the needs of older people with dementia who form a growing proportion of residents. Here the design of homes seeks to compensate for and maintain changing capabilities through colour coding, wanderers' gardens, individualised bedrooms and the therapeutic use of visual and aural stimulation which seek to reinforce self-control and self-identity (Dunlop, 1994).

Alongside these changes in the physical environment, there has been a continued concern to develop practice in homes which allows a more individualised or person-centred approach to care within group settings. From the 1970s onwards discussions have taken place concerning the rights of older people to choose how they live their lives in care, the need for staff to pay greater attention to 'getting to know' residents – their past lives and their present needs. One of the most common findings among quality of life studies in residential homes is the desire expressed by older people for staff to see them as themselves behind their ageing bodies, spending time talking with them and enabling people to maintain autonomy and control, even though they may be unable to carry out activities of daily living. The quality of residents' lives is also reflected in their relationships with other residents and how they spend their time (Reed and Payton, 1997). Much is known about 'what should or could happen in care settings' and at present it would be fair to say that examples of good and bad environments stand alongside each other. Even to this day evidence is still presented of care staff whose time is taken up with physical caring tasks; and of residents with little choice and little privacy, who have lost contact with their former lives and their former selves (Peace et al., 1997).

In the 1980s our knowledge of the physical and social environments was made public through developments in the regulation of care settings. While private and voluntary sector residential care homes have been registered with local authorities since the Second World War, and nursing homes even earlier (Peace et al., 1997), it was really the growth of the private sector in the early 1980s which led to the development of a more comprehensive system of regulation involving inspection as well as registration. This was encoded in the Registered Homes Act 1984 and its accompanying regulations, guidance and code of practice (Department of Health and Welsh Office, 1990). Later the NHS and Community Care Act, 1990, brought local authority provision into this system through the setting up of 'arm's length' inspection units. Regulation has meant that homes must now meet conditions of fitness concerning – fit people to run homes; fit buildings and fit care plans – and that issues of quality control and quality assurance are given a much higher profile (Peace et al., 1997).

In contrast, sheltered housing for older people has not been subject to regulation, although more recent developments which provide housing with care – a hybrid of sheltered housing and residential care – are commonly registered with the local authority and/or health authority. The history of sheltered housing since the 1950s runs in parallel to that of the residential sector but finds its roots in housing policy and the need both to address social aspects of accommodation and, at the same time, to encourage the release of what was seen as under-occupied family-sized housing (Peace et al., 1997). Developed predominantly in the public sector, there has been a range of provision from old people's bungalows (known as Category One) to the more common grouped housing for older people (bedsits or one bedded flats) with or without access to a warden living on site and/or an alarm system. Today sheltered schemes are in a period of change. More commonly seen as a 'home for life' by older occupants, some schemes have incorporated increasing levels of care services.

It can be argued that as residential care homes and nursing homes extend their range of accommodation and sheltered housing schemes offer increased levels of care services, then what may evolve is a form of residential living which may provide an acceptable home which engenders the sense of ownership (Peace et al., 1997). But will this possibility become a reality? At present people moving into residential care and nursing homes commonly do so in their mid-80s – they have often been living alone at home receiving multiple care services and may make the final move from hospital. In this case they may make that major transition from their own home at a point when they are most vulnerable and arguably 'not in control' (Norman, 1980). In contrast those older people moving into sheltered housing do so at a younger age (mid-70s), when they are 'in control' of the move and are able to re-establish themselves in their new surroundings perhaps more easily (Peace and Johnson, 1997).

Residential Living or Institutional Care?

How then do these non-domestic settings stand up to the characteristics of institutionalisation? In terms of the public nature of daily living it is true that there have been developments in providing residents and tenants with more private space. In residential care and nursing homes residents more commonly have a 'room of their own'. But space is an expensive commodity, and this is reflected in the tensions which exist between some proprietors and regulators over seeing single rooms as a standard of quality provision (ADSS, 1991). Nevertheless, it has been shown to be something that is desired by older people (Willcocks et al., 1987) and as such has been taken on board to differing degrees, though as with any market system the best provision goes to those who can pay the most.

Private space, of course has the potential for personalisation. But as just noted, for some older people this move is unplanned and they may have already lost many possessions. Others find it difficult to cram a lifetime into one room, but some succeed (Counsel & Care 1991; Gubrium, 1993). However, as we saw in the domestic setting having a private space is one thing, having privacy is another. Having privacy says something about control over space and over who has access to your space. This is still not always the case in many residential care homes and nursing homes, and there is continuing evidence that as people become more physically and mentally dependent on others then control becomes more easily eroded. While residential practice has changed to some extent, staff still find it easier to oversee a group of people sitting in a public lounge than they do scattered individuals in their own rooms, especially when they themselves are few in number.

In sheltered housing and those residential settings which have adopted an apartment design, the physical environment can provide a buffer between tenant and paid carers. Having a 'proper' front door means other people have to negotiate their access with the individual – it gives territorial rights. It also says something about the risks people are willing to accept by being in control of their own space, even though this risk may be alleviated to some extent through alarm and call systems. These are aspects of daily life which people accept in their own homes and which have been demonstrated to work within non-domestic situations.

But while the design of a care setting may assist in the maintenance of degrees of personal control, it will also need to be reinforced by the care practices of staff. For people who need the support of others to make real choices over how they live their lives, then staff need to be both enablers and doers, with the balance set through discussion. It is the imbalance in the power of staff over residents which can tip what may be experienced as residential living into institutional care (or control?) (Peace et al., 1997). The relationship between paid carers and residents has to be based on a mutual respect gained through an understanding of past and present history. For older people, their home provides much of this history which may be lost in the move to a non-domestic setting. Re-creating this sense of identity becomes crucial for the maintenance of autonomy and well-being. This is about enabling people to remain engaged at whatever level in situations where their dependencies are no longer concealed within the confines of their own home but often made very public.

As also noted, non-domestic care settings are now regulated. At the level of policy, regulation is concerned with both the standard of care provided and the protection of vulnerable individuals. It is also about accountability for the spending of public money on paid care (by whatever means) (Day, Klein and Redmayne, 1996). At the day-to-day level, regulation can be experienced as more or less intrusive. It is perhaps most noticeable in relation to the physical environment where – for example – fire doors may impede access and look 'non-domestic', or where kitchen areas may be 'out of bounds' to an unauthorised person. But it also involves paid carers in a wide range of record keeping which does not occur in the domestic environment. In some ways regulation is bound to formalise organisations and in this sense re-enforce the non-domestic nature of these settings – but how it is managed can make a great difference to how individuals experience this aspect of their environment. If they can become involved in the process themselves then it may enhance their sense of mastery over the environment (see Kellaher and Peace, 1993).

Conclusions

This chapter began by stating the ideological principle that *'receiving care at home is infinitely better than in institutions'*. For some older people the privatisation and individualisation of living arrangements may lead to greater social isolation and exclusion. This is partly due to a constriction of life space as a consequence of poorer health, but it is also about restricted access to community resources. One consequence is an increasing investment in attachment to things and the meaning of objects and spaces as triggers to memories in the absence of people and on-going participation. The pain which can be caused by the relocation to alternative care environments late in life is symptomatic of this investment and acts as a signal to future generations. In this way it is not the alternative care setting which is necessarily at fault rather the very fact of relocating the self.

This brief exploration of domestic and non-domestic settings in relation to care shows that a 'homely environment' embodies something which is of itself created by individuals within an historical and social context. The timing and circumstances surrounding transitions between places of accommodation and care is crucial in understanding attachment; for if individuals can maintain control over decisions regarding changes in place, they may re-create their 'homely environment'; if they cannot, then they may suffer through relocation (Norman, 1980). The maintenance of control can also be influenced by a number of factors outlined here which if recognised could make such change less stressful. These include issues of privacy, autonomy and accountability.

Control and privacy

For many older people who live alone, particularly older women, their home has become their own private space where physical or mental frailties may be both concealed from the outsider and supported through a familiar meaningful environment. While living alone has become a particular feature of old age for present generations, current trends show that this will be a more common experience for many throughout the life course (ONS, 1997). Thus the experience of private space has become a common feature of everyday life and this has been reflected in the design of non-domestic care settings.

But in all settings the important issue in relation to privacy, both in terms of territorial space and personal space, becomes the maintenance of boundaries and control over access. While the domestic home may be regarded by most as their defensible space, for the older person in need of daily care, the home is open to others – family members, home carers, community nurses, cleaners. Just how carers – informal and formal – perceive their role and relationship with the older person influences how they handle crossing the threshold into someone else's space.

Indeed some have argued that the intrusion by service providers into the homes of some housebound individuals can be seen as a form of institutionalisation at home, making the private public (Gavilan, 1992). Issues of boundaries and access are equally important in other circumstances, for example, in day care settings the temporary nature of caring may make space appear neutral – after all people return to their own homes at the end of the day – but what about the ownership of specific areas, tables and chairs, or how intimate tasks such as bathing may be handled in a public setting?

Control and Autonomy

The recognition of how control over space enables the individual to maintain autonomy needs further exploration. Many older people see the domestic setting as having been, and continuing to be, central to the creation of their social roles throughout life. For people receiving care services at home, the gendered nature of carework and housework is particularly important. Many of today's older women may feel that the home is the place where they have controlled the action and the routines, even though men may have taken over tasks within the home later in life. It is not surprising then that comments are commonly heard that 'home carers do not do things the way I would have done' or that services are inflexible and do not fit in with the 'way people wish to live their lives' (Kellaher, 1997). These become the compromises of later life to be set alongside staying at home. The question becomes 'is it easier for the individual to maintain their authenticity at home?'. In non-domestic care settings control over actions, routines and spaces can often be weighted in favour of staff who find it easier to see this as a work environment expecially if their responsibility to watch people and 'make sure they are all right' outweighs the individual's right to privacy, decision making and personal responsibility. Finding an authentic role within a non-domestic care setting may feel out of reach for some residents, made worse by the way in which relocation often breaks links with past lives and past carers. However, it would be wrong to propose that this was the only view, as some people find that interacting with others enables them to re-kindle former roles lost through the constriction of life space which living alone in later life may confer.

Control and accountability

A final area highlighted here is the issue of accountability and the regulation of care settings and care services. In terms of creating 'homely environments' for care, systems of regulation can operate both to set and raise standards, and in doing so impose certain conditions on daily living through areas such as fire safety or food hygeine. In this way provision can seem more public than private. However, regulation provides a necessary safety-net and a system of re-dress, and where attention is paid to a person-centred approach to care, sensitive management of regulatory procedures such as inspection can prevent it from being seen as intrusive. Some level of watching seems an inevitable part of caring for someone else and this relates to care provided in domestic as well as non-domestic settings. The regulaton of domestic services within people's own homes remains a problematic area[4] with the onus firmly placed on service providers to maintain and develop standards and on those purchasing services to make informed choices. However, much depends on whether the purchaser is a local authority or a private individual, and at what point the competent individual making choices over the provision of services in the home becomes the vulnerable adult.

This discussion highlights something of the complexity surrounding the seemingly simple assumptions concerning homely environments for care and the polarisation of home and institution. A majority of us will live out our lives within domestic settings, but in future many more will need to make informed decisions about accommodation and care in later life and combinations of care arrangements which may move between domestic and non-domestic settings. Recognising some of the differences and similarities between these types of environment will enable us to move forward in understanding the relationship between people and places for care.

Notes

1. Doyal (1995) comments that 'in most developed countries births have now been removed from home. Ninety-eight per cent of British women currently deliver their babies in hospital, despite the lack of evidence that this is safer than a home birth' (Campbell and Macfarlane, 1990: 134).

2. For example, different cultural and religious practices can also affect the use of space. In some Muslim households, women do not enter the men's space when guests are present; and in many households of other cultures, such as Hindu, Rastafarian and Sikh, men and women tend to socialise separately (National Federation of Housing Associations, 1993).

3. In 1950, 53% of the housing stock in Britain was private rented, 29% owner-occupied and 18% public rented; in 1994 this had changed dramatically – 10.1% private rented, 67.6% owner-occupied and 22.2% public rented (Peace and Johnson, 1997).

4. At present domiciliary services are not subject to regulation although many inspection units operate a system of voluntary registration.

References

Ackers, and Abbott, P. (1996) *Social Policy for Nurses and the Caring Professions.* Buckingham: Open University Press.

Allen, G. (1989) 'Insiders & outsiders: boundaries around the home', in G. Allan and G. Crow (eds), *Home and Family: creating the domestic sphere*. London: Macmillan.

Altman, I. and Low, S.M. (eds) (1992) *Place Attachment*. Plenum Press: New York.

Arber, S. and Ginn, J. (1991) *Gender and Later Life: A Sociological Analysis of Resources and Constraints*. London: Sage.

Association of Directors of Social Sources (1995) *A Room of One's Own*. Northallerton: ADSS.

Audit Commission (1985) *Managing Social Services for the Elderly More Effectively*. London: HMSO.

Audit Commission (1986) *Making a Reality of Community Care*. London: HMSO.

Barton, R. (1959) *Institutional Neurosis*. Bristol: John Wright.

Bowlby, J. (1969) *Attachment and Loss*. London: Hogarth Press.

British Council of Organisations of Disabled People (1996) *Demolishing Special Needs*. London: BCODP.

Campbell, R. and Macfarlane, A. (1990) 'Recent Debates on the Place of Birth', in J. Garcia, R. Kilpatrick and M. Richards (eds), *The Politics of Maternity Care: Services for Child-bearing Women in 20th Century Britain*. Oxford: Clarendon Press.

Centre for Policy on Ageing (1984) *Home Life: A Code of Practice for Residential Care*. London: Centre for Policy on Ageing.

Counsel & Care (1991) *Not Such Private Places: A Study of Privacy and the Lack of Privacy for Residents in Private and Voluntary Residential and Nursing Homes in Greater London*. London: Counsel and Care.

Dalley, G. (1996) *Ideologies of Care: Rethinking Community and Collectivism*. London: Macmillan.

Davis, A. (1987) *Managing to care in the Regulation of Private Nursing Homes*. Birmingham: Health Services Management Centre and Pattern Press.

Day, P., Klein, P. and Redmayne, S. (1996) *Why Regulate? Regulating Residential Care for Elderly People*. Bristol: The Policy Press in association with Joseph Rowntree Foundation.

Department of Environment (1993) *English Housing Conditions Survey 1991*. London: HMSO.

Department of Health (1989) *Caring for People: Community Care in the Next Decade and Beyond*. Cmnd 849. London: HMSO.

Department of Health & Welsh Office (1990) *Making Sense of Inspection*. Training Package for Registration and Inspection of Staff. London: HMSO.

Doyal, L. (1995) *What Makes Women Sick*. Basingstoke: Macmillan.

Dunlop, A. (1994) *Hard Architecture and Human Scale: Designing for Disorientation*. Dementia Services Development Centre, University of Stirling.

Gavilan, H. (1992) 'Care in the community: issues of dependency and control – the similarities between institution and home', *Generations Review*, 2 (4): 9–11.

Goffman, E. (1961) *Asylums*. London, Harmondsworth: Penguin Books.

Gubrium, J. (1975) *Living and Dying in Murray Manor*. New York: St Martin's Press.

Gubrium, J. (1993) *Speaking of Life: Horizons of Meaning for Nursing Home Residents*. New York: Aldine de Gruyter.

Gurney, C. and Means, R. (1993) 'The meaning of home in later life', in S. Arber and M. Evandrou (eds), *Ageing, Independence and the Life Course*. London: Jessica Kingsley Publishers.

Haskey, J. (1996) 'Population review (6) families and households in Great Britain', *Population Trends*, 86, Autumn: 7–24.

Higgins, J. (1989) 'Home and institution', in G. Allen and G. Crow (eds), *Home and Family: Creating the Domestic Sphere*. London: Macmillan.

Holland, C. (1996a) *'Battling it: Older Women's Agency and Housing'*, paper given at the Women's Studies Network, Pontypridd, July.

Holland, C. (1996b) *'A Room of One's Own'*, paper presented at the Annual Conference of the British Society of Gerontology, University of Liverpool, September.

Holland, C. and Peace, S. (1997) *'Small Homes: "the Corner Shop' of Residential Care'*. Paper presented at the Annual Conference of the British Society of Gerontology, Bristol, September 1997.

Ittelson, W.H., Proshansky, H.M., Rivlin, L.G. and Winkel, G.H. (1974) *An Introduction to Environmental Psychology*. New York: Holt, Rinehart and Winston, Inc.

Jerrome, D. (1996) 'Continuity and change in the study of family relationships', *Ageing and Society*, 16 (1): 93–104.

Kellaher, L. (1997) 'User inspiration: How users of services can contribute to service responsiveness and sensitivity'. In Camden Social Services, *The Report of the Independent Sector Forum Conference. User Involvement in Monitoring and Quality*. September 5. London.

Kellaher, L. and Peace, S. (1993) 'Rest assured: new moves in quality assurance for residential care', in J. Johnson and R. Slater (eds), *Ageing and Later Life*. London: Sage. pp. 168–77.

King's Fund Centre (1980) *An Ordinary Life: Comprehensive Locally-Based Residential Services for Mentally Handicapped People*. London: KFC.

King, R.D., Raynes, N. and Tizard, J. (1971) *Patterns of Residential Care*. London: Routledge and Kegan Paul.

Laing, W. (1995) *Laing's Review of Private Healthcare 1995*. London: Laing and Buisson Publications.

Laing, W. (1996) *Laing's Review of Private Healthcare 1996*. London: Laing and Buisson Publications.

Matrix (1984) *Women and the Man Made Environment*. London: Pluto Press.

Miller, E.J. and Gwynne, G.V. (1972) *A Life Apart*. London: Tavistock.

Morris, P. (1969) *Put Away: A Sociological Study of Institutions for the Mentally Retarded*. London: Routledge & Kegan Paul.

National Federation of Housing Associations (1993) *Pensioners Face Worse Affordability Problems*. London: NFHA.

Norman, A. (1980) *Rights and Risks*. London: Centre for Policy on Ageing.

Office for National Statistics (1997) *Social Trends 27*. London: Stationery Office.

Peace, S. (1986) 'The design of residential homes: an historical perspective', in K. Judge and I. Sinclair (eds), *Residential Care for Elderly People*. London: HMSO.

Peace, S. (1993) 'The living arrangements of older women', in M. Bernard and K. Meade (eds), *Women come of age*. London: Edward Arnold.

Peace, S. and Johnson, J. (1997) 'Living arrangements', in M. Bernard and J. Phillipson (eds), *Social Policy of Old Age*. London: Centre for Policy on Ageing.

Peace, S., Kellaher, L. and Willcocks, D. (1982) *A Balanced Life: A Consumer Study of Residential Life in 100 Local Authority Old People's Homes*. Research Report No. 14. Survey Research Unit, Polytechnic of North London.

Peace, S., Kellaher, L. and Willcocks, D. (1997) *Re-evaluating Residential Care.* Buckingham: Open University Press.

Phillipson, C. (1990) *Delivering Community Care Services for Older People: problems and prospects.* Stoke on Trent: Keele University, Centre for Social Gerontology.

Reed, J. and Payton, V. (1997) 'Understanding the dynamics of life in care homes for older people: implications for de-institutionalising practice', *Health and Social Care in the Community,* 5 (4): 219–90.

Residential Forum (1996) *Creating a Home from Home: A Guide to Standards.* London: NISW.

Saunders, P. (1990) *A Nation of Homeowners.* London: Unwin Hyman Ltd.

Sixsmith, A. and Sixsmith, J. (1990) 'Places in transition: the impact of life events on the experience of home', in T. Putnam and C. Newton (eds), *Household Choice.* London: Futura.

Towell, D. (1988) *An Ordinary Life in Practice.* London: KFC.

Townsend, P. (1962) *The Last Refuge.* London: Routledge & Kegan Paul.

Townsend, P. (1986) 'Ageism and social policy', in C. Phillipson and A. Walker (eds), *Ageing and Social Policy.* London: Gower.

Twigg, J. (1997) 'Deconstructing the "social bath": help with bathing at home for older and disabled people', *Journal of Social Policy,* 26 (2): 211–32.

Wall, R. (1984) 'Residential isolation of the elderly: a comparison over time', *Ageing and Society,* 4 (4): 483–505.

Weaver, T., Willocks, D. and Kellaher, L. (1985) *The Business of Care: A Study of Private Residential Homes for Old People.* CESSA, London: Polytechnic of North London.

Willcocks, D., Peace, S. and Kellaher, L. (1987) *Private Lives in Public Places.* London: Tavistock Publications.

Women's Design Service (1991) *Designing Housing for Older Women.* London: Women's Design Service.

9

CAREGIVING, CAREWORK AND PROFESSIONAL CARE

Celia Davies

While the concept of the unpaid carer has firmly emerged on to the agenda of public policy in recent years, forms of paid care have received only sporadic attention. Yet those who do paid and those who do unpaid care often share a difficulty of putting the work that they do into words, and it may be helpful to examine them together.

'Caring' is defined here as *attending, physically, mentally and emotionally to the needs of another and giving a commitment to the nurturance, growth and healing of that other*. This can mean just 'being there for' someone, not necessarily listening, not necessarily even being physically present, but being known to be available, checking the situation out from time to time and being ready to respond if asked. The definition deliberately fuses labour and love (Graham, 1983), but it also carries an implication for each. First, as far as the labour side of caring is concerned, if the essence of caring work is 'committed attending' in the way the definition suggests, then the work cannot easily be translated into a set of identifiable and predetermined tasks. The close observation that a carer undertakes attunes her or him to the minute differences that guide action. Nothing is predictable in advance; uncertainty is a feature of caring and flexibility of response is a central requirement. Second, as far as the matter of 'love' is concerned, the emotional work that is implied here involves not so much affection, as a commitment to the creation of a sustained relationship with the other.

Caring in this sense, takes place in a variety of interpersonal relations and in different institutional settings. For the purposes of this chapter, I will distinguish *caregiving, carework* and *professional care*. 'Caregiving' refers mainly to the caring that is done on an unpaid basis within networks of family and friends. 'Carework' is used to refer to a variety of paid jobs in the health and personal service sectors and also to some jobs in the informal economy. The jobs of care assistants of various kinds in the home or in residential care, of home helps, of domestic servants and of childminders are included here and have a number of obvious characteristics. They remain largely women's work, they exist outside any sustained training framework, and they attract a low status and low regard. I will return to these later after looking first, as my main focus, at *'professional care'*, referring to work which is not only paid for, but also presumed to be based on a scientifically grounded and thorough training.

Professional care – nurses' voices

The example of professional care drawn upon here is nursing. In 1992, the Royal College of Nursing (RCN), the largest single professional association of nurses in the UK, took as the focus of its campaigning the question of the worth and the value of nursing. Influenced by a widely discussed and important text on caring – not, however, much known outside nursing circles (Benner and Wrubel, 1989) – one result was an exercise inviting its members to write in with events and incidents demonstrating what, for them, was unique and worthwhile about nursing practice. A publication was subsequently drawn up that presented 50 of these accounts, interspersed with a commentary from the College (Royal College of Nursing, 1992). The dilemma, the college argued, was that good nursing was rather like invisible mending – much of it could not be seen. An insider view, therefore, was necessary to clarify for others just what nursing truly entailed. Four of these accounts are presented here as illustrative, perhaps, of professional care in nursing.

> I was a student nurse and I was being taught by the enrolled nurse how to pass a nasogastric tube on a patient. The lady we were working on was quite poorly. She had lung cancer and had had fluid drained from her pleural cavity twice that week. . . . The enrolled nurse explained to her exactly what we were going to do and how much better she would feel. He was quite clear about how unpleasant the tube could be when it was going over the back of her throat. He then explained it again to me and she watched like a hawk, holding the tube he had given her in her hand. After all the preparation, he proceeded to put the tube up to her nose, and lifted her two hands and wrapped them round his. 'At any time when you want, you can stop this,' he said. So she did, three seconds later. The second time, he was just as patient. Eventually, with tears pouring down her face, she pushed at his hand to 'help' the tube going right down her throat. After she was all tidied up and settled, and some of the bile had been drained off, we all held hands for a second, and he made her laugh by inviting her to help with the intubation of any other patient who might need it. (Student nurse)

When you look after old people who have Alzheimer's disease, it is sometimes possible to tell that there is something wrong with them, even if there is no measurable change in their condition. It may be a tiny change in appetite or wakefulness that is too minute to be worth reporting, a change in temperament, or bowel habit, that is still within the normal range, but you know that there is something wrong. They can be quite clearly 'coming down with something'. It's not just a hunch, but if you know the patient and keep a close eye on them you can predict what is going to happen. That's why it's good to have an experienced nurse looking after old people. (Care of the elderly nurse)

Bill had Huntingdon's Chorea and he used to stagger about all over the place with his arms flailing. . . . On one occasion he inadvertently struck one of the patients who responded by hitting back and there was a tussle which the nurses had to sort out. I took him to the day room with me. He was clearly quite distressed. . . . I managed to persuade him to lie down on the sofa. He was still moving about a lot in his agitation. I got him to curl round one of the cushions and sat very close to him rubbing the back of his neck and stroking his hair at the base of his skull. I had seen his wife doing this before and it seemed a natural and comforting thing to do and before long he had dropped off to sleep. It is not something they taught me at the school of nursing but it felt right and it worked. (Mental health nurse)

We had a drunk in one night who was shouting and bawling in pain. He was a biker who had come off his bike when it had hit a wall. You know how sometimes you feel about drunks – he was making all this row while the quiet ones lie still and bleed to death – nevertheless, there was something about the abrasions on his face that made me think he must have had a real bump on the head, so I held his head and neck still while the other staff got the clothes off him and splinted the broken legs. Even in X-ray he was cursing and trying to sit up. We put on the lead aprons and held him down. He was known locally as a drug abuser and we wondered if he really only wanted some pethidine. I made sure he had some anyway. The relief was instantaneous, too quick, still I'm glad we got it for him. It quietened him down and it turned out that he had fractured his neck, one sudden false move would have paralysed him. (Accident and emergency charge nurse)
(Royal College of Nursing, 1992; various pages)

A number of themes in professional care can be singled out from these excerpts. First, there is the question of the formal knowledge acquired through systematic training. The importance of such knowledge is clearly evident in these excerpts as well as elsewhere in the RCN publication. It is there, for example, in the case of a nurse who clearly had more experience in coronary care than her medical colleagues and this worked to the benefit of the patient, in the case of the nurses who puzzled about a set of symptoms and eventually was able to diagnose porphyria, and in an incident where the nurse recognized the significance of repeated swallowing in a barely conscious patient. Yet there are few cases overall that could be classed in an obvious way as a celebration of the mastery of the principles of textbook knowledge; instead they are about weighing this knowledge against an understanding of the full circumstances of a patient, continuing to observe and puzzle when something is not quite as expected. Nurses remember with pride spotting something that others might have missed. In some instances this comes as a result of years of experience; often, however, it is a result of patient, minute and detailed observation that takes place in the sustained close relationship that the nurse has with the patient, and that has been singled out in this chapter as the defining characteristic of caring work.

Emotional commitment to patients, caring about outcomes, building a relationship so as to learn more about the person and hence adjust the environment and the care plan are a second theme in these quotations and in the publication as a whole. The commentary refers to the way in which nurses need both technical and interpersonal skills and will make an emotional commitment. It also notes that the nurse takes 'the risk of coming very close to the patient', explaining that this can entail forming 'an intimate but not intrusive relationship, using touch, massage, and gentle encouragement to help patients find new hope or comfort in distress' (Royal College of Nursing, 1992: 2). Why the term 'risk'? Arguably, it is a recognition of the crossing of the boundary between the rational action that is seen as appropriate for the public domain and the intimacy that is more common in the private and domestic one – and of the way in which caring encompasses both.

Thirdly, there is the sheer impossibility of rigid job demarcations when the paramount issue is to remain alert to the needs of others and to find appropriate ways to meet these. This comes out here in a wide array of other incidents. It is there, for example, in the evident pride of the nurse who performed last offices for a Jewish woman on a Friday when the Rabbi was not available and was then asked days later by the Orthodox Jewish family to do the same for her husband. It is present too in a number of cases where nurses who deal with clients with learning disabilities devise innovative routines for daily living that will provide a framework and give a sense of progress for all concerned. The role of the nurse, the commentary explains, has to be infinitely flexible 'because the primary task is to act in the interests of the patient according to the nurse's professional judgement' (Royal College of Nursing, 1992: 25). Yet, it is rather more than this. The nurses in these examples are attending to the whole situation and the resources it offers, they are prepared themselves to become engaged and to seek to engage others, and doing this in ways that do not always neatly map on to the hierarchical relations and the boundaries of job descriptions as specified by the organisation.

Professional care refers to a form of public caring work that is undertaken by those who have enjoyed a systematic and formal training. We might expect that the formalisation of care that is involved in these instances would offer a clear identification of skills and an appropriate reward structure that matches increments in skills together with mechanisms to avoid overidentification with the cared for, and an altogether firmer sense of the boundaries of responsibility in caring work. If we regard nursing as the paradigm case here, however, a very different picture emerges. Nurses find it difficult to settle on a definition of their work, argue that it is devalued and misunderstood, and frequently complain that they are not able to 'do nursing' in the institutional settings in which they find themselves.

One author who has considered the question of caring and nursing quite directly is Nicky James, whose work on care of the dying offers a range of insights into caring work in the public and private domains (James, 1989, 1991, 1992). In the main, however, the theme of professional care emerges obliquely, for example, in discussions of professionalisation as a gendered historical process (Hearn, 1982; Witz, 1992). Waerness provides a highly pessimistic comment, suggesting not only that caring values tend to 'get lost' when brought into the bureaucratic public arena, but that any formal training involving scientific knowledge will further exacerbate this and suppress the values of caring (Waerness, 1992: 223). She adds that 'nursing science' cannot be a solution to the problems of strengthening the values inherent in the rationality of caring, 'at least as long as this science is based in the generally accepted notions of scientific knowledge and learning'.

Caregiving and carework

Professional care offers one frame of reference and illustrates the elusive nature of the concept. What of the other two categories suggested here? *Caregiving* refers mainly to the caring that occurs within networks of family and friends on an unpaid basis. Caregiving is usually carried out under conditions of isolation from other carers, where, though there may be breaks from or intervals in caring, there is little in the way of a vocabulary to name the work and its demands, and nothing in the way of a regulatory framework that limits the physical load or hours. While the judges/assessors of the caregiving may be one (the cared for) or many (the wider family network), caregiving remains a private matter, not set in any wider consensus about what is reasonable and what is competent care. In these instances, caregiving is often emotionally intense. It can be highly rewarding at a personal level; it can also be draining and exhausting. The caregivers can lose a sense of having a separate self, start living for and through the other – with all the feelings of resentment and guilt that this is likely to evoke. Discussions of caregiving in this context frequently take on a strongly moral cast; they are about whether or not the caregiver is a sufficiently virtuous person rather than about whether s/he has skills in competent caring.

Carework is used in this chapter to refer to a variety of paid jobs in the health and personal service sectors and also to some jobs in the informal economy. The jobs of care assistants of various kinds in the home or in residential care, of home helps, of domestic servants and of child-minders are included here and have a number of obvious characteristics. They remain largely women's work, they exist outside any sustained training framework, and they attract a low status and low regard. All this is consistent with a blindness to the skill base that is involved. Equally important, however, is the conflict that such work sets up when incorporated into a regular bureaucratic control system. This has been described particularly vividly by Kari Waerness in the case of home helps, whose work is organized in such a way as to allow them to give flexible and versatile services to a small number of clients in their own homes over a long time period. She found that home helps exhibit a strong personal attachment to the clients, and this is the feature that they most enjoy and see as integral to the work. They can be acutely aware, however, that the values that they bring to their work and the experi-ence and skill that they draw upon do not strictly 'make sense' in the public sphere in which they operate (Waerness, 1992: 221–3). Other studies, for example of care assistants in hospitals and residential settings, confirm this picture, emphasising also the often unacknowl-edged therapeutic role that such workers play as they build close relationships with patients and clients (see, for example, Hart, 1991; James, 1989, 1991, 1992; Diamond, 1990).

Gender, rationality and caring

The difficulties in conceptualising caring and the lack of a well-differentiated vocabulary surrounding it that have emerged from the material of the previous section suggest that it is not only in caregiving work and carework but also in professional care that it is difficult to put practice into words. Writers such as Hilary Graham (1983) and Kari Waerness (1992) from within the caring debate, and sociologists such as Margaret Stacey (1981) and Arlene Kaplan Daniels (1987) from within the study of work more generally, all point to the theoretical legacy of a social science fashioned by men that has elevated a notion of scientific rationality, denied a place for emotions and in this way restricted the very definition of work. This section argues that we cannot move further towards a specification of the 'logic of caring' until we have a clearer understanding of the social processes that have given rise to its denial and repression, both in practical and in theoretical terms. To do this we need to attend to the cultural content of gender, specifically to the *metaphors of masculinity* that give a sense of vision and purpose to the public world and that underlie the separation of home and work and inform the notions of bureaucracy and profession.

Work on masculinity is now burgeoning and taking many forms, not all of which enjoy the support of feminists. It may help if we understand masculinity and femininity not as attributes of individuals but as cultural representations; we may also want to see the construction of femininity not as separate and complementary to the power and the privileging of masculinity but as something given a negative construction as 'other'. Then it may be possible to steer a path between some of the difficulties and begin to explore gendering of social institutions in a way that sheds light on the dilemmas of caring, particularly the ambiguities and paradoxes of professional care. The following paragraphs give a brief sketch of this.

Theorists of difference in psychology and psychoanalysis offer a model of gendered developmental pathways that has a clearly agreed outline. The path to masculinity entails an experience of separation from others, the creation of a strongly bounded sense of self, an emphasis on individuality, a wish for power, agency and action, and for being a subject – making a difference in the world. The path to femininity by contrast, involves a continuing experience of connection with others, a focus on interdependence, and a sense of self in reference to and in relation to others rather than as always autonomous and apart (see for example: Benjamin, 1988; Chodorow, 1989; Gilligan, 1982; Miller, 1984; Van Herik, 1982). The priority given to the first of these pathways gives rise to a masculine world, one populated by bounded selves. It is a world in competition. Each strives autonomously in pursuit of individual interests; impulses towards others are at base violent, coercive and cruel. If the world is full of 'hostile strangers', forms of order and the establishment of stable patterns of power over others are of paramount importance. Masculinity, understood in this way as a cultural project, becomes obsessed with establishing relations of domination among men and ensuring their stability and predictability. By these means the fear of other men can be contained. The public world that men have created, with its visions of rational action and its rules of behaviour, responds directly to this. The separation of this public world from a private one, where emotions, including enthusiasms and commitments, are allowed to reign, where vulnerabilities can be to some extent exposed and explored, is a solution to the demands of masculinity.

It is in the hands of Roslyn Bologh (1990) in particular, in her feminist reinterpretation of Max Weber as a man and as a theorist of bureaucracy and politics, that this abstract notion of masculinity and its dependence on and intimate relation to femininity has come vividly alive. Teasing out Weber's masculinist vision of the truly manly man, the restrained and heroic leader who has espoused a cause and acts with restraint in pursuit of it, she paints a sympathetic portrait both of the limits of a rational vision of action in the world and of the tragedy of masculinity. In imposing his will and taking personal responsibility, the manly man must endure the distrust of others. Given the importance of the cause, he will sometimes have to sacrifice ethics, ignore the welfare of others and perhaps use violence. He must examine his conscience, and maintain his dignity and his distance, sometimes keeping silence, always keeping his own counsel. He is, if you like, cold, calculating and ruthless in his relentless rationality. Yet he is more than this. He is not simply exercising strength and power. This is mediated and redeemed by commitment to an end, which requires him to relinquish the sympathy of others. Weber sees here a constant struggle for true heroic greatness, its tragedy being that it can only ever be achieved at the high points of life. The manly ideal, then, is a not only a tough job specification, it is a set of principles of personal conduct where a man can take pride in his achievements but must live constantly with the secret of his own frequent failure.

The point in all this for those who would understand caring is that the public world, or at least the masculinist fiction of it, is devoid of caring. Culturally, it is built on this absence, it celebrates it. The 'civilizing process' brings autonomous self-controlled individuals into orderly relations with each other in pursuit of agreed goals. Emotions, enthusiasms and vulnerabilities will get in the way. These, however, have not been expunged, but have been confined to the private sphere and assigned to women. 'Women, like unrepressed children,' Bologh observes, 'are expected to express enthusiasm, liveliness, sympathy, delight' (1990: 259). She explains:

> Our very concept of what it is to be a man . . . presupposes repression: a certain conception of and relation to women, a relation in which women are expected to fulfill men's personal and domestic needs, needs which are then not recognised as essential to being a man. . . . The very existence of the public world as we know it, presupposes, yet denies that it presupposes, the private world, and the kind of person, woman, who is defined in terms of that world. This is not the same as saying the two are separate and complementary. Rather they are forcibly divided and the division is maintained by repression. (Bologh, 1990: 242)

Thus, masculinity's version of rational action conceives itself as autonomous and independent of the other. In practice, as is already clear, while denying the other, it also needs and assumes it. Femininity, repressed in this way, now appears not so much as something benign and childlike, but as something that is to be feared as a temptation, something that, in other words, is seductive but contemptible. Caring is caught in this matrix of repression and fear.

Weber's classic account of bureaucracy makes renewed sense when seen as a resolution of the problem of organising that attends to these cultural issues of masculinity. Offices are hierarchically arranged and coordinated and are specialised. Rules are the key feature of bureaucracies. Bureaucratic decisions depend not on any personal judgement concerning the details of the case, but on knowledge of and application of the rules. The primacy of the rules renders the process orderly and predictable. All officials will act in the same way; they will not be swayed by personal mood or by anger, ridicule or other emotional display on the part of others.

These criteria from Weber's early account still form the starting point for much organisational analysis and management thinking today. They involve impartiality of decision making; there is no room for the passionate personal plea or the elaboration of circumstances that would particularise. There is a stress on impersonality; the official is detached from the decision, remaining 'outside of' or 'above' it, using a routine decision process that will be reviewed in a routine way. The hierarchy is a means of resolving any uncertainty or dispute; the bureaucracy speaks with one voice, expecting loyalty and deference not to individuals but to the offices that they occupy. Impartiality, impersonality and hierarchy create a stable and predictable order in which the interests of men as hostile strangers are tightly controlled. These three also preserve the relations of strangers. Intimacy and the exercise of emotion are no part of the vision that is bureaucratic organisation. Formality and distance are seen as the only route to a rational decision. Loyalty is to be had, but the kind of energy that comes from passionate commitment is missing. It is not just the routines of bureaucracy that render it bereft of caring, it is its embrace of impartiality, impersonality and hierarchy, and the unacknowledged celebration of masculinity that this entails.

Two steps beyond Bologh are necessary if we are to relate this more closely to caring. First, we need to see that the profession, far from being based on principles antithetical to bureaucracy, is itself a further expression of masculinity in the sense that it has been described here. The professional encounter, at first sight so particularised and contextualised, turns out to encompass, though not in identical form, the features of impartiality and impersonality previously discussed in relation to bureaucracy. What is apparently attention to the fullest circumstances of each separate client/case is in practice a sifting of information in terms of a diagnostic model and a translation into categories of action that fit the established competencies of the professional. Impersonality comes in the guise of proper professional detachment. The 'bedside manner' of the doctor, for example, keeps emotion firmly under control. Professionals offer a detached 'understanding' when clients, in what can be a highly charged context, frequently apologise for their fears and their tears. There are often also rules of eligibility to receive services that operate at a distance from the professional encounter itself and ensure that skills can be employed in an impersonal way. Individual autonomy stands at the very heart both of cultural concepts of masculinity and of professions. But, whereas in the case of the bureaucracy, autonomy is rationed on hierarchical lines, in the case of the profession it is earned by dint of heroic effort – the lengthy training that yields the prize of mastery over knowledge, and the lengthy apprenticeship that means that a person does not become a fully fledged professional until a relatively late age.

The second step needed here is to see that the relation of denial and repression of femininity and the principles that femininity stands for operate not only in the division between public and private spheres but *within* the public sphere. In regard to bureaucracies, Rosemary Pringle's (1989) study of secretaries is central to this argument. It is because secretaries attend to needs that are personal and emotional, and because they carry out work that is underconceptualised, devalued and ignored, that their bosses can continue to act in a disembodied way and can continue to present their decision-making processes in terms of the abstract ideal that has been described. Masculine rationality, she argues 'tries to drive out the feminine but does not exist without it'. A parallel fiction surrounds the professional. Take, for example, the appearance of the hospital consultant in the outpatient department or on the ward round. This involves a direct encounter with the patient, but it is a fleeting encounter. It is sustained through bureaucratic recording systems that are the work of others, through much preparatory and often considerable follow-up work with patients by others. It is only through the adjunct work of others (Tancred-Sherif, 1989), primarily in this case, nurses, that the work of the medical profession can take on its active, agentic and distant and controlling character. The profession, therefore, turns out to be predicated on a denial of the feminine, even in an area where pain and vulnerability are at their most obvious and overt.

The project of putting care onto the agenda takes on a very different aspect in the light of the material in this section. It is not that caring has been somehow overlooked, and can be retrieved and added to a pre-existing framework. It is rather that the denial of caring is central to the construction of the public world. Bringing in caring means unmasking the binary gendered thought that bolsters masculinity. This is true of caregiving, carework and professional care. A first step to the revalorisation of care that many feminists seek is a deconstruction of the existing concept of care; a process that requires us to deconstruct the masculinity that gives it shape.

Care in context

An abstract argument like that presented here also needs to be applied in a more local historical context. In Britain, the context is the restructuring of health and welfare that came to fruition with the National Health Service and Community Care Act of 1990, and the creation of responsibilities not simply to deliver care but to commission and purchase it from a range of providers ostensibly in competition with each other. Elsewhere, too, a similar emphasis on managerialism and on market-oriented mechanisms for care delivery has come into play (see Chapter 8). Caregiving, carework and professional care are profoundly affected by this restructuring of welfare – involving, for example, new providers in the shape of voluntary and profit-making agencies in the community, the casualisation (in some cases) of a careworker labour force, and possibilities of self-employment for some professional carers and of payment for some unpaid home carers.

In the light of the foregoing discussion, three factors can be singled out. First, 'new managerialism' – as it is often called in the UK, with its cost-driven 'performance culture', its businesslike job titles, its reference to competition between providers and its stress on customer choice in a quasimarket – turned out to herald a new set of social relations with many of the same masculinist characteristics as the old. Like the bureaucrat and professional, the new manager remains distant and controlled. He takes a critical stance towards the arguments and established practices of others, and follows his own convictions without being swayed by appeals to sympathy or particular cases. The key difference between the masculinity of managerialism and that of bureaucracy or professionalism is that the new arrangements, by stressing market competition, laid bare the notion of hostility and warring, encouraged it, celebrated it and aimed to work with it, rather than seeking to contain, hide or transcend it in some way.

Second, it may well be that the very overt celebration of masculinity in new managerialism provides the conditions for a backlash. Interestingly, and in terms that hark back to the idea of 'hostile strangers', some writers have begun to refer to a new culture of 'distrust' (Harrison et al., 1992: 68). Commentators have also suggested a 'retreat into technique', in that although all appears to be rational and neutral, the first and controversial step (of defining the specific nature of the service need) has not been addressed. These blind spots, it can be suggested, relate centrally to the necessary uncertainty surrounding care and the assessment of need for care and to the questions of interdependence, uncertainty and vulnerability that masculinist visions reject.

On a related point, this model, in a way much less true for the bureaucratic or the professional one, is beginning to be questioned in direct gender terms. Thus, for example, we hear health service staff referring to new managerialism as a style that is aggressive, harsh and confrontational. There is now a form of 'gender talk' in the National Health Service that was quite unknown a decade ago. It refers disparagingly to the 'men in suits' and questions the relevance of a 'grey suit' mentality that brings to bear an economic calculus that is devoid of human warmth and sympathy and that distances itself from the suffering that those in the front-line of health care must face on a daily basis and the personal dilemmas that this creates for them in carrying out the work of caring.

All this creates scope – and this is the third point– for new alliances in questioning emerging assumptions about forms of health care. There are the older NHS administrators, loyal to the principles that under-pinned the service in the 1940s, disaffected with the changes that managerialism has brought in train. Their doubts sometimes come together with those of younger middle managers, many of them now women, who feel that there are alternatives to a 'macho management' style and a work culture that entails such long hours and high stress. There are some doctors – particularly younger men and women – who are finding in the new culture of criticism of the medical profession hope for a 'new professionalism', one less arrogant and more accepting of the contributions that other professionals and indeed the patient/client/user can make. There is a further line of questioning coming from local government that is asking whether the ethos of public service and the notion of welfare have not been lost in managerial reforms and are now in need of reinvention. And, interestingly, with the arrival of a Labour government in 1997, talk has turned to a 'third way' between markets and the old relations of both bureaucracy and, to some extent, professionalism also. The relation of nurses to these disparate strands of criticism is at present dispersed and uncoordi-nated. Some nurses have embraced with enthusiasm the new managerialism and, aided by its link with equal opportunity policies, have taken advantage of routes into general management that have opened up for them. Others are wanting to rethink what is meant by professionalism, to find more confident ways of expressing the caring that they do – seeing only too clearly that deskilling is on the cards for them unless they are able to take a new initiative. Now is a moment of potential for alliances among these groups and for academic research that supports such alliances.

Community care, the social policy theme that prompted feminist concern with the nature of care and its impact on women's lives a decade ago, is back on the agenda, and new care providers and new relationships are being advocated and rapidly put into place. In the 1980s much academic effort around community care policy concentrated on the unpaid work of *caregiving*. Changes in that policy and changes in our understanding of caring suggest that it is time now to make a move, to extend the focus to include *care work* and *professional care* and to address the dilemmas that women are expressing in these areas. Underpinning any such move, this chapter has argued, there needs to be a firm understanding of the metaphors of masculinity and femininity that at every level of activity shape the vision of what it is that is to be achieved. There is an urgent intellectual task to show how dichotomies might be transcended, and how competence and caring could come into a new alignment for the new century. If we accept this task, we will be part of a new debate about the nature and significance of care on the welfare agenda. We shall surely all benefit.

References

Benjamin, J. (1988) *The Bounds of Love*. New York: Pantheon.

Benner, P. and Wrubell, J. (1989) *The Primacy of Caring: Stress and Coping in Health and Illness*. New York: Addison Wesley.

Bologh, R.W. (1990) *Love or Greatness: Max Weber and Masculine Thinking – A Feminist Inquiry*. London: University of California Press.

Chodorow, N. (1989) *Feminism and Psychoanalytic Theory*. London: Yale University Press.

Daniels, A.K. (1987) 'Invisible work', *Social Problems*, 34: 403–15.

Diamond, T. (1990) 'Nursing homes as trouble', in E. Abel and M. Neilson (eds), *Circles of Care: Work and Identity in Women's Lives*. Albany, NY: SUNY Press.

Gilligan, C. (1982) *In a Different Voice: Psychological Theory and Women's Development*. London: Harvard University Press.

Graham, H. (1983) 'Caring: a labour of love', in J. Finch and D. Groves (eds), *A Labour of Love: Women, Work and Caring*. London: Routledge and Kegan Paul.

Harrison, S., Hunter, D., Marnock, G. and Pollitt, C. (1992) *Just Managing: Power and Culture in the NHS*. London: Macmillan.

Hart, L. (1991) 'A ward of my own: social organisation and identity among hospital domestics', in P. Holden and J. Littlewood (eds), *Anthropology and Nursing*. London: Routledge.

Hearn, J. (1982) 'Notes on patriarchy, professionalization and the semi-professions', *Sociology*, 16: 184–202.

James, N. (1989) 'Emotional labour', *Sociological Review*, 37: 15–42.

James, N. (1991) 'Care, work and carework: a synthesis', in J. Robinson et al. (eds), *Policy Issues for Nursing*. Buckingham: Open University Press.

James, N. (1992) 'Care = organisation + physical labour + emotional labour', *Sociology of Health and Illness*, 14: 488–509.

Miller, A. (1984) *Thou Shalt Not Be Aware: Society's Betrayal of the Child*. New York: New American Library.

Pringle, R. (1989 [1988]) *Secretaries Talk: Sexuality, Power and Work*. London: Verso.

Royal College of Nursing (1992) *The Value of Nursing*. London: The College.

Stacey, M. (1981) 'The division of labour revisited or overcoming the two Adams', in P. Abrams et al. (eds), *Practice and Progress: British Sociology, 1950–1980*. London: Allen and Unwin.

Tancred-Sherif, P. (1989) 'Gender, sexuality and the labour process', in J. Hearn et al. (eds), *The Sexuality of Organization*. London: Sage.

Van Herik, J. (1982) *Freud on Femininity and Faith*. Berkeley, CA: University of California Press.

Waerness, K. (1992 [1984]) 'On the rationality of caring', in A. Showstack Sassoon (ed.), *Women and the State*. London: Routledge.

Witz, A. (1992) *Professions and Patriarchy*. London: Routledge.

10

THE EMERGENCE OF CARE AS A POLICY

Julia Johnson

Few would dispute that the concept of care is central to social welfare policy in Britain in the 1990s. Indeed, it has figured in legislation for many decades. For example, children could be 'received into care' or made the subject of a 'care order'; older people can be deemed to be in need of 'care and attention' or of 'continuing care'; people leaving psychiatric hospitals can be provided with 'after care'. In 1989 the government produced a White Paper entitled *Caring for People* which was the basis of the National Health Service and Community Care Act 1990. Yet, despite the predominance of the concept of care in welfare legislation and policy guidance, it remains ill-defined. The 1989 Children Act provides 55 definitions in its interpretation section (s. 105), but the definition of care is not one of them. It seems that 'care' is simply assumed to be a universally accepted and understood objective of social welfare policy.

During the 1980s, the government's emphasis on care by the community prompted a large amount of research into informal care. The feminist concern was the impact of this policy on women – that care by the community really meant care by women. As a result, the nature of informal caring relationships has received considerable attention and the concept of care in this context has been subjected to detailed analysis by researchers (see, for example, Parker, 1990; Twigg and Atkin, 1994). When the question is asked 'what is care?', the answer tends to be referenced to this literature (see for example Bornat et al., 1997). Although not unconnected, care as a policy concept has received less attention, as evidence of the 1989 Children Act indicates.

There is evidence, however, that while care has featured for a long time in welfare policy, its symbolic and ideological significance has changed over time. For example, the index to Peter Townsend's *The Last*

Refuge (1962), a critical study of Britain's old people's homes undertaken in the late 1950s, does not include an entry for 'care'. A later book on the same subject (Willcocks, Peace and Kellaher, 1987) includes over twenty entries under the heading of 'care' in its index. Furthermore, care staff in *The Last Refuge* are referred to as 'care attendants', whereas, Willcocks and her colleagues (1987) refer to them as 'care assistants'. Now, in the 1990s, it is not uncommon to hear care staff in residential care homes being referred to as 'carers'. These differences suggest not only that care has become an increasingly popular concept but also that what it represents has changed.

Today's social welfare policies have their origins in the Elizabethan Poor Law. But the provision of care was not an explicit feature of this. Rather the Poor Law was aimed at the *relief* of destitution. Following the Poor Law Amendment Act of 1834, a distinction was drawn between the deserving and the undeserving poor: the former were provided with 'outdoor' relief, the latter with accommodation in the workhouses. The poor and the destitute gradually became categorised into different groups who became the objects of different policies – for 'lunatics', 'the feebleminded', 'orphans', 'the infirm', 'the old' and so on. A review of the historical development of these different policies demonstrates differences in the meanings that have been attached to the concept of care. The purpose of this chapter is to explore these changing meanings within the context of welfare policies for children and adults.

Children and care

Prior to the introduction of legislation to control their economic exploitation on the labour market, children were regarded as economic assets. What was important was 'obedience' and 'respect' for parental authority rather than parental care and the welfare of children. However, with the passing of legislation to control child labour and to make their education compulsory, the concept of childhood became more constructed and the responsibility of families to care for children more established. Towards the end of the nineteenth century, legislation was introduced which allowed the Poor Law guardians to assume parental rights over 'deserted' children, and later over those whose parents were deemed to be unfit to have 'control' of a child by reason of 'mental deficiency', 'vicious habits' or 'mode of life'. In addition, the first of many statutes aiming to deter the ill-treatment of children, through criminal penalties, was introduced in 1889. Even under the Victorian Poor Law, the workhouse was regarded as an unsuitable environment for children and they could be 'boarded out' by the Poor Law guardians with foster parents and, by 1913, it was illegal to keep a child over the age of three years in the workhouse for more than six weeks. Thus, during the nineteenth century, what we now regard as ordinary parental and family responsibilities became the model for the provision of care. The late nineteenth century legislation relating to the care of children set the seeds for subsequent child welfare policies.

As Hendrick (1994) has pointed out, in the development of welfare policies, children have been regarded as both victims and threats: victims of ill-treatment, neglect or exploitation, and threats through lack of control or ill-health. Hence children have been seen as needing both care and control to prevent them from becoming either victims of, or threats to, society. Furthermore, a careful reading of some of the post-war legislation relating to children suggests that it is the 'normal' family that is regarded as the proper locus of such care and control.

By the mid-twentieth century, the concept of care had become firmly established in child welfare policy. The Curtis Report (1946), which paved the way for the 1948 Children Act, was concerned to identify ways by which children who were deprived of a 'normal home life' could be brought up under conditions best calculated to compensate them for the loss of parental care. It recommended that children should be 'boarded out' with foster parents in preference to being placed in institutional care. The 1948 Act created children's departments, employing 'child care officers', to cater for the needs of deprived children. This Act placed a duty upon local authorities to 'receive into care' voluntarily children who were orphaned, abandoned or lost, or whose parents were either temporarily or permanently unable to care for them because of physical or mental ill health or incapacity or other circumstances preventing the provision of 'proper accommodation, maintenance and upbringing'. In addition, reception into care had to be 'necessary in the interests of the welfare of the child'.

Grounds for the local authority assuming parental rights over a child in care included the child being abandoned or having a parent or guardian who 'suffers from some permanent disability' rendering them 'incapable of caring for the child' or who 'is of such habits or mode of life as to be unfit to have the care of the child'. Further grounds for the assumption of parental rights were added in 1963 (Children and Young Persons Act): the term 'abandoned' was refined to include children whose parent or guardian's whereabouts remained unknown for not less than twelve months, and 'mental disorder' (under the meaning of the 1959 Mental Health Act) was added as a possible reason for rendering a parent unfit. These reasons for receiving children into care or assuming parental rights give us some clue as to what was thought to constitute proper parental care. If a parent was deemed unfit, the local authority would provide substitute care. While care itself was not defined, the 1948 Act stated that it was the duty of the local authority to 'further the best interests' and 'afford the opportunity for proper development of character and abilities' of a child 'in care'.

The influence of the work of John Bowlby (1951) on child care policies during the 1950s and 1960s was considerable. He studied the effects of maternal deprivation on child evacuees during the Second World War and concluded that early separation anxiety could lead to later delinquency. Although his emphasis on the importance of mothers was later criticised, his work on attachment and loss (Bowlby, 1980) has continued to exert a powerful influence on child care policy and practice. The promotion of bonding and the avoidance of separation anxiety have remained fundamental to what is regarded as proper child development, care and control.

Bowlby's work reinforced the idea that the 'delinquent' child was in need of reform rather than punishment. It was not until 1969, however, that both troubled and troublesome children and young people were brought under one umbrella through the Children and Young Persons Act, 1969. This Act enabled offending children, to be the subject of civil care proceedings in court rather than criminal prosecution. Under care proceedings, a 'Care Order' could be made or a 'Supervision Order'. Reflecting the move away from punishment towards care, Approved School Orders were abolished and Approved Schools were redesignated as Community Homes. Conditions that had to be satisfied for the court to make a care order included any of the following : that the child or young person's 'proper development' was being 'avoidably prevented or neglected' or their health being 'avoidably impaired or neglected' or they were being 'ill-treated'; that they were being 'exposed to moral danger'; that they were 'beyond control' of their parent or guardian; that they were 'not receiving efficient full-time education'; or that they were 'guilty of an offence'. In addition, the child had to be 'in need of care or control which he is unlikely to receive unless the court makes an order . . .' (s. 1.2). It became the duty of the local authority to receive into its care any child made the subject of a care order. It also became a duty, where a supervision order was in force, for the supervisor to 'advise, assist and befriend'. Although somewhat speculative, it might be suggested that 'care' and 'supervision' in this context represented the two sides of 'normal' family care – the mother role and the father role.

It was during the mid-1970s that child abuse was 'rediscovered' following the death of Maria Colwell, a child who was returned home after being in foster care and subsequently killed by her step-father. This heralded something of a shift away from the prevention of neglect to the protection from abuse. It also led to the 'permanency' movement as enshrined in the 1975 Children Act. The permanency lobby questioned the assumption that children are best cared for where possible by their parents. The imperative to finally re-unite children with their parents, it argued, could lead to children 'drifting' in care without secure bonds, or worse still to be returned to dangerous homes. The new Act reduced the rights of natural parents and allowed potentially more security for foster parents through increased rights to adoption (Hendrick, 1994: 240). However, what some might describe as the 'moral panic' that arose over child sexual abuse in the 1980s, had an opposite effect. The 'Cleveland Affair', when around 200 children were taken into care on the grounds of suspected sexual abuse, put even middle-class parents under the threat of state intervention. On the one hand, therefore, local authorities were being accused of failing to protect and adequately care for children in their care; on the other they were being criticised for being over-interventionist and undermining parental responsibility.

Arguably, the 1980s was a turning point in child care policy, particularly as far as the notion of care was concerned. Once care, wherever it was located, was perceived as a potential threat to the welfare of children, policy moved towards the concept of protection rather than care. With the introduction of the 1989 Children Act, the idea of children being 'received into the care of the local authority' was dropped and replaced by the notion of children being 'looked after' in local authority accommodation. This Act is underpinned by the principle of *parental responsibility* and promotes *partnership* between social services departments and parents. Under the Act, which repeals much that went before it, the local authority has a duty, (a) to safeguard and promote the welfare of children within their area who are in need, and (b) so far as is consistent with that duty, to promote the upbringing of such children by their families. Need is defined as being unlikely to achieve or maintain a reasonable standard of health or development or to have the opportunity to do so. It also includes the likelihood of impairment of health or development if services are not provided, or being disabled. Services include 'assistance in kind' or, in exceptional circumstances 'in cash' (Vernon, 1993: 37). The local authority has a duty to provide 'day care' for pre-school age children and 'after hours care' for school age children (s. 18). The local authority must also provide accommodation if 'suitable accommodation or care' is not available (s. 20). Criminal 'care orders' were abolished by this Act but civil 'care orders' and 'supervision orders' remain, although a court may only make such orders if the child is likely to suffer significant harm which is due, or likely to be due, to their not receiving reasonable care or to their being beyond parental control. New orders were created ('Assessment Orders' 'Protection Orders' and 'Recovery Orders') for local authorities to fulfil their duty to investigate, and exercise their powers to protect children who are suspected of being at risk of significant harm.

The emphasis of the 1989 Act appears to be on prevention, so that children can be properly cared for by their own families. However, as Hendrick points out (1994: 227), the category of *children in need* can become a residual one, particularly in a climate of economic retrenchment, so that those deemed to be 'in need' are only those 'at risk'. Ironically then, in practice, the Act, far from focusing on prevention and minimal intervention to promote the welfare of children and families, is potentially highly interventionist focusing largely on protection, surveillance and regulation. There has been a subtle shift in policies for children from providing substitute or supplementary care for those in potential need to protecting those at risk.

Adults requiring care

Much of the legislation relating to the care of different categories of adults – older people, disabled people, people with learning difficulties or mental health problems – is shared in common. And like policies relating to children, different adult groups have also been treated as both victims and threats. There are, however, some important differences in the meanings attached to 'care' for these different groups of adults.

In the eighteenth century 'lunatics' were housed in madhouses, workhouses and bridewells to protect society from 'the mad'. In the nineteenth century, asylums were built to offer 'moral treatment' to these lunatics, but they soon became overcrowded and poorly resourced and the ethos of treatment gave way to one of custody. However, the idea of caring for people with mental health problems outside of the asylum also has it roots in the nineteenth century. For example, Devon County Asylum, in the 1850s, used two houses in its grounds for 'tranquil patients' and, in 1879, the Mental After Care Association was established to 'facilitate the readmission of the poor friendless female convalescents from the Lunatic Asylums into social life' (Murphy, 1991). The Mental Treatment Act 1930 set the seeds of national community care policies in the setting up of out-patient clinics and in its requirement that local authorities should provide 'after-care' for ex-patients. The notion of after-care in the field of mental health services (as with the probation service) has stuck. Care it would seem was something that was provided not in hospitals (or indeed prisons) but in the community.

The Mental Health Act 1959 made it mandatory for local authorities to provide both 'care' and 'after-care' facilities such as residential homes, day care and other services. The distinction drawn between the 'care' and 'after-care' seems to suggest that care is a preventive strategy, provided to people living in the community. 'After-care', on the other hand, is a rehabilitative strategy for ex-hospital patients. The Mental Health Act 1983, which replaced the 1959 Act requires Health Authorities and Social Services Departments, in co-operation with voluntary agencies, to provide 'after-care services' (s. 117) for patients who had been discharged from hospital after being detained for treatment. The code of practice stated that a 'care plan' for after-care should be drawn up (s. 118) and a subsequent circular required the health service 'to implement the care programme approach for people with mental illness, including dementia . . .' (HC(90)23/LASSL(90)11). By the mid-1990s, with the massive run down of long-term psychiatric hospital beds and the severe under-resourcing of community alternatives, community care for people with mental health problems was deemed to be failing. A number of high-profile violent incidents led to the passing of the Mental Health (Patients in the Community) Act 1995: after-care for those who have been compulsorily detained in hospital was replaced by 'supervised discharge orders', and health authorities are required to keep 'supervision registers'. Hence, just as there has been a drift in policies for children towards supervision, surveillance and protection and away from care, so with adult mental health services.

At the beginning of the twentieth century, policies for people with learning difficulties were heavily influenced by the eugenics movement and its concern to control the sexual reproduction of 'mental defectives'. The Radnor Commission *Report on the Care and Control of the Feebleminded* 1908 (which preceded the Mental Deficiency Act 1913) argued that 'there are strong grounds for placing . . . mental defectives from each sex in institutions where they will be retained and kept under effectual supervision . . .'. The emphasis was on segregation and supervision, to protect society from the perceived potential threat of the spread of 'mental deficiency'.

During the 1960s and 1970s an influential literature emerged on institutional care (Barton, 1959; Goffman, 1961; Townsend, 1962; Robb, 1967; Morris, 1969; Meacher, 1972; Miller and Gwynne, 1972). This literature, combined with a number of reports of inquiries into the conditions in 'mental' and 'mental subnormality' hospitals (Ely, Farleigh, Whittingham) and concerns about the costs of long-term hospital provision, raised serious doubts about institutional care. Institutions were clearly places where people could be subjected to abuse and ill-treatment, or where individual potential was frequently unrecognised or undeveloped. These doubts led to a shift towards community care policy, and to the development of the philosophy of 'normalisation' for people with learning difficulties. Normalisation, in its various guises, was based on the idea that people should be enabled to lead as 'normal' a life as possible in 'ordinary' settings in the community. Numerous policy documents emerged during the 1980s which reflected this basic philosophy of care (eg. King's Fund Centre, 1980).

The National Health Service and Community Care Act 1990 was the first enactment of 'community care' as policy. The White Paper that preceded it (DoH, 1989) expressed the belief that 'community care offers the best form of care available' (para. 1.8), and its proposed changes were intended to 'enable people to live as normal a life as possible in their own homes or in a homely environment in the community' and to help people 'to achieve maximum possible independence and . . . their full potential' (para. 1.8). The Act introduced the 'community care assessment' as a formal mechanism for assessing an individual's need for care. Again care is not defined but it is represented by a variety of facilities and services provided, to individuals as part of a 'package of care'. These include home-based services such as meals and personal assistance, they also include day care, hostels and other kinds of supported residential facilities including residential care homes and nursing homes.

The 1990 Act is an umbrella piece of legislation in the sense that it changed the way in which need is assessed and care is provided, but services continue to be provided through a variety of existing statutes. Residential accommodation, for example, is still provided through the National Assistance Act 1948 (as currently amended by the NHS and Community Care Act). This requires local authorities to provide or arrange residential accommodation for those 'who by reason of age, illness, disability or any other circumstances are in need of care and attention which is not otherwise available to them' (s. 21). The 1948 Act also includes the power to compulsorily remove people from their homes to institutional care in order to 'secure the necessary care and attention' if they (1) are suffering from a grave chronic disease or being aged, infirm or physically incapacitated, are living in insanitary conditions, and (2) are unable to devote to themselves and are not receiving from other persons proper care and attention (s. 47). Whereas policies for children are linked to the need for care and 'control', those for adults are linked to the need for care and 'attention'. This is an issue to which I will return later.

Prior to the National Assistance Act which brought an end to the Poor Law, the old workhouses had become Public Assistance Institutions (PAIs). The new Act of 1948, however, introduced the concept of residential *homes*. It was the intention of Aneurin Bevan who presented the Act to parliament in 1948 that residential homes for older people, unlike the former PAIs, would be like hotels for the working classes. Residents would continue to receive a pension out of which they would pay for their accommodation and care. It was also intended that residential care homes would be small scale and homely, although, as late as the early 1960s this was still far from being the case (Townsend, 1962). Nevertheless, even though the old ethos of 'attendance' rather than 'care' prevailed in practice for more than a decade, the 1948 Act was a dramatic policy break with the past and introduced the 'residential care home' as a community care facility. Like children 'in care', adults in residential care homes would be provided with substitute homely or family care.

Non-residential services are also provided under a variety of enactments. The 1948 National Assistance Act allowed for the provision of such services by placing a duty on local authorities to make arrangements for promoting the welfare of 'persons who are blind, deaf or dumb (or who suffer from mental disorder of any description) and other persons who are substantially and permanently handicapped by illness, injury or congenital deformity or such other disabilities as may be prescribed by the minister'. In 1968 (under the Health Services and Public Health Act), older people were added to the list when local authorities were given the power, but not the duty, to promote the welfare of 'old people' through the provision of meals on wheels, home helps, transport services, adaptations to the home and social work support. In other words, local authorities could exercise their discretion in the case of older people and were not obliged to provide services. And authorities were guided to exercise this discretion circumspectly. An obvious explanation for this is that older people are regarded as a potential threat to the economic well-being of society, through the size of potential demand for services. Thus they are frequently construed as a 'burden' on society. It is only disabled people (including disabled older people) who are entitled to services as of right. Like the 1989 Children Act, where there is an implicit distinction between *all* children and those defined as *children in need*, so certain adult groups, those disabled or infirm, have been targeted for intervention on grounds of need.

Prior to the creation of social services departments through the 1970 Social Services Act, social services for people with mental health problems and learning difficulties were provided and organised by local mental welfare departments, while those for disabled people and older people were provided by welfare departments. Following the 1970 Act, these two departments together with children's departments were amalgamated: mental welfare officers, welfare officers and child care officers became generic social workers. At the same time, the home help service, which had been provided by local authority health departments, was transferred to social services. So, within the ambit of social services, there emerged two distinct categories of work: social work and social care. The 1970s saw a huge growth in social care – in the provision of domiciliary care services to people at home. It was during the 1980s that the home help service was gradually transformed from 'home helping' to 'home caring'. Increasingly, ordinary domestic tasks such as cleaning were given a low priority, and personal care tasks such as helping people to bed and preparing meals gained priority. The community care reforms of the 1990s completed this transformation and much of what had previously been the work of the district nursing service has become social care work. As both primary and secondary health care are increasingly focusing on acute medical care, so care work has become the disputed territory between nursing and social services.

While the kinds of care services provided for adults under the new community care legislation remained the same, the National Health Service and Community Care Act 1990 dramatically changed how those services would be provided. A critical feature of the Act was that it split the purchase of services from the provision of services. As far as community care was concerned, this meant that local authorities became 'enabling' authorities responsible for assessing people's needs and arranging packages of care from a variety of providers (mainly private and voluntary agency suppliers). Hence care became a commodity available on the 'care market' to be purchased, contracted for, charged for, and managed by a 'care manager'. Local authorities are no longer 'caring' authorities but assessors and managers of care. The separation of the assessment of need from the provision of care services is an effective way of rationing resources and targeting those in greatest need. Again, as in the case of children, those deemed to be in need may end up being a residual category of people consisting only of those 'at risk'. And, those at risk are those who need protection.

It was during the 1980s that a focus on abuse began to emerge with the publication of Mervyn Eastman's book *Old Age Abuse* (1984) and by the 1990s several social services departments were developing guidelines on 'elder abuse'. But concerns were also emerging about the abuse of people with learning difficulties. By the mid-1990s several organisations had been set up to combat 'elder' and 'adult' abuse and, as with child care, the term 'protection' had gained considerable currency.

The emergence of 'carers'

The NHS and Community Care Act 1990 embodied the political ideology of a series of Conservative governments, first elected in 1979. From the early 1980s onwards, the government began to dismantle the welfare state which it regarded not only as inefficient but also as a 'nanny' state that undermined self-sufficiency and self-help. With regard to caring in the community, its attitude was summed up in an early White Paper, *Growing Older*, which stated that:

> Whatever level of public expenditure proves practicable, and however it is distributed, the primary sources of support and care for elderly people are informal and voluntary. These spring from the personal ties of kinship, friendship and neighbourhood. They are irreplaceable. It is the role of public authorities to sustain and, where necessary, develop – but never to displace – such support and care. Care in the community must increasingly mean care by the community. (DHSS, 1981: 3)

It is clear that the main responsibility for care was seen to lie with ordinary individuals in the community, particularly the family, and this theme was reiterated in a variety of official documents relating to community care throughout the 1980s. As mentioned at the beginning of this chapter, these developments prompted a considerable amount of research (much of it government funded) into what became termed 'informal care', and it was during this time that the concept of 'carers' emerged (Bytheway and Johnson, 1997). In 1981, the White Paper *Growing Older* did not use the term 'carer' when talking about informal care but, by 1989, the term had been adopted in official policy documents: one of the key objectives for service delivery in the White Paper *Caring for People* was 'to ensure that service providers make practical support for carers a high priority' (1989: 5). In 1995, through the Carers (Recognition and Services) Act, a 'carer' (someone providing over twenty hours a week care on a regular basis) became a legal category. The Act distinguishes between three types of informal carers: 'carers', 'young carers' and 'parent carers'.

There are two strands to the history of the emergence of 'carers': that of pressure groups seeking to improve the situation of those looking after disabled and older people, and that of researchers and policy makers who have been concerned to develop the policies and practices of service and support agencies. In 1959, the National Council for the Single Woman and her Dependants was set up to campaign on behalf of the many single and widowed women who were looking after older or infirm relatives. Later, in 1981, a separate organisation, the National Association of Carers was formed to widen the net to include other types of informal carers. By the following year, the National Council for the Single Woman and her Dependants had 'opened its doors' to men and married women and renamed itself the National Council for Carers and their Elderly Dependants. Competition between the two organisations was short-lived and, in 1986, the two merged to form the Carers National Association which became a powerful pressure group for carers and was instrumental in bringing about the new carers legislation in 1995.

Alongside the development of these organisations was the campaign to extend Invalid Care Allowance (ICA) to married women. ICA was introduced in 1975 to compensate full-time informal carers for lost earnings. It was only payable to men and single women since it was assumed that married women would be at home anyway and not in employment. This anomaly raised awareness not only of the denial of employment opportunities to women but also of their unpaid and unacknowledged contribution to informal caring. The Equal Opportunities Commission wrote one of the first authoritative reports on the subject in 1980 and it employed the term 'carers' to describe 'those adults who are responsible for the care of the sick, handicapped or elderly' (EOC, 1980; 1). Further research studies followed and many reports and seminars were given titles such as 'Caring for the Carers' and so the term 'carer' became established in the professional vocabulary. In 1986, ICA was eventually extended to include married women and it was only then that it could be construed as a payment for care rather than a benefit to (partially) replace lost earnings.

During the early 1990s, some people, notably disabled people, started to reject the notion of care and being cared for. Morris (1991) for example cogently argues that care means control and what disabled people want is equality and independence. This she argues can only be achieved by the provision of support (sometimes involving personal assistance) to enable disabled people to participate fully and equally in society. The disabled people's movement strongly supported the Direct

Payments Bill (enacted in 1996) which allows local authorities to provide cash payments to disabled people so that they can arrange and purchase their own 'personal assistance'. Such arrangements allow disabled people to avoid being 'cared for' through the local authority. The disability rights movement has also raised questions over the focus on the needs and rights of informal carers. Some have argued that this focus has detracted attention from the real issue – the need for 'care' in the first place, and by implication, for 'carers' (Morris and Keith, 1995). What is required, they argue, is equal access to ordinary services and support facilities that would remove the need for care and dependency on carers.

Dependence and independence

Dependence is a crucial issue in relation to care policy, and it is the notion of dependence that the 'independent living movement' has challenged. The focus of the 1948 National Assistance Act was on all adults in need of 'care and attention' and the emphasis was largely on the provision of residential care. No doubt, the notion of 'attention' was a hangover from the Poor Law institutions and PAIs which were staffed by 'attendants' and 'supervisors'. In the early years of residential care homes, as pointed out earlier in this chapter, 'care attendants' provided care and attention. While the use of the word attention no longer features in modern community care policy documents, the link between care and attention remains. But, with the passage of time, this link has been increasingly been confined to older people.

Townsend (1981) has argued that residential care homes are a symbol of dependency. Residential care has been rejected by people with learning difficulties, disabled people and mental health service users. 'Independent living schemes' are almost exclusively available to these groups of service users: shared houses in the community or cluster flatlets staffed by 'support workers'. Only 3% of special housing for older people is of this nature, for example, Abbeyfield Housing (McCafferty, 1994). Sheltered housing for older people is staffed by 'wardens' and residential care homes by 'care staff' – they are not staffed by 'support workers'. Thus care has come to signify dependence.

Where a clear link remains between care and attention is in the case of the Attendance Allowance. This non-taxable and non-means tested cash benefit was introduced in 1971 for any disabled person over the age of 16 years who required attendance. Eligibility is assessed on the basis of the degree to which 'help' is needed 'with personal care', even if such help is not actually provided (DSS, nd: 7). Interestingly, in 1992, a new allowance was introduced, the Disability Living Allowance. This replaced Attendance Allowance and Mobility Allowance for disabled adults under the age of 65. Those over the age of 65 may continue to claim Attendance Allowance but are not entitled to the Disability Living Allowance or its mobility component. Apart from being a cost-saving measure, there is an implicit assumption in this new development about dependency: the Disability Living Allowance is aimed at supporting independence, whereas the Attendance Allowance is for attending to the dependent. Independent living it would appear is the prerogative of people under the age of 65 years. Indeed, the Independent Living Fund (now wound down), which was set up in 1988 for disabled people to purchase their own personal assistance was only available to people under 65 years, as are Direct Payments now. Attendance Allowance then, like residential care, has become a symbol of dependence – and it is older people who are the main recipients of these benefits and services.

Conclusions

What can we conclude from this resumé of care as policy?

First, care in its development as a policy concept for both children and adults is something for which families are primarily responsible. It is modelled on notions of good parental practice and is best provided in homely environments.

Second, it is clear that care is a benign policy. As Macintyre argued twenty years ago, care represents humanitarian rather than organisational values (Macintyre, 1977). In policy, however, it rarely features on its own, it is linked to control, supervision, attention, and protection, and thereby becomes a kind of humanitarian adjunct to these more oppressive imperatives. Although something of an over-simplification, a review of care policies for different user groups suggests that children have been most frequently the subject of 'care and control', mental health service users and people with learning difficulties of 'care and supervision', and disabled people and older people of 'care and attention'.

Third, care is a form of power and control because it is provided by others and deemed to be what is in a person's best interests. Care is provided to people in need. Neglect, desertion, ill-treatment, impaired health and development, being in moral danger, being out of control or troublesome, being without advice, assistance or friendship may all be deemed symptomatic of the need for care.

Fourth, care is sequentially linked to other relationships and to individual 'moral carers' within institutions (Goffman, 1961). It precedes and follows treatment and punishment and is provided before and after school. More specifically, it is an entity into which one may be received or placed.

Fifth, recent developments in state policy as a whole have reconceptualised care as a commodity for which people can be assessed and deemed eligible. It can be ordered, planned, progammed, managed, purchased, charged for, provided in the form of various services, and marketed.

What this resumé also shows is an historical shift in priorities from caring for the dependent to providing support to sustain independence, or at least reduce dependence on the state, and to providing protection for the vulnerable. In this sense it might be argued that care as a policy concept is in decline. Certainly the evidence of the views of the disability movement indicates that those in receipt of care are not always happy about the consequences for their social identity. But this may have more to do with the vocabulary of practice than the rhetoric of social policy.

Government social policy is concerned as much with public expenditure as with meeting needs. The concept of dependence is perceived to imply costs and this is reflected in the continuing anxiety – if not to say panic – within government about the population 'dependency ratio': the total number aged below 16 and above 65 set against the total number of people of 'working age'. If care is increasingly associated with dependence, then this suggests that the idea of 'cutbacks in care' will become a further development in the continuing complex history of care as policy.

References

Barton, R. (1959) *Institutional Neurosis*. Bristol: John Wright and Sons.

Bornat, J., Johnson, J., Pilgrim, D., Pereira, C. and Williams, F. (eds) (1997) *Community Care: A Reader*. London: Macmillan.

Bowlby, J. (1951) *Maternal Care and Mental Health*. Geneva, WHO; London: HMSO.

Bowlby, J. (1980) *Attachment and Loss: Volumes 1–3*. London: The Hogarth Press and The Institute of Psychoanalysis.

Bytheway, B. and Johnson, J. (1997) 'The social construction of carers', in A. Symonds and A. Kelly (eds), *The Social Construction of Community Care*. London: Macmillan.

DoH (Department of Health) (1989) *Caring for People*. London: HMSO.

DHSS (Department of Health and Social Security) (1981) *Growing Older*. London: HMSO.

DSS (nd) *The Guide to New Benefits for Disabled People*. DS 706, Department of Social Security.

Eastman, M. (1984) *Old Age Abuse*. Mitcham, Surrey: Age Concern England.

Equal Opportunities Commission (EOC) (1980) *The Experience of Caring for Elderly and Handicapped Dependants*. Manchester: Equal Opportunities Commission.

Goffman, E. (1961) *Asylums*. New York: Anchor.

Hendrick, H. (1994) *Child Welfare: England 1872–1989*. London: Routledge.

King's Fund Centre (1980) *An Ordinary Life: Comprehensively Locally Based Residential Services for Mentally Handicapped People*. London: King's Fund Centre.

McCafferty, P. (1994) *Living Indepedently: A Study of the Housing Needs of Elderly and Disabled People*. London: HMSO.

Macintyre, S. (1977) 'Old age as a social problem', in R. Dingwall, C. Heath, M.

Reid and M. Stacey (eds), *Health Care and Health Knowledge*. London: Croom Helm.

Meacher, M. (1972) *Taken for a Ride*. London: Longman.

Miller, E.J. and Gwynne, G.V. (1972) *A Life Apart*. London: Tavistock Publications.

Morris, P. (1969) *Put Away: A Sociological Study of Institutions for the Mentally Retarded*. London: Routledge and Kegan Paul.

Morris, J. (1991) *Pride Against Prejudice: Transforming Attitudes to Disability*. London: The Women's Press.

Morris, J. and Keith, L. (1995) 'Easy targets: a disability rights perspective on the "children as carers" debate', *Critical Social Policy*, 15 (2/3): 36–57.

Murphy, E. (1991) *After the Asylums: Community Care for People with Mental Illness*. London: Faber and Faber.

Parker, G. (1990) *With Due Care and Attention: a Review of Research on Informal Care*, 2nd edn. London: Family Policy Studies Centre.

Robb, B. (1967) *Sans Everything: A Case to Answer*. London: Nelson.

Townsend, P. (1962) *The Last Refuge*. London: Routledge and Kegan Paul.

Townsend, P. (1981) 'The structured dependency of the elderly', *Ageing and Society*, 1 (1): 5–28.

Twigg, J. and Atkin, K. (1994) *Carers Perceived: Policy and Practice in Informal Care*. Buckingham: Open University Press.

Vernon, S. (1993) *Social Work and the Law*, 2nd edn. London: Butterworths.

Willcocks, D., Peace, S. and Kellaher, L. (1987) *Private Lives in Public Places*. London: Tavistock Publications.

11

CHANGING HEALTH CARE

Linda J. Jones

This chapter will define and explore two models of health care, the 'welfare' paradigm and the 'market' paradigm, assessing how far there has been a decisive shift from the public service ethos enshrined in the former to the privatised, competitive approach of the latter. It will briefly review the emergence of a national, public health service in the 1940s and the challenge presented to this service by market approaches such as competitive tendering, contracting and private health provision. In doing so, it will consider the extent to which the meaning of 'care' within the health sector has been recast and highlight how the language of health care has altered.

The concept of care within the health sector has always been complex and diverse, encompassing intensive nursing of critically ill people within specialist units, the provision of in-, out- and day-patient services in hospitals, primary care and domiciliary support for those with chronic sickness. Most of us are familiar and comfortable with this broad view of 'care' as a service-based concept, accepting that it spans a wide range of contexts and different types of intervention across the health sector. The implication is that although what constitutes 'health care' in any given situation may change, the values and central importance of care as a relationship between carer and cared for in the cause of health remains unchanged.

Yet there are strong grounds for questioning the contemporary relevance of this view of 'care'. The caring relationship, while still of great importance in health care, has come under threat from an approach to health provision which has redefined health as a commodity that can be bought and sold. In addition, structural changes within the health sector over the past 20 years, such as the rise of day surgery, shorter hospital in-patient stays, and skill-mix have offered a challenge to established ways of caring. Health care has undergone a partial transformation, through the rise of the internal market, the privatising of some services and the growth of the private sector. In these circumstances, how far are we justified in suggesting that the view of health care as a public good has been successfully challenged by a quite different view of health care as a commodified, private good? Or, to put it another way, we need to ask whether we have been witnessing the replacement of a 'welfare' paradigm of health care with a 'market' paradigm, and what this may mean for caring relationships.

The 'welfare' paradigm

At its inception in the 1940s the British National Health Service commanded almost universal public support. Health care, it was argued, was a public good and the main objective, to which most subscribed, should be to protect it by providing better (and more) services. Unlike social services, public housing or income support, health care was used by all citizens. Anyone could fall sick and therefore everyone needed a comprehensive service which provided treatment without stigmatising patients. The National Health Service enshrined the equal right of all citizens to receive treatment and care according to need from doctors, nurses and other health professionals. 'Care' within this 'welfare' paradigm had an institutional focus – on the hospital and the long-stay institution – and was characterised by dependency: waiting, receptivity, compliance and other aspects of patienthood.

The 'welfare' paradigm of health was widely accepted in the postwar years as the appropriate model for health services in the UK. Its principles were noted by Allsop (1995) as: collectivism, comprehensiveness, universalism and equality of access, to which she added 'professional autonomy' to highlight the power exercised by clinicians. Services were organised centrally by the democratically accountable state, with central government in overall control of finance and policy development. Hospitals and health authorities came into public ownership and general practitioners became independent contractors, providing primary medical services. The system was largely financed out of general taxation. Almost all types of services were provided for the whole population which were free at the point of use and as nearly as possible of a uniform standard. Clinical freedom to assess health needs, diagnose and treat patients drove the system.

Underpinning the 'welfare' paradigm of health were ideas about the efficient use of labour and the responsibilities of postwar capitalism. *The Beveridge Report* of 1942 argued for a 'cradle to grave welfare state' that gave all citizens a minimum level of social security and thus defeated the 'five giants': idleness, want, disease, ignorance and squalor. Central to this strategy was 'full employment' which enabled the rest of the welfare system to work through keeping up the levels of taxation and insurance contributions, and central to full employment policies was the good health of the population. The notion of public health and health care as investments in prevention, which would bring their rewards in the shape of a fit and productive citizenry, had roots in the nineteenth century Victorian public health movement (Jones, 1995). This was restated and extended in the deal between labour and capital that underpinned the establishment of the welfare state. It was assumed that once the initial process of diagnosis and treatment of the sick had been carried out (together with provision of adequate housing and a healthier environment) health costs would begin to stabilise, although politicians were aware of the inbuilt pressures of public demand and rising expectations (Bevan, 1952).

The language of welfare

The language which described the 'welfare' paradigm of health was derived from paternalist welfare principles. The medical profession, in the shape of the general practitioner and the hospital doctor, was the legitimate driving force of the 'service', supported by 'administrators', 'almoners', 'nurses' and other 'professions supplementary to medicine'. Treatment was given to individual 'patients' who were cast as largely passive and dependent, or required to be active only in certain, pre-scribed ways – such as in revealing their personal histories to clinicians (Armstrong, 1993). Characteristically, care meant 'being cared for' and 'attended to' in a hospital bed by professionals who made all the essential decisions.

A curative model of medicine was dominant, with 'acute care' being viewed as more prestigious than 'chronic care', reflecting the much greater percentage of the health care budget spent on funding acute hospital beds than on long-term care. Little mention was made of community-based care. The 'chronic sick' who included those with mental and physical disabilities, were housed in long-stay hospitals, often large-scale instituituions built in Victorian times. The health service, in fact, operated largely as a 'sickness' service, responding to presented health problems. Costs, and attempts to control them, were always central to health care systems but they did not intrude directly upon the doctor-patient relationship.

The challenge to the 'welfare' paradigm

The language of crisis first gathered pace in relation to the welfare state in the 1970s (Mishra, 1984; Deakin, 1987). Economic factors, such as inflation, the oil crisis and new technology, combined with social and demographic changes – such as greater longevity – to reinforce an ideological shift from Keynesian to market liberal philosophy. In Keynes' view, the state had a key role to play in protecting employment and stimulating demand in times of slump. To market liberals – the 'New Right' as they came to be called – such policies represented unwarranted intrusions by the state which hampered the free play of the market and would be costly failures.

State welfare began to be characterised by the New Right as an increasing burden. In particular, the state faced the problem of funding provision of health care and of pensions for the growing numbers of retired citizens. The retention of 'full employment' (a central Keynesian principle) came to be seen as of secondary importance compared with the fight against inflation. Criticism centred on the inflationary impact of supposedly excessive levels of state spending on social security, education and health. The public sector was conceptualised as extravagant and unproductive, as parasitic on tax-paying citizens and on a productive private sector (Jones, 1994).

The argument was less about expenditure as such than about efficiency and productivity. All through the 1980s, as the battle over welfare raged, welfare expenditure in the UK held steady or expanded (Hill, 1992) as a result of the sharp rise in unemployment and accompanying rise in benefit payments. The crisis of welfare was framed as a fiscal crisis in which an intolerable burden of increasing dependency was seen as threatening to overwhelm the taxpayer and stifle the spirit of individual enterprise. But behind this critique lay a more fundamental questioning of welfare state principles. Deakin, writing in 1987, commented:

> There is now widespread uncertainty, covering all shades of opinion, about the future of welfare and the objectives that it should be seeking to achieve . . . Some of the questions opened up . . . are about tensions between rival objectives for social policy, exposed by the decline in the economy and the changing relationship between social policy and the broader objectives set by government, and the purposes that the state's presence in the field of welfare are intended to serve and whether it is capable of securing them. Some about means: whether welfare can be better provided through the market or informally. . . . Others are about ends: whose interests welfare is intended to serve and who has really benefited from its expansion. (Deakin, 1987)

Such debates came to reflect deeper ideological and philosophical uncertainties about the legitimacy and desirability of state-run welfare provision. These were expressed on the political left as well as by the New Right. The continued existence of health inequalities despite over 30 years of a free, universal health service was documented (Townsend and Davidson, 1982). Left-wing critics cited the dominance, inflexibility and unresponsiveness of health professionals to patient needs (Doyal, 1979; Rodmell and Watt, 1986). A radical new literature on caring emerged at the beginning of the 1980s which demonstrated how far, in spite of a national health service, state welfare depended on the unpaid labour of women to support long-term sick and disabled people (Nissel and Bonnerjea, 1982; Finch and Groves, 1983; Graham, 1986). The policy of shifting care from long-stay hospitals into community settings, while it was seen as progressive and overdue, also emphasised the lack of adequate community care provision and increased pressure on these informal carers.

Those on the political left favoured more equal, effective and responsive public services (Walker, 1984). The New Right solution was a market approach. Hayek (1944) had argued that collectivism could only destroy freedom and oppress the citizen; the main role of the state should be to safeguard the freedom of the individual, not to provide welfare services which could be better obtained through free market competition. Rational producer and consumer choices would ensure that supply balanced demand, and therefore that a free, self-regulating market could deliver any and all commodities that were required: from toothpaste to palliative care. Following Hayek, the New Right rejected the Keynesian approach with its commitment to full employment through state intervention in macro-economic policy. In doing so, it was able to capitalise on the philosophical critique of the role of the state and the demolition of state socialism in Eastern Europe.

The challenge to the health sector was less profound than to other parts of the welfare system, partly because the moral distinction between deserving and undeserving citizens was less evident in health than elsewhere. The health sector seemed strangely insulated and even complacent as debates about the general role and scope of welfare became more acrimonious in the 1970s and 1980s. Nonetheless, by the later 1980s the National Health Service was being critically reviewed and pruned back. Part of the new rhetoric in health which facilitated this process was the increased emphasis on individual 'lifestyle' and personal responsibility to keep healthy. For example, the government White Paper, *Promoting Better Health*, claimed:

> much distress and suffering could be avoided if more members of the public took greater responsibility for looking after their own health . . . and were persuaded of the importance of protecting their health; of the simple steps needed to do so; and of accepting that prevention is better then cure. (DHSS, 1987)

The shift to a 'market' paradigm

Upward pressure on health care budgets intensified in the 1980s and early 1990s as increased longevity, technological innovation, professional power, inflation and consumer demand acted together to stimulate health sector growth. The health sector needed around 3% growth per annum to keep up with the growing demands made by elderly patients. On the provider side the rate of technological change was striking, in particular the rapid rise in day surgery, in new surgical techniques which were less traumatic and did not require long hospitalisation, and in out-patient care. In most UK hospitals, for example, 43% of planned surgery was being done on a day-case basis by the early 1990s, and it was calculated that the average district general hospital would be able to serve a 50–100% bigger population by the end of the 1990s (Newchurch, 1993). Non-invasive surgery reduced hospital-stay lengths and costs, and it was claimed that as few as 28 high-technology hospitals, supported by locality hospitals for day cases, could provide all of the UK secondary and tertiary care. However, these savings were more than matched by the costs of technological innovation and the pressure to make new treatments available to all categories of patients.

The drive for cost cuts

By the early 1990s health services everywhere found themselves under pressure from spending cuts, creeping privatisation and extensive restructuring. In the UK the health sector was being prepared for a market approach in the late 1980s. Compulsory competitive tendering for ancillary services in health care, management reforms, clinical audit and efficiency savings all pre-dated the 1990 National Health Service and Community Care legislation (Jones, 1994). Domestic, catering and laundering services became candidates for competitive tendering, a generic drug list was introduced, and health authorities' in-house direct labour was required to bid for contracts against private external contractors. In the late 1980s a greater degree of managerial control was introduced through the Griffiths reforms, along with attempts to make clinicians more accountable and cost sensitive (DHSS, 1984).

The private health sector itself was stimulated through changes in planning regulations, tax relief on insurance payments by older people, and changes in consultants' contracts which enabled them to undertake more private work (Rayner, 1987). Health authorities were required to establish cost improvement programmes, and hospitals were encouraged to generate extra income from commercial activities, from the sale of land and property, from the creation or extension of pay beds and private wards, and from deals with the private health sector. New Right health and community care legislation also gave health authorities powers to raise money directly through charitable donations and fund-raising. During the 1980s, £150 million was raised in this way (Social Trends, 1996).

Rationing became a more widespread feature of health care systems at a clinical and health authority level, through waiting lists, age criteria and so on. The high cost of tertiary care made some form of rationing essential, and it has largely been clinicians who have rationed on medical grounds, making judgements about survival, entitlement and quality of life. Politicians avoided becoming directly involved; but by introducing charges in the 1980s, for example, for eye tests and dentistry, they effectively rationed some forms of health care by cost and income.

The enshrining of market principles

These policies reflected more than the pressing need to contain costs. They indicated an ideological mission to 'roll back the welfare state' and establish a health market. In this sense the changes in the health sector in the late 1980s signalled a changing paradigm. The passing of the 1990 National Health Service and Community Care Act, which established a purchaser-provider market system in health and community care, respresented a new stage in consolidation of a market approach.

Plans for the restructuring of health care were floated in the government White Paper *Working For Patients* which claimed that 'the organisation of the NHS – the way it delivers health care to the individual patient – also needed to be reformed' (Department of Health, 1989). Arguing that costs were rising too fast and standards and costs were too variable across the country, the White Paper proposed delegating to the local level 'as much power and responsibility as possible'. This would involve establishing NHS 'hospital trusts' with self-governing status within the health service and encouraging general practitioners in the larger group general practices to become 'fund-holders' with control over their own budgets. Health authorities and GP fundholders would become purchasers of health care for their populations, with the NHS trusts and general practices as the providers of services. Thus some general medical practitioners would become both purchasers and providers of care, but elsewhere a purchaser-provider split would emerge.

The NHS trusts became free floating businesses within the health sector, detached from district and regional control and accountable to the NHS executive. District health authorities planned for population needs and purchased the care; family health services authorities (FHSAs) oversaw the work of GPs, dentists and opthalmic opticians. In 1995 legislation was passed that allowed FHSAs and health authorities to merge so that one overarching body assessed and commissioned health care. Regional health authorities became recast in 1996 as NHS regional executives, shifting from a strategic planning function to an executive function. The internal market of purchasers and providers was born.

Within primary care there was a drive towards a total fundholding system in the mid-1990s. *A Primary Care Led NHS* (DoH, 1995), the government's vision for primary care in the future, emphasised both the need to control rising costs and the role of the internal market in providing greater choice. It envisaged a variety of alternative models of primary care, including that of a salaried general practitioner working within a trust or commercial enterprise – a notion that raised the spectre of the 'privatisation' of general practice.

In addition there was a shift in community care based on a similar purchaser-provider split. Local authorities became purchasers, with very tight restrictions designed to force them to shed their erstwhile role as providers of social care. This, compounded by the difficulty of shifting adequate resources from secondary to primary health care, meant that public residential services have been poorly supported. Instead the private health care industry has consolidated its growing role as provider of so-called 'community based' residential care (Wistow et al., 1994). The private nursing homes and residential homes were the main beneficiaries of a purchaser-provider split in social care provision, partly because the state reined back the provision of public sector alternatives. Domiciliary based care has been slower to develop, in spite of the evidence that older and disabled people value life in their own homes.

The linguistic shift in health policy

Accompanying the shift to a 'market' paradigm was a linguistic revolution. As health policy makers borrowed organisational principles and practices from the private sector, the terminology of private sector management became more prominent. Managers and a culture of managerialism replaced public sector administration. The 'welfare' paradigm emphasised the professional service ethic: expert giving and lay receiving of treatment. In the market culture patients became 'customers' or 'consumers', and health care became the 'healthcare' industry. Health inequalities were recast as 'variations' or 'differences' and were marginalised on the health agenda until the mid-1990s. A dazzling new array of management-speak, including terms such as 'total quality management' and 'downsizing', was adopted (Pattison, 1997).

The image of the 'welfare' health service, enshrined in the receptive patient being cared for in the hospital bed, was challenged by the rise of day surgery and outpatient treatment, which projected the image of a more active consumer, fitting in treatment around everyday life and engaging in a significant degree of self-care. In contrast to institutional care, community care embodied notions of self-care, support for everyday living in ordinary surroundings and the de-professionalisation of caring.

The economic turn in health sector language has become noticeable, with the increasing use of a vocabulary and analogies drawn from private enterprise: 'healthgain', health as an 'industry' and a 'market'; hospitals which became 'trusts' and 'enterprises'; 'skill-mix'; measurement of 'inputs, outputs and throughputs'; assessment of 'risk'. In one of the leading professional health care journals in the UK, *The Health Service*

Journal, the term 'healthcare', in particular linked with 'industry', has replaced 'health care' even among academic contributors. Throughout the UK national press the use of the term 'healthcare' has been growing and this new way of describing the sector is exclusively co-located with 'trust', 'group' and 'NHS' (COBUILD, 1996).

Language and imagery are important in identifying and influencing how people think about health care. The definition of healthcare as an 'industry' as opposed to a 'service' suggests a very different type of provision. The image conjured up by the term 'healthcare industry' is one of enterprise culture and 'privatisation', pursuing goals of greater productivity and profitability, whereas 'service' is primarily about types of provision. The former aligns health with other industries and with the private sector; the latter links health to other parts of the public sector. Pursuing the industrial analogy carries a further implicaton. It casts healthcare as a commodity to be bought and sold. Health care, in contrast, implies a relationship between carer and cared for. 'Healthcare' might therefore be signalling a disengagement from the service ethic.

On the other hand, it could be argued that the market approach signals a greater concern for the user of health services. A central aspect of the shift to healthcare has been a recasting of the patient as a consumer. Consumer satisfaction is vital to industrial success, and one important aspect of market reforms has been the policy requirement to 'listen to local voices' and to increase consumer choice (DoH, 1993; DoH, 1995). 'Empowerment' and 'participation' have also been 'buzz' words in the 1990s, and this contrasts with the image of the patient passively waiting to be treated that is associated with a service ethic.

Evaluating 'market' principles

What has been the effect of introducing market principles into health care? Three issues are worth highlighting here: the loosening of loyalties to the NHS by patients and staff; the growth of the private and voluntary sector; and increased levels of patronage.

Public and private choices

The language of consumer choice was not merely a political rhetoric but to some extent expressed public dissatisfaction with welfare paternalism and its inflexibility. Just as some users of social care have been critical of the dependency creating idea of care (see Chapter 6 in this volume) so the rise of consumer movements and the spread of community health, self-help and myriad private and voluntary groups in health were partly a product of growing disenchantment with bureaucratic provision. Have market principles worked to empower users and put pressure on health providers to offer more sensitive and appropriate services? While much has been made of the need to 'listen to local voices' and involve local people in determining health needs, there is little hard evidence that public consultation or user participation has really influenced health care delivery. On the other hand, the shift in community care provision to contractualism and a purchaser-provider split has the potential to deliver user empowerment and involvement in a way that traditional professionally dominated services have not (Means and Smith, 1994).

Surveys in the late 1980s and early 1990s revealed high levels of support for continued government responsibility for health care and suggested that the New Right had failed to weaken support for a national health service (Crewe, 1989). However, one effect of fund-holding has been to create some elements of a two-tier system in which referral choices and opportunities for treatment are greater for some patients (Glennerster et al., 1994). Such breaches of equal access may provoke 'consumerist' responses and further undermine the public health service. There is some evidence that public attachment to the 'welfare' paradigm has been weakened. Opinion polls in the early 1990s, for example, indicated that the responsibility for providing some treatment, such as that for people with AIDS, should not be funded solely from taxation but also from charitable sources (*Social Trends*, 1996). Sixty-one per cent of people in 1996 agreed with the statement that they 'should take more responsibility for their own health' as compared with 41% in 1995 (*Social Trends*, 1996).

More people are taking out private insurance or paying privately to jump the queue. By 1995 the penetration level of private health and medical insurance had reached 18%, of which half was from individual contributors (Chartered Institute of Marketing, 1996a). Private health facilities grew rapidly in the 1980s, and health care staff increasingly worked across the public-private divide, 'normalising' the market system. In 1986 most private hospitals were independent and charitable. By 1996, 64% of private hospitals were 'for profit' and clustered in groups, of which the largest were BUPA, BMI and Compass (Chartered Institute of Marketing, 1996b). By 1995, 19.8% of the hospital and nursing home market was supplied by the private sector, compared with 9.9% in 1986 (*Social Trends*, 1996). This suggests that although people give public support to a national service, they are increasingly prepared to pay for treatment, either through insurance or on a 'one-off' basis. 'Going private', if the queue is too long, seems to have become much more acceptable.

Private sector growth

The New Right supported a policy in which the state ensured basic health coverage through taxation or social insurance but allowed or actively encouraged people to buy non-essential health care themselves. 'Hotel' type hospital accommodation, plastic surgery and, more controversially, abortions and expensive, hard-to-evaluate treatments fell into this latter category, and the mid-1990s saw increasing determination by financially hard pressed health authorities to resist demands that all and every type of treatment should be provided.

There was also growing use by purchasers of a public-private mix of providers, the latter being both commercial and not-for-profit (Ovretveit, 1995). Health authorities increasingly negotiated clinical contracts with the private sector. By 1994, 20% of all elective surgery, which included 28% of hip replacements and 20% of heart surgery was undertaken by the private sector. The private finance initiative encouraged public sector trusts to make deals with private companies to build new infrastructure, undertake new types of service provision and develop joint leading edge research and clinical interventions.

On the one hand, it is argued that public management of health services can sit easily side by side with the growing system of private financing of health. In this view public regulation is the key and, wherever the finance comes from, the system can serve public ends provided it is publicly regulated. Ovretveit (1995) argues that many countries have entered a 'phase of mixing the best of public and private'. Others would claim, however, that such changes fundamentally undermine the principles of a national health service and that full public ownership, management control and public sector employment of health care staff have all been considerably eroded by market principles.

There is also the fear that private companies are in the process of 'softening up' the public sector, and standing by ready to inherit as trusts and enterprises hit hard times. The spread of corporate for-profit health care has been noticeable for a decade or more. Rayner (1987) noted the expansion of multi-national health corporations in the United States into the UK in the 1980s. One feature of private health care in the United States has been vertical integration. This involved the accumulation of purchaser and provider roles in one company, a trend becoming apparent in the UK (Chartered Institute of Marketing, 1996b). Provision of health care through a string of nursing homes or hospitals is one stage; the purchase of hospital supply companies, drug companies, insurance provision and so on completes the chain from primary producer to front-line provider of care. The freeing of restrictions on multi-nationals in the 1980s and the encouragement of private health insurance encouraged major investment by these companies in the UK. However, some public sector hospitals may be in a good position to undercut the private sector by offering private beds and health care at substantially lower prices because of their economies of scale (Ovretveit, 1995).

There is as yet no decisive evidence that market principles have made health care systems more efficient or effective. They have been extremely costly to set in place: UK hospital trust management running costs are around £0.5 million a year each (Newchurch, 1993). Great financial savings were made as a result of contracting out services to private tender, but arguably these have shifted costs elsewhere – to the individuals forced to take pay cuts and see their conditions of service deteriorate. Related to this were substantial changes in the division of labour in health care and a drive towards 'skill-mix' by the trusts. Not only were the boundaries blurred between doctors and nurses, with the emergence of new types of specialist and advanced practitioners taking on quasi-medical roles, but skill-mix became more apparent within nursing. The professionalisation of nursing through Project 2000 has accelerated the shift towards assistant carers – auxiliaries, health care assistants and so on – who now provide much of the hands-on care in hospitals which trainee nurses provided in the past. A shift towards community-based care and the growth of private residential and nursing homes increased the demand for a cheap health care labour force. Almost 20% of health workers in the UK now work outside the NHS and many of these are low-paid, part-time semi- or unskilled women. In addition, there are growing numbers of social care workers delivering domiciliary care to clients.

The democratic deficit

Regulated purchasing alone has not enabled democratic accountability to be sustained. While purchasers were exhorted to 'listen to local voices', carry out 'local needs assessments' and purchase for 'health-gain', there were few checks in the system to ensure that this was done effectively. There was a lack of democratic accountability within the NHS, from government appointed regional chairs through to the boards of hospital trusts and the role of the GPs. Until 1990 there was some representation on regional and district health authorities from local authorities and communities. Regional Health Authorities were then phased out, with regional offices of the NHS Management Executive taking over their residual functions. Until 1984 consensus management did ensure that occupational groups had some representation on health authorities, but since then they have no necessary access. Until 1974 community health services and public health were under the control of democratically elected local authorities.

The upshot was a lack of accountability at local level, apart from such monitoring as the Community Health Councils (CHCs) were able to do. The NHS was of course democratically accountable to parliament, via the Secretary of State for Health. The minister could be questioned, and the running of the NHS was scrutinised by the Select Committee on Health, the Public Accounts Committee and the Audit Commission. But this was the same minister who agreed the appointment of the chairs of the health authorities and family health services authorities, appointed the chair and non-executive directors of the NHS trust boards, and appointed the chair and non-executive members of Regional Health Authorities – who in their turn oversaw the appointment of district chairs and managers. The opportunity for patronage in the UK health service, and for making 'political' appointments, expanded enormously.

Conclusion – beyond the market paradigm

The market paradigm, with its emphasis on choice and efficiency through managed competition, seemed to carry all before it in the mid-1990s. The definition of 'care' within this paradigm became more restricted, driven by competitive tendering, contracting and other structural changes. The boundary between health and social care was gradually redrawn so that long-term care became reconceptualised as a private good. The revision of the conceptual vocabulary of health care emphasised its commodification and helped to weaken public adherence to the welfare paradigm. Commercial medicine and private health insurance became more widely acceptable.

Health care was effectively recast within a framework in which competition and a private-public mix of service provision were viewed as the way to achieve equity, access and comprehensiveness. Social solidarity, one cornerstone of the 'cradle to grave' philosophy of the 1940s welfare state, was under threat.

One of the strongest arguments put forward by health reformers was that public demand could decreasingly be satisfied by a health care system wholly dependent on public finding. Private investment and an internal market approach could 'liberate' health care systems to increase patient choice and 'consumer sovereignty'. Money would 'follow the patient', efficient providers would be rewarded by growth and the inefficient would disappear. Thus, health care would become both much more efficient and more responsive to public needs. In doing so, the welfare principles of equity, comprehensiveness and access, if not solidarity (a term much distrusted by neo-liberals), would be satisfied.

How far did the decisive victory of the Labour Party signal a rejection of this rhetoric and a decisive break with the market paradigm? The incoming Labour government of May 1997 certainly rejected some aspects of market principles. In place of competitive fund-holding it committed itself to locality commissioning for health care and locality purchasing, whereby primary health teams as a group purchase health care and medical services. It questioned the competitive basis of the 1990 reforms, arguing that the huge management costs of structuring the internal market represented a drain on the system and pledging to free this resource for patient care (Department of Health, 1997). It reined in the private finance initiative and placed much more emphasis on public health. Poverty and health inequality were put back onto the health agenda and school and workplace health improvement targeted (*The Guardian*, 7.7.97).

These changes acknowledged that market principles had not delivered on equity and effectiveness. They had increased the total amount spent on health care, but too much had gone, it was argued, into paying for restructuring and for the running costs of the new health care businesses. What was striking about the Labour government's pledges was the commitment to draw back from what were seen as the excesses of the market paradigm and to focus on cooperation – the return, perhaps, of social solidarity. Yet it also faced many of the same problems that weakened the welfare paradigm in the first place: escalating health care costs, expanding public expectations, expensive technological innovations, rising staff costs and a shortage of available new financial resources.

In these circumstances it remains doubtful whether the welfare paradigm will be fully reinstated. In the first place, many of the structural changes of the 1980s and 1990s are irreversible without the commitment of major new financial resources, which are unlikely to be found. Second, private health care is much stronger than it was before the 1980s and its growth is likely to continue, although perhaps at a slower pace. Indeed, the government's acceptance of the public-private mix of health care has been signalled by the continuation of the private finance initiative, albeit pruned back. Third, notions of effectiveness and efficiency will continue to be of central importance. In relation to this issue, a return to the welfare paradigm is unlikely to be sought, since it was characterised by profession-defined and dominated services – with the patient, the cared for person, constructed as a passive recipient rather than an active consumer.

Neither welfare nor market models resolve two key issues facing the health sector: repairing the democratic deficit and prioritising health. There were more local surveys, rapid appraisals and focus groups in the NHS than ever before in the 1990s, yet there were also more opportunities for patronage. There was evidence of health professionals' greater willingness to share power with patients and to acknowledge their right to participate in and be more fully informed about their own treatment and care. At the same time, much caring work was privatised and undertaken either by private commercial or not-for-profit agencies or by unpaid carers. Creating greater democracy within the health sector will require the dismantling of patronage systems, greater local accountability and a more active engagement with users. Greater transparency within trusts, more lay representation and open political debate about hard issues, such as rationing care, represent positive ways forward. The greatest potential for user participation may lie with new approaches, such as 'Citizens' Juries', where citizens make decisions which the health authority agrees in advance to consider fully and either implement, or explain fully why they have not done so (Sergeant and Steele, 1988).

The second issue concerns the pursuit of better health. In both the welfare and the market paradigms health was equated with health care. In the welfare paradigm health was the goal but provision of sickness services, in particular, medical services, came to predominate. In the New Right's health care reforms this orientation to health as a product to be purchased was extended. More people took out private insurance or paid privately for immediate attention. The penetration level of private health and medical insurance approached 20% (Chartered Institute of Marketing, 1996a). Yet 'health' and 'healthcare' are not synonymous. The consumption of more and more healthcare does not necessarily bring health, and it certainly distracts attention from the causes of ill health.

If health rather than health consumption is the main objective, there is a need to 'focus upstream' and prioritise prevention (McKinlay, 1979), acknowledging that the encouragement to individuals and families to spend a greater proportion of their income on health care may be misplaced. The Labour government, by developing a revised public health strategy early in its first term of office, acknowledged that more effort should now be directed to measures to combat some of the underlying causes of ill health: poverty, unemployment, poor housing, a polluted environment (*The Guardian*, 14.7.97). This strategy draws on the welfare model but extends the responsibility of the health sector to provide leadership in order to improve the health of the whole population. No longer is it enough to conceive of health services as providing care and care for sick people. A move towards a new 'health' paradigm requires a move away from both the welfare concept of health care and the market concept of healthcare to a view of health as more than the absence of disease.

References

Allsop, J. (1995) *Health Policy and the National Health Service*. London: Longman.
Armstrong, D. (1993) 'From clinical gaze to regime of total health', in A. Beattie, M. Gott, L.J. Jones and M. Sidell (eds), *Health and Wellbeing: A Reader*. Basingstoke: Macmillan.
Bevan, A. (1952) *In Place of Fear*. London: Heinemann.
Beveridge, W.H. (1942) *Social Insurance and Allied Services*. Cmd 6404. London: HMSO.
Chartered Institute of Marketing (1996a) *Trends in Health Care*. London: Chartered Institute of Marketing.
Chartered Institute of Marketing (1996b) *The Private Health Care Sector*. London: Chartered Institute of Marketing.
COBUILD (1996) Personal communication.
Crewe, I. (1989) 'Values: the crusade that failed', in D. Kavanagh and A. Seldon, *The Thatcher Effect: a Decade of Change*. Oxford: Oxford University Press.
Deakin, N. (1987) *The Politics of Welfare*. London: Methuen.
Department of Health (1989) *Working for Patients*. Cmnd 555. London: HMSO.
Department of Health (1993) *Working Together for Better Health*. London: HMSO.
Department of Health (1995) *Towards a Primary Health Care Led NHS*. London: HMSO.
Department of Health (1997) *The New NHS – Modern, Dependable*. London: The Stationery Office.
DHSS (1984) *Griffiths Management Enquiry*. London: HMSO.
DHSS (1986) *Primary Health Care*. London: HMSO.

DHSS (1987) *Promoting Better Health*. London: HMSO.

Doyal, L. (1979) *The Political Economy of Health*. Basingstoke: Macmillan.

Enthoven, A.C. (1985) *Reflections on the Management of the NHS*. London: Nuffield Provincial Hospital Trust.

Enthoven, A.C. (1988) *Theory and Practice of Managed Competition in Health Care Finance*. Amsterdam: Elsevier.

Finch, J. and Groves, D. (1983) *A Labour of Love: Women, Work and Caring*. London: Routledge and Kegan Paul.

Glennerster, H., Matsaganis, M., Owen, P. and Hancock, S. (1994) 'GP fundholding: wild card or winning hand?', in R. Robinson and J. Le Grand (eds), *Evaluating the NHS Reforms*. London: King's Fund Institute.

Graham, H. (1986) 'Caring for the Family', Research Report No. 1. London Health Education Council.

Ham, C., Robinson, R., Benzeval, M. (1990) *Health Check: Health Care Reforms in an International Context*. London: Kings Fund Institute.

Hayek, F.A. (1944) *The Road to Serfdom*. London: Routledge and Kegan Paul.

Hill, M. (1992) *Health Policy in Britain*. London: Macmillian.

Jones, L.J. (1994) *The Social Context of Health and Health Work*. London: Macmillan.

Jones, L.J. (1995) 'Business ethics and political power', in H. Jones and J. Lansley (eds), *Social Policy and the City*. Aldershot: Avebury. pp. 15–31.

Lupton, D. (1995) *The Imperative of Health*. London: Sage.

McKinlay, J.B. (1979) 'A case for refocusing upstream: the political economy of illness', in E.G. Jaco (ed.), *Patients, Physicians and Illness*. New York: Free Press.

Means, R. and Smith, R. (1994) *Community Care: Policy and Practice*. Basingstoke: Macmillan.

Mishra, R. (1984) *The Welfare State in Crisis*. Brighton: Harvester Wheatsheaf.

Mishra, R. (1990) *The Welfare State in Capitalist Society*. Brighton: Harvest Wheatsheaf.

Newchurch and Company (1993) *Strategic Change in the NHS – Unleashing the Market*. London: Newchurch and Company.

Nissell, M. and Bonnerjea, L. (1982) *Family Care of the Handicapped Elderly: Who Pays?* London: Policy Studies Institute.

Office for National Statistics (1996) *Social Trends, 26*. London: HMSO.

Ovretveit, J. (1995) *Purchasing for Health*. Buckingham: Open University Press.

Pattison, S. (1997) *The Faith of the Managers*. London: Cassell.

Pierson, C. (1991) *Beyond the Welfare State*. Oxford: Basil Blackwell.

Rayner, G. (1987) *Banking on Sickness*. London: Pluto Press.

Rodmell, S. and Watt, A. (1986) *The Politics of Health Education*. London: Routledge.

Saunders, P. (1994) *Welfare and Inequality*. Cambridge: Cambridge University Press.

Sergeant, J. and Steele, J. (1988) *Consulting the Public*. London: Policy Studies Institute.

Townsend and Davidson (1982) *Inequalities in Health: The Black Report and The Health Divide*. Harmondsworth: Penguin.

Walker, A. (1984) *Social Planning: A Strategy for Socialist Welfare*. Oxford: Basil Blackwell.

Wistow, G. Knapp, M., Hardy, B. and Allin, C. (1994) *Social Care in a Mixed Economy*. Buckingham: Open University Press.

12

WHAT MAKES FOR GOOD CARE?

Ann Brechin

We see repeatedly in different chapters in this book that care is a slippery and contested concept. Also for something so fundamental to human relationships and the survival of the human species, it seems extraordinarily difficult to do well. This chapter attempts the task of exploring what 'good care' might be and how it can come about, across a wide spectrum of care relationships. The focus is not on the social policy issues, in terms of the legislative framework of community care, for example, although such frameworks do have a significant impact on the care that is delivered. Rather the focus here is at the inter- and intra-personal level. What is it that is going on between people when good care is happening and what is happening for the individuals involved, whether as carers or cared-for, in that process? What factors challenge and damage such processes and, conversely, what might be involved in enhancing and sustaining them?

Care is used both loosely and specifically as a concept. This is true in terms of what acts are involved and in terms of the participants, their roles and the context. It is also true in terms of the motivations involved and the aims and purpose of care. How to describe, let alone evaluate 'good care' is therefore very problematic. Indeed the very notion of care as encapsulated in community care legislation is challenged on the grounds that it implies a dependency role for those deemed 'in need of' care, which runs counter to the whole spirit of independent community-based living (Morris, 1994). Without ignoring such issues, care is used here to include a wide range of interpersonal exchanges, from emotional or practical support to direct physical care, all of which involve a transaction between people in which one gives and one receives. This potential power imbalance, between giver and receiver, in such a relationship is at the root of many problems associated with care and care relationships. How that is negotiated and understood is of great importance.

It will be apparent that in some circumstances care is mutually rewarding, coterminous with personal and social expectations and not overwhelming to the personal identity or needs of the carer or the person cared for. In some other circumstances, the reverse may be true. There will be many factors at work here, and the distinctions may not depend on generalising about straightforward differences. For example, one could not say that caring for one's own children is straightforward and that good care is easy to achieve, whereas caring for a severely disabled group of elderly people is problematic. The important factors will *cross-cut* these circumstances and situations. The intention here is to focus on fundamental aspects of care relationships and care processes in order to identify commonalities of caring. This means including, therefore, informal and formal care in health, social care or family settings and the whole spectrum of identified 'client' groups as well as children – or indeed any of us to the extent that we all, from time to time, need some care in our lives.

'Good care' is most commonly described these days in terms of enhancing quality of life – that is, in terms of the outcomes for those who are cared for. There is also an extensive literature looking at what is involved in delivering good care from the point of view of the carers, whether informal or paid. It is also possible to try to look at both aspects, in essence at the interrelationship between carer and cared-for. This is the main focus this chapter will take. It will suggest that in evaluating the quality of care, it may be essential to look at both the carer and cared-for experiences in parallel. Indeed, the nature of the care relationship and the processes involved in sustaining that relationship can be seen as being at the heart of any understanding of what constitutes and what encourages 'good' care.

The contexts in which the care is happening remain a significant part of the story and cannot be ignored. Chapter 8, for example, brings the setting firmly into the foreground. Much that is written about care and caring is in the framework of a primarily social policy analysis. That is, the main factors and context and tools of analysis brought to bear are at the level of the impact of policies and of service structure transitions on the roles and relationships of key players. This chapter, while drawing on that extensive and important thinking, will try to focus more on a psychological exploration of the care relationship. The intention here is not to dismiss the factors surrounding and to some extent forging the care relationship, rather it is to bring the spotlight to bear on the actual processes and experiences involved in caring.

Forms and functions of care

As an academic (and political) topic, 'care' has so far defied attempts to find a neat and agreed definition. What it seems to generate are issues for debate and rather discursive attempts to outline the areas care might include. It is generally agreed to include 'caring for' and 'caring about' (Parker, 1981; Graham, 1983) in the sense of covering both the caring tasks involved and the emotional aspect. Whether or not these are integrally related or separable, however, becomes a contested issue particularly in relation to perceptions of women as emotionally involved carers. Dalley (1988), for example, argues that the insistence on seeing the two aspects as inherently bound up in women's nature have distorted the picture and inhibited a proper analysis of the more complex and problematic reality. In many ways, this starting point, with its ideological focus on natural caring instincts forming a backdrop to the introduction of community care policies, has got in the way of a fuller analysis covering informal and formal, paid or professional caring. Attempts to address both in the same breath are relatively few.

One analysis which does this has been developed by Celia Davies (1995) and is represented in Chapter 9 in this book. She frames a three-way distinction: 'caregiving', primarily informal among family and friends; 'carework', mostly low-paid and female dominated work, with low-status and minimal training, but demanding quite a high level of skill which goes unrecognised; and 'professional care', based on systematic and formal training, but with nevertheless minimal identification of what precisely is meant by caring skills. This sets the scene for a valuable exploration of the hidden assumptions bound up in gender stereotypes and gendered language which, the author argues, restrict progress in our understanding. In particular, these restrict our ability to resolve the apparent dichotomies between task-based caring and emotional-labour based caring (the caring for or caring about split (Graham, 1983) or 'labour versus love', as Davies bills it). Her definition of care, striving to integrate these strands, is that it involves 'attending, physically, mentally and emotionally to the needs of another and giving a commitment to the nurturance, growth and healing of that other'.

Taking a rather different tack, Twigg and Atkin (1994) suggest five elements of caring, although some of these seem more like contexts or influences than elements. They include 'the performance of tasks of a supportive nature which go beyond the normal reciprocities common between adults'; a sense of kinship obligation; the emotion associated with caring, including the emotional labour involved in the provision of emotional support and encouragement as a direct element of caring; co-residence, in the sense that 'sharing a household radically affects the experience of caring . . . and the important ways in which caring is about the consequences of a relationship'; and 'a feeling of being responsible for the cared-for person'.

By touching on contexts and influences here, Twigg and Atkin bring into focus the issues around the moral basis and justification for caring. This aspect, which might be typified as being about the impact and implications of the caring relationship, is frequently interpreted negatively in terms of the burden of care on the carers (Finch and Groves, 1980; Glendinning, 1983). It is also seen negatively in terms of the imbalanced power relationship, particularly where assumed 'responsibility for' the cared-for person can be seen to directly impinge on their independence and autonomy (Morris, 1994). In Morris's view 'taking charge of' is a more apt description of what happens in practice, than the more commonly cited 'caring about', with associated and powerfully distorting perceptions of people as dependent and in need of others to take responsibility for their well-being. Chapter 6 explores this further and argues that conceiving of disability in terms of 'difference' rather than in more negatively loaded terms such as abnormality or dependence could help to challenge such disabling forms of care.

An approach to defining care which has been less pursued is the categorisation of care activities. Hopson (1981) developed a framework in which he described six 'strategies for helping'. Perhaps 'helping' takes a broader sweep than 'care' would generally be assumed to include, but I would argue that, in practice, care can and does include all these elements.

1. Direct action, involving doing something to or on behalf of the other person;
2. Giving advice, involving offering an opinion on the best course of action for the other person to take;
3. Giving information, which may provide a basis for the other person to make more informed choices;
4. Providing instruction, to assist the acquisition of skills;
5. Systems change, to influence the context surrounding the person;
6. Counselling, helping the individual to explore problems and choices. (Hopson, 1981)

He sees these as varying from one to six in terms of their powerfulness to support longer-lasting change. The first two, direct action and giving advice, he sees as potentially de-skilling. Therefore while they may help in an immediate way, the net result could disempower the individual. The second two, giving information or instruction, are, he argues, likely to be empowering in relation to the particular situation or problem, but may or may not have a wider relevance for the individual. The last two, improving the system or context, or helping the individual to explore and problem solve, should, he suggests, have a longer lasting and more transferable impact.

I would not entirely agree with this analysis, which may arise from his focus on shorter term help rather than longer term care. Direct action interventions can, even Morris would agree, be entirely empowering if they free the individual to have more control over other aspects of their life. I would also like to argue for some adjustments in the categories, in particular to introduce a primary focus on advocacy into the 'systems change' item. I think there are also a couple of key areas missing from the list including what might broadly be seen as the 'physical therapies', and a hard to define area, which is about sharing or supporting daily-living or leisure activities and generally doing things together in an enabling way – perhaps 'supportive companionship' might be an apt term for this.

What I would agree with is the importance of the promotion of empowerment as a key measure of the success of any caring or helping process. It is not, however, self-evident what care should be directed towards achieving, and cultural variations in the perception of desired outcomes provide one example of the contested purposes that may exist. Historically too, there have been widely varied interpretations of what care should deliver (Brechin and Swain, 1990). It has shifted from what was essentially a 'sick role' model, in which the carer was expected to provide comfort and sustenance, which the patient was expected to receive passively, but with gratitude. It has also shifted on from the 'eternal pupil' model in which achieving full potential through supported learning and continued development was the expectation and the carer role became primarily developmental and educational. In the current climate, influenced by the normalisation movement, self-advocacy and now the Community Care and National Health Service Act of 1990, (HMSO, 1990) caring ostensibly aims towards supporting rights and choices in the context of an ordinary life in the community.

The reality is that, as Hopson's list shows, some of these forms of caring are not alternatives, but have to continue to exist alongside each other, being variously appropriate at different times and in different circumstances. Care can be seen as delivering comfort and protection from some of life's demands and stresses – an implied lifting of burdens – as in, for example, the provision of relief from pain and stress for dying people, or more contentiously the 'protection' of vulnerable people from risk or harm. At the other end of the scale care may be seen as directed towards enhancing autonomy (the capacity for self-determination), rights, control and freedom of choice, with a varying emphasis on the degree of responsibility and developmental effort to be taken on by the cared-for individual.

It may, however, be possible to see these quite different care purposes within one frame of reference and to judge them against that. The *common purpose* might be seen as the enhancement of autonomy in the context of supported living (promoting control and choice *and* the necessary support to lead an ordinary life). The provision of relief or protection (from pain, effort, hunger, loneliness, danger) or the promotion of learning (skills, communication, daily life tasks) would be the potential building blocks which might form part of the strategy to achieve the common purpose. Such concepts of supported living stem primarily from work in the learning disability field, but would seem to have relevance to all care work. Care is responsive, I would suggest, to the particular needs and circumstances and preferences of the individual and should be directed towards improving the balance for that individual between neediness and autonomy.

In the case of a child this is easy to envisage. The effective care and sustenance of a developing child requires meeting needs for warmth, food, bodily care, etc., but this has to be managed and adapted alongside the enhancement of personal growth, relationships, skill development and a general sense of selfhood and ability to control and interact with the social and physical environment. Should parents forget this, as they are wont to do from time to time, growing children will normally waste no time in reminding them that a sense of autonomy is firmly on their agenda, as well as having meals available on tap. While easy to envisage in the case of caring for children, the tensions are perhaps nowhere more clearly apparent. Whether natural parents, foster care or residential child care is involved, and whatever difficulties or disabilities the children may or may not have, maintaining the balance between direct care and fostering autonomy requires great artistry.

Where the need for care is more prolonged or more complex than it is for a growing child or young person, maintaining the right balance of care becomes even more crucial. Children will redress imbalances; they will normally have at least a peer group to refer to for equity. For people who are chronically sick or dying, or disabled, ageing or in need of care 'beyond the normal reciprocities common between adults', it is easy to see how Jenny Morris's picture of disempowering, taking-charge type of care can occur. But it is possible for the 'common purpose' to be held in the frame. Chapters 3 and 7 show how the emphasis on respect for the individual wishes and needs of sick or dying people can revolutionise the nature of the care offered. The administration of pain relief, or the protective care needed for someone with Alzheimer's disease, can indeed become a process associated with denial of autonomy and loss of control; but it can also be fully integrated with a care approach designed to empower even the dying or dementing individual. The implication is that the provision of direct relief will only avoid the trap of paternalism and disempowerment over time if it is offered as a building block in the promotion of autonomy and supported living.

Defining and evaluating 'good care'

Any attempt to define 'good care' must be explicit about what the purpose of the care is assumed to be. As outlined above, the emphasis will shift with time and circumstance, but there is a widely shared consensus across the health and social care domains, that care should be aiming at *promoting autonomy in the context of supported living*. This holds true across across most service-user groups: older people, disabled people, including particularly those with learning disability and people with mental health problems. It is interesting to recognise how easily the notion extends to be relevant also for chronically sick or dying people, for children or young people, even for those experiencing acute trauma or illness. This is not so surprising, perhaps, when the concept is so congruent with ordinary human needs.

Evaluation of care has primarily occurred in the context of reviewing the quality of new community care-based services, particularly residential and day services (for example, Wolfensberger and Glenn, 1975; Peace, 1993; Perry and Felce, 1994; Raynes et al., 1994; Knapp et al., 1992; Felce and Perry, 1995). In line with the shifts from medical to educational and then to a supported living focus for care, the emphasis has shifted explicitly from a focus on the delivery of care and the quality of the processes involved to an evaluation of outcomes, normally viewed in terms of the quality of service users' lives. Such assessments of life quality can and do cover a wide range of areas. Five 'domain headings' are suggested by Felce and Perry under which such quality of life evaluations are typically conducted (Felce and Perry 1995). They label these physical well-being, material well-being, social well-being, development and activity, and emotional well-being and cite examples of studies under each of these headings.

Enabling people to have access as far as possible to normal patterns of living and normal relationships and to make choices for themselves was the emphasis of Nirje (1969, 1980) in the early days of the normalisation movement and it is this thinking that has underpinned the shift to 'quality of life' outcome measurement. The shift was radical in assuming an absolute right to normal living, not a right dependent on acquiring skills or patterns of behaviour, or on recovery from illness, in order to qualify. This is reflected in the second major shift in evaluation, from an interest in and focus on, the development of people's skills and how far they have changed or 'improved' their functioning, to an emphasis on how successfully 'supported access' to choices within ordinary living has been provided no matter what the level of skill or ability. The 'supported access' implies whatever is necessary and appropriate for the individual, including physical adaptations, emotional support, explanation, or fully supported participation.

'Bad care' at the extreme end of the scale is somewhat easier to define on the face of it, although it does become apparent from the scandals which routinely hit the headlines that those closely involved, and not just the perpetrators of abuse in care relationships, may still find it hard to be sure about whether what is happening is acceptable or not – or at least whether it should be ignored or not (Wardaugh and Wilding, 1993; Levy and Kahan, 1991; Westcott, 1991; Martin, 1984). Moving away from extremes of neglect or abuse, whether sexual, physical or emotional, bad care can be seen as falling at the other end of a continuum, from care which enhances autonomy and supports ordinary living, to care which is destructive of selfhood, self-esteem or self-confidence and which undermines the capacity to make choices within the context of an ordinary life.

Care as a process and relationship

It was suggested earlier that evaluation of care has shifted from a focus on how care is delivered to a focus on the outcomes of care. Care itself, however, involves a process built around a central relationship and, without taking account of the experiences and feelings involved in that process and the relationship directly, any evaluation will reveal only part of the story. If we want to understand 'good care' in the sense of care which brings positive consequences for those who are involved, then we must take account of the process and the relationship itself and not just see care as an instrumental means to an end.

An exploration of the positive satisfactions reported by informal carers (Grant and Nolan, 1993) suggests that the concomitants (as they term them) of caring can be considered as integral to the process and relationship. They describe three clusters of satisfaction or reward which encompass the range of satisfactions mentioned by carers. They found these to be unrelated to the degree of burden or stress of caring involved. These were 1) satisfactions deriving from the inter-personal dynamics between carers and dependents; 2) satisfactions deriving from the intra-personal dynamics of the carer; 3) satisfactions deriving from the desire to avoid some kind of negatively perceived external consequence for the dependant. Much of the detailed feedback from carers conveyed a sense of the significance of the relationship itself underpinning expectations about caring roles, respect for the feelings and wishes of the person being cared for and the pleasure involved in meeting their needs.

Reading the quotes from the informal carers gives a sense of a good fit with the purposes of care outlined earlier. This is care aimed at promoting autonomy and supporting ordinary living. Professional and other paid care seems to have gone through a very complex route to arrive back at delivering something approaching the same kind of personally tailored, empowering care; although it is worth remembering that the sample of carers who responded to the survey were inevitably self-selecting, and others may well not have come across as so warmly in tune with their care relationships. The shift, though, to empowering care inevitably does make very different demands now on carers. Care work has shifted from being about 'looking after' someone who is seen as unable to care for themselves; it has also moved on through the 'developmental model' in which the purpose of caring was primarily educational and aimed at improving the level of skill, ability and functioning; it is now best typified as the 'supporting self-advocacy' model in which the role is facilitative, enabling and as inconspicuous and normative as possible. Such changes have major implications for the caring process for both paid and unpaid carers and may warrant more attention than they have had so far (Smith and Brown, 1992).

Carers and those who are cared for will have needs and interests that are in conflict with each other in a myriad of ways. That is part of the human condition. Social organisation mediates and manages such conflict according to evolved rules, mores and legislation. Otherwise there might well be even more scandals. This is not to suggest that everyone involved in caring is wicked or motivated by evil design. But it is to suggest that there are pressures of self-interest at work which mitigate against offering care in the best interests of the other (Wardaugh and Wilding, 1993). Good care can only be achieved by continually working against those pressures, first by recognising them and then by building systems and support structures which help us to overcome them. This is true whether the focus is on long-term community care, on support for terminally or chronically ill patients, or on acute interventions.

Dimensions of good and bad care: a simple model

In focusing on the care process as well as the outcome and in seeing it as part of a relationship, we draw attention to the possibility that any evaluation of quality of care should address the experience of both parties to the care. Inspections and outcome-focused quality assessments can provide important safety checks to ensure that, on balance, people are achieving certain desirable 'outputs' from the care they are receiving. For example, it could be demonstrated that someone has educational opportunities, is developing new skills, or is taking part in a range of appropriate social activities. This will suggest, although it will not prove, that the care is adequate and probably better than the care provided where someone is failing to achieve those outcomes. It doesn't tell us very much, if anything, however, about the nature and con-comitants of the actual caring (the inter- and intra-personal experiences) going on within the care process. Just how good is the care, and how good might it be, and who or what is good? Do we need to know – indeed can we find out – which members of staff are involved in good care relationships and with which residents?

Similarly, the analyses of caring in terms of the burden of stress, the satisfactions, the emotional labour involved, the often devalued nature of the work, can tell us something of the likely impact on the process of caring, but does not directly provide us with an assessment of the quality of the care. At the point of burn-out, or absenteeism, or where abuse or neglect occurs, we can safely say that the carer has failed or is failing to provide good care. But how do we focus on the in-between range to evaluate the quality of the caring process itself? How can we

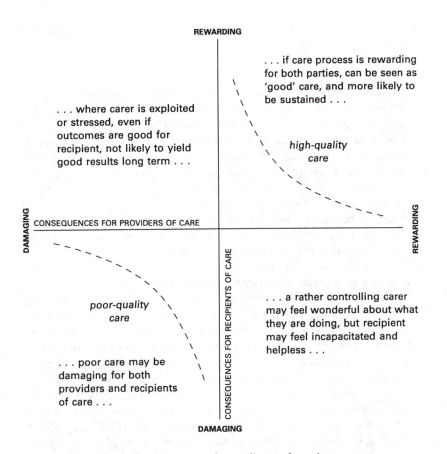

Figure 12.1 *Quality of care in terms of rewarding or damaging consequences for providers and recipients of care*

describe a spectrum of quality of care from good to bad in such a way as to usefully include what seem to be a range of important factors?

The model to be proposed here, suggests very simply that such a spectrum needs to address the perspective of both the carer and the recipient of care concurrently. On this model, care would only be deemed to be good if the consequences were good from the point of view of both parties. If this is represented by two axes on a graph with one dimension representing the range from 'rewarding' to 'damaging' (or positive to negative) for the recipient of care and the other dimension representing the same range for the carer, then the model would suggest that good care will be represented in the area of the graph reflecting scores towards the positive end on both axes (see Figure 12.1).

Before embarking on a discussion of how 'rewarding' or 'damaging' might be defined, it may be useful to say a little more about the rationale for such a model in relation to a concept of good care.

There are a number of assumptions which underlie this suggestion which need to be made explicit:

1   It is assumed that if the care process is rewarding for both parties, it can be reasonably seen as an example of 'good care' and is also more likely to be sustained and to continue to be successful.

2   The outcome of care could be rewarding for one person and not the other. A rather controlling carer, for example, may feel wonderful about what they are doing, but the recipient may feel incapacitated and helpless. In the opposite case, where the carer is exploited or stressed, even if the outcomes are good for the recipient of care, it is assumed that this is not likely to yield good results long term, nor is it likely to be as effective in the short term. It seems reasonable to argue then, that this is a 'less good' care process than if both parties experience positive consequences.

3   It seems reasonable to suppose that there will be interactive effects between the level of reward or damage to each party in the relationship, although these will be complex. For example, by expending greater efforts, the carer may improve the care/support delivered, but at a cost to him/herself. Thus on the model the carer would move down the axis towards the 'damage' end, while the recipient of care moves up. Conversely by reducing the level of demand to the carer, moving him or her up, then, towards the 'reward' end, the outcome for the recipient might become worse, resulting in a move down their axis to a level of reduced reward. There may also be another kind of interaction at work creating a positive, or negative impetus. The better the outcomes, the more likely both parties are to feel satisfaction and vice versa. This would be more inclined to push both up or both down, rather than drive one up at the cost of driving the other down. The model allows these interactive effects to be noticed and taken into account.

4   Extending our understanding of the process of care by modelling it in this way and checking out predictions could help to make more explicit and raise questions about the nature of good and bad care relationships and how to achieve and sustain good ones. Providing good care cannot be achieved according to any recipe, and can only be developed and evaluated against a model that allows for the active participation of the two parties involved. In other words, there can be no absolute measure of what good care practice should look like, it can only be judged relative to the needs, wishes and style of the person receiving the care. What is right for one person may be quite wrong for another. This may vary particularly across time and circumstance and across age, gender and cultural differences. The model builds in its own integral template by making the inter-relationship of the two parties central.

Coming back to the dimensions of the model, what should be implied by the polar extremes of 'rewarding' and 'damaging'? The proposals sketched out here form only a basis for further work and are not intended to be definitive. What they do attempt is a drawing together of ideas and evidence from different realms of work, using in particular the clustering framework offered by Grant and Nolan (1993) to suggest the key consequences or concomitants of care that should be looked at. This is extended and adapted from their focus on informal carers' experiences to encompass paid and professional carers and also the experiences of those who are cared for.

Three core areas are suggested as contributing to any evaluation of quality of care:

1   The first area would focus on the facilitation of choice or opportunity and would be a measure of the extent to which the care relationship enhanced or limited the range of options available or accessible. Both parties to the care would have views on this as well as more objective measures being possible, and from Grant and Nolan's work it is clear that avoidance of more negatively perceived options is one aspect of a positive outcome. This could be an important variable in a more direct sense for the carer too. Their role as carer may reasonably be expected to enhance their options, either directly as a result of the role and status it affords them, through the work, the relationship and the activities or through payment received for work done. More commonly the caring role is seen in terms of loss of freedom and restriction of lifestyle and where this is the case, it needs to be part of any evaluation.

2   The second area would look at the interpersonal processes involved. The nature of the relationship, the interactions occurring and the roles being played out form the core of the day-to-day reality of any care process. The style and the underlying meanings (the macro-communications as well as the minutiae of communications and interpersonal contact) will be fundamental to how the care process is experienced. This contact is the essential means by which any physical care is mediated as well as forming the heart of any emotional care.

3   The third element is the intra-personal experience (what happens within rather than between individuals) and would focus essentially on the impact of the caring relationship on self-esteem. There are important issues to do with such things as sense of personal identity, agency, empowerment, and self-confidence, which would be an important part of judging the extent to which any care relationship and process is rewarding or damaging. The impact on the self-esteem of the person being cared for and the impact on the self-esteem of the carer seem self-evidently central to defining the success or otherwise of the relationship and process.

Psychological factors and quality of care

It is not difficult to find relevant literature and research which address aspects of the above framework. Counselling and psychotherapy have a great deal to offer to any analysis of intra and inter-personal processes, for example, most of which is quite directly relevant to care relationships (for example, Rogers, 1969; Yalom, 1980; Hobson, 1985). There is a growing literature on the emotional labour involved in paid care work (Menzies, 1970; Smith, 1992; Aldridge, 1994; Kristjandottir, 1992; Pike, 1990; Davies, 1995; Anderson, 1997) and a long history of research into the experiences of informal carers, particularly parents looking after disabled children, but increasingly now extending beyond that (e.g. Quine and Pahl, 1986; Bowers, 1987; Kahana and Young, 1990; Qureshi, 1992, 1986; Grant and Nolan, 1993). There is also now a growth of literature offering insights into the experiences of 'service-users' on the receiving end of care (Atkinson and Williams, 1990; Read and Reynolds, 1996). The intention here is to begin to sketch out some of the potential insights which emerge from the above formulation/model to see whether they hold up to scrutiny.

This involves the introduction of two further concepts (again neither of them new), which may help with the sketching. One is the concept of 'a working alliance' evolved from the notion of an equality-based therapeutic alliance in psychotherapy (Bordin, 1979 and 1994, Dunkle and Friedlander, 1996) and applied in relation to working partnerships in care (Brechin and Swain, 1990) through ideas developed to underpin Shared Action Planning (Brechin and Swain, 1987). The basis of that thinking is that the nature of the new partnerships in care, in which empowerment rather than dependency is the primary aim, involves the establishment of something like a working alliance. This is a very different form of partnership from that entailed in a traditional medical/sick-role relationship or in a teacher/pupil/educational relationship. We may be able to learn something from the elaboration of this concept about the way in which care can be better or worse (rewarding or damaging) and what circumstances or factors may sustain or threaten it. We may also learn how to make better judgements about the quality of the care on this basis.

The second concept is 'difference'and in particular the 'construction of difference'. In one sense any long-term care relationship is predicated upon difference, whether the difference is between parent and child, or the presence or absence of impairment or health problem or some other difference, making care of one person by another seem necessary and appropriate. Within family care relationships, such difference may become almost invisible to the participants because who they are and their family roles may predominate. (Not always so, of course, and difference may be heightened when an onset of difficulty, illness or impairment is relatively sudden.) In paid care, difference is the defining characteristic. The acknowledgement of difference becomes in effect the passport to care, through the formal process of 'needs assessment'. How that 'difference' in either setting is construed by both parties to the care will have a potentially powerful impact on the care process, and vice versa, in that the quality of the care process may impact upon the construction of 'difference'.

It is interesting to think about what might tend to happen when long-term caring is failing. On the model, this would have the evaluation scoring falling downwards on the axes, and might reflect problems with outcomes, with the interpersonal interactions or with intra-personal experiences or with all three. If the caring has to be maintained at all costs, there are likely to be some rather destructive psychological pro-cesses coming into play. As satisfactions for the carer erode, the need to justify the stress and effort may lead to an increased distancing from the person cared for associated with an increase in negatively perceived 'difference'. To justify and sustain caring for another, it is probably necessary to see them as in need of your care. In order to see them as in need of your care, it may be necessary to see them as different from you. Seeing them as very similar to you is ideologically desirable in terms of normalisation and a necessary basis for a working alliance. That may, however, make it difficult to give the necessary energy or focus to identifying and meeting their needs, especially if that has to be sustained intensively or over an extended period of time. It is also inherently contradictory. Constructing a de-valued difference can also be a way of shoring up a weakened self-esteem at the expense of the other person. The more someone is seen as particularly difficult, disabled, or chal-lenging, the more acceptable it becomes for the carer to feel unable to cope. Locating the problem, in the form of de-valued difference, more firmly in the individual, shifts some of the burden of responsibility from the carer. If one examines care relationships, care environments, caring roles, it is easy to see how many factors can threaten the carer's identity. It is also easy to see how a process of constructing a de-valued difference (or accentuating, elaborating, generalising from difference) can protect or shore up the threatened identity.

Ignatieff (1993) draws on this process of constructing difference from psychoanalytic theory: a process which helps to protect and shore up identity, by defining the 'other' as somehow less than or worse than the self. Down the years, patronage, paternalism and professionalism can all be seen as operating in this kind of direction. Ignatieff applies this in a rather different context, examining at one point the processes by which Yugoslavs who had been friends one day became enemies the next. He draws on a Freudian concept, 'the narcissism of minor difference' and builds a compelling account of how the preservation of identity becomes dependent on constructing a negatively differentiated identity for 'the other'. It is about *post hoc* rationalisation, at one level, but he is describ-ing it in terms of deep-seated emotional processes. Such increased differentiation will undermine, of course, any working alliance that might have existed. For that to remain operational, the relationship must be based on a form of mutual respect and a sense of equality.

Difference is not, however, an absolute; nor is it necessarily negative. It is a constructed concept and in this perhaps lies a potential salvation of care and caring relationships which have run into difficulties. It is possible to acknowledge difference, without it being seen as problematically representative of the whole person. This is the 'people first' argument: that disability, age, childhood, race involve differences, but not differences which obliterate common humanity.

To arrive at this possibly more sophisticated position requires a process which could be understood as a process of deconstructing rather than denying or ignoring difference. The concept of 'equal people', for example, does not deny real differences which exist, however difficult they may be to define. Rather it brings into the foreground commonalities of humanity, shared aims and wishes, human needs and human rights; an entitlement to ordinary human pleasures and lifestyles.

This process of 'deconstructing difference' can be seen as operating at a cognitive level, but also as describing the aims and outcomes of good quality care. Rather than care which 'constructs and de-values difference', increasing disadvantage, stigma and a spoiled identity, good quality care should 'deconstruct difference', not by eliminating it, but by supporting lifestyles, opportunity and agency appropriately within a relationship which is satisfying for both parties. What this suggests is that efforts, through training, support and management structures need to be directed towards a deconstruction of difference in such a way as to protect and enhance the ability of both parties to sustain a working alliance within the care relationship. Good care would be expected to flow from this.

Conclusion

The reference in the last paragraph to training, support and management structures could be extended to include other aspects of the context in which care occurs. It reminds us that the context is a powerful determinant of what happens at the end of the day, as care is transacted between people. What has been suggested here is that we also need to look closely at care processes and relationships to understand what it is that happens when things go right and when things go wrong. There is a considerable consensus around what care might ideally be trying to achieve in terms of outcomes. Less attention is paid to the complexities of the underpinning processes of care, the feelings engendered and what the critical psychological factors may be in determining quality of care.

The model outlined here focuses attention on what might be seen as key criteria in the quality of care processes and relationships. The intention is that the model should be relevant across several divides. This is not to ignore the significance or the importance of addressing such divides, but to attempt to arrive at a conceptualisation that may help with the identification of some fundamental similarities in care work and experiences in very different contexts. Thus the model aims to have relevance across areas of informal and formal care, or, in Davies' terms (1995), across caregiving, carework and professional care. At the same time it aims to encompass a wide range of service user-groups and settings. Thirdly, it includes the range of care tasks, from direct physical care, for example, to advocacy. And finally it allows for both 'labour' and 'love' aspects of care – both caring for and caring about.

Two fundamental features of 'good care' are proposed: namely the formation of a working alliance and engagement in a process of deconstructing difference. In line with this dual focus, it is suggested that any assessment of quality should bring into central account the experience of both the carers and those in receipt of care. Both are party to the care relationship and both influence the care process and outcome. The experiences of both, therefore, matter and jointly determine the quality of care.

References

Aldridge, M. (1994) 'Unlimited liability? Emotional labour in nursing and social work', *Journal of Advanced Nursing*, 20: 722–28.

Anderson, M. (1997) 'The importance of ambivalence: caring for people with learning disabilities who engage in self-injurious behaviour'. Unpublished PhD thesis, Open University: Milton Keynes.

Atkinson, D. and Williams, F. (1990) *Know Me as I Am: an Anthology of Prose, Poems and Paintings by People with Learning Difficulties*. London: Hodder and Stoughton.

Bordin, E.S. (1979) 'The generalisability of the psychodynamic concept of the working alliance', *Psychotherapy: Theory, Research and Practice*, 16: 252–60.

Bordin, E.S. (1994) 'Theory and research on the therapeutic working alliance: new directions', in A. Horvath and L. Greenberg (eds), *The Working Alliance: Theory, Research and Practice*. New York: Wiley.

Bowers, B.J. (1987) 'Intergenerational caregiving: adult caregivers and their aging parents', *Advances in Nursing Science*, 9 (2): 20–31.

Brechin, A. and Swain, J. (1987) *Changing Relationships: Shared Action Planning with People with a Mental Handicap*. London: Harper and Row.

Brechin, A. and Swain, J. (1990) 'Creating a "working alliance" with people with learning difficulties', in A. Brechin and J. Walmsley (eds), *Making Connections: Reflecting on the Lives and Experiences of People with Learning Difficulties*. London: Hodder and Stoughton.

Dalley, G. (1988) *Ideologies of Caring: Rethinking Community and Collectivism*. Basingstoke: Macmillan.

Davies, C. (1995) 'Competence versus care? Gender and caring work revisited', *Acta Sociologica*, 38: 17–31.

Dunkle, J.H. and Friedlander, M.L. (1996) 'Contribution of therapist experience and personal characteristics to the working alliance', *Journal of Counseling Psychology*, 43 (4): 456–60.

Felce, D. (1996) 'Ways to measure quality of outcome: an essential ingredient in quality assurance', *Tizard Learning Disability Review*, 1 (2): 38–44.

Felce, D. and Perry, J. (1995) 'The extent of support for ordinary living provided in staffed housing: the relationship between staffing levels, resident dependency, staff-resident interactions and resident activity patterns', *Social Science and Medicine*, 40: 799–810.

Finch, J. and Groves, D. (1980) 'Community care and the family: a case for equal opportunities?', *Journal of Social Policy*, 9 (4): 487–514.

Glendinning, C. (1983) *Unshared Work? Parents and their Disabled Children.* London: Routledge and Kegan Paul.

Graham, H. (1983) 'Caring: a labour of love', in J. Finch and D. Groves (eds), *A Labour of Love: Women, Work and Caring.* London: Routledge and Kegan Paul.

Grant, G. and Nolan, M. (1993) 'Informal carers: sources and concomitants of satisfaction', *Health and Social Care*, 1: 147–59.

HMSO (1990) *National Health Service and Community Care Act.* London: HMSO.

Hobson, R.F. (1985) *Forms of Feeling: The Heart of Psychotherapy.* London: Tavistock Publications.

Hopson, B. (1981) 'Counselling and helping', in D. Griffiths (ed.), *Psychology and Medicine.* London and Basingstoke: British Psychological Society and Macmillan.

Ignatieff, M. (1993) *Blood and Belonging: Journeys into the New Nationalism.* London: Chatto and Windus.

Kahana, E. and Young, R. (1990) 'Clarifying the caregiving paradigm: challenges for the future', in D.E. Biegel and A. Blum (eds), *Aging and Caregiving: Theory, Research and Policy.* Beverly Hills, CA: Sage.

Knapp, M., Cambridge, P., Thomason, C., Beecham, J., Allen, C. and Darton, R. (1992) *Care in the Community: Challenge and Demonstration.* Aldershot: Ashgate.

Kristjandottir, H. (1992) 'Empathy: a therapeutic phenomenon in nursing', *Journal of Clinical Nursing*, 1: 131–40.

Levy, A. and Kahan, B. (1991) *The Pindown Experience and the Protection of Children: the Report of the Staffordshire Child Care Inquiry 1990.* Staffordshire: Staffordshire County Council.

Martin, J.P. (1984) *Hospitals in Trouble.* Oxford: Basil Blackwell.

Menzies, I.E.P. (1970) *The Functioning of Social Systems as a Defence Against Anxiety.* London: Tavistock Institute of Human Relations.

Morris, J. (1994) 'Community care or independent living?', *Critical Social Policy*, 40 (1): 24–45.

Nirje, B. (1969) 'Towards independence', in *11th World Congress of the International Society for the Rehabilitation of the Disabled*, Dublin.

Nirje, B. (1980) 'The normalisation principle', in J. Flynn and K. Nitsch (eds), *Normalisation, Integration and Community Services.* Baltimore: University Park Press.

Parker, R. (1981) 'Tending and social policy', in E.M. Goldberg and S. Hatch (eds), *A New Look at the Personal Social Services.* London: Policy Studies Institute.

Peace, S.M. (1993) 'Quality of institutional life', *Reviews in Clinical Gerontology*, 3: 187–93.

Peace, S.M., Kellaher, L. and Willcocks, D. (1997) *Re-evaluating Residential Care.* Buckingham: Open University Press.

Perry, J. and Felce, D. (1994) 'Outcomes of Ordinary Housing Services in Wales: Objective Indicators', *Mental Handicap Research*, 7: 286–311.

Pike, A. (1990) 'On the nature and place of empathy in clinical nursing practice', *Journal of Professional Nursing*, 6 (4): 235–41.

Quine, L. and Pahl, J. (1986) 'Parents with severely mentally handicapped children: marriage and the stress of caring', in R. Chester and P. Divall (eds), *Mental Health, Illness and Handicap in Marriage.* Rugby: National Marriage Guidance Council.

Qureshi, H. (1986) 'Responses to dependency: reciprocity, affect and power in family relationships', in C. Philipson, M. Bernard, and R. Strang (eds), *Dependency and Interdependency in Old Age: Theoretical Perspectives and Policy Alternatives.* London: Croom Helm.

Qureshi, H. (1992) 'Informal care by families of young adults with mental handicap and severe behaviour problems'. Unpublished PhD thesis, Manchester: University of Manchester.

Raynes, N.V., Wright, K., Sheill, A. and Pettifer, C. (1994) *The Cost and Quality of Community Residential Care.* London: David Fulton Publishers.

Read, J. and Reynolds, J. (1996) *Speaking our Minds: An Anthology.* Basingstoke: Macmillan.

Rogers, C. (1969) *On Becoming a Person: A Therapist's View of Psychotherapy.* London: Constable.

Smith, P. (1992) *The Emotional Labour of Nursing.* London: Macmillan.

Smith, H. and Brown, H. (1992) 'Inside-out: a psychodynamic approach to normalisation', in H. Brown and H. Smith (eds), *Normalisation: a Reader for the Nineties.* London: Routledge.

Twigg, J. and Atkin, K. (1994) *Carers Perceived: Policy and Practice in Informal Care.* Buckingham: Open University Press.

Wardaugh, J. and Wilding, P. (1993) 'Towards an explanation of the corruption of care', *Critical Social Policy*, 37: 5–31.

Westcott, M. (1991) *Institutional Abuse of Children: From Research to Policy.* London: NSPCC.

Wolfensberger, W. and Glenn, L. (1975) *Programme Analysis of Service Systems: Handbook and Manual*, 3rd edn. Toronto: National Institute of Mental Retardation.

Yalom, I.D. (1980) *Existential Psychotherapy.* New York: Basic Books Inc.

INDEX